Digital Finance

Zhiyi Liu · Wenxuan Hou

Digital Finance

How Innovation Reshapes the Capital Markets

Springer

Zhiyi Liu
Shanghai Artificial Intelligence Social Governance Collaborative Innovation Center
Shanghai, China

Wenxuan Hou
School of Business
University of Edinburgh
Edinburgh, UK

ISBN 978-981-99-7304-0 ISBN 978-981-99-7305-7 (eBook)
https://doi.org/10.1007/978-981-99-7305-7

This Springer imprint is published by the registered company Springer Nature Singapore Pte Ltd.
The registered company address is: 152 Beach Road, #21-01/04 Gateway East, Singapore 189721, Singapore

Paper in this product is recyclable.

Preface

Part 1: Defining Digital Finance

Digital finance[1] is a form of financial services and transactions that relies on digital technologies, including mobile devices, the internet, and blockchain, among others. It provides and delivers various financial services and products through digital channels, such as digital payments, digital lending, and digital investments. The rise of digital finance can improve the inclusiveness and efficiency of financial services, reduce transaction and operational costs, enhance transparency, and promote the innovation of new business models and products. However, it also brings new challenges and risks, such as cybersecurity issues, data privacy protection, and regulatory compliance difficulties.

In order to better understand how digital finance is transforming the financial industry, we also need to consider its impact on financial efficiency and costs. Digital finance can improve the efficiency and reduce costs of financial services by reducing reliance on physical infrastructure and lowering transaction expenses. However, the rapid development of digital finance has also raised some concerns, such as cybersecurity, data privacy, and regulatory compliance

Digital finance does not have a single definition, but researchers generally agree that its emergence has brought new opportunities and challenges to the financial industry. As a means of inclusive finance, digital finance helps narrow the gap in accessing financial services, especially for those groups that are difficult to reach by traditional financial systems. At the same time, digital finance can also improve the efficiency of financial services, reduce transaction and operational costs, and bring benefits to both financial institutions and consumers. However, it also brings new risks and challenges, including cybersecurity issues, data privacy protection, regulatory compliance, etc., which require us to take appropriate measures to manage and respond.

---

[1] Schueffel, P. (2016), "Taming the beast:a scientifific definition of fintech," Journal of Innovation Management.

Part 2: The Evolution of Digital Finance

The roots of digital finance can be traced back to the 1970s when the United States developed the world's first Electronic Funds Transfer (EFT) system, laying the groundwork for the digitization of financial services.

However, the real turning point that gave birth to the diversified forms of digital finance came from the technological revolution of the internet in the 1990s and the popularization of mobile technology in the 2000s. These two major technological trends fostered the birth of new forms of digital finance, such as mobile money and online payment systems.

Clearly, the formation of digital finance is not an isolated event but rather the result of various driving factors working together. Among them, the role of technological innovation is particularly prominent, as it has enabled the expansion of digital channels and platforms for delivering financial services, including but not limited to mobile payments, online lending, and peer-to-peer lending. Compared to traditional financial services, these emerging forms of services have distinct advantages, offering faster transaction speeds, lower costs, and greater convenience in accessibility.

Another driving force behind the development of digital finance is inclusive finance. The goal of inclusive finance is to provide financial services to those who were previously excluded from the formal financial system. With the growth of digital financial service channels and platforms, achieving this goal has become increasingly feasible.

Furthermore, consumer demand is also a significant driver of digital finance development. Modern consumers seek faster, more convenient, and easily accessible financial services, and technological advancements enable financial institutions to meet these demands by offering digital financial services.

Finally, regulatory reform plays a significant role in driving the development of digital finance. With the establishment of new regulatory frameworks for digital payments and the formulation of guiding principles for mobile banking, the advancement of digital finance has received significant impetus. These regulatory reforms provide financial institutions with a framework to offer digital financial services to their customers.

In summary, the development of digital finance is driven by various factors, including technological innovation, inclusive finance, consumer demand, and regulatory reform. These elements have collectively propelled the emergence of new forms of digital financial services, such as mobile money, online payments, and digital lending, fundamentally changing how people access financial services and conduct transactions.

Part 3: The Importance of Digital Finance in the Modern Economy

After gaining an understanding of the scope, development, and influencing factors of digital finance, let's now discuss its significance in the modern economy.

The role of digital finance in the modern economic system is increasingly prominent, mainly due to its ability to achieve financial inclusion, enhance financial service efficiency, reduce operational costs, and pave the way for new business models and product types.

Digital finance offers possibilities for financial services to those who were previously marginalized by the formal financial system, such as low-income families, small businesses, and rural communities. Services like payment solutions, savings accounts, and credit facilities, which were previously inaccessible or costly, can now be provided through digital finance. This advancement helps reduce poverty and stimulates economic growth.

Furthermore, there exists a symbiotic relationship between inclusive finance and digital finance. Digital finance serves as a powerful tool to drive inclusive finance, enabling more people to access financial services. In turn, inclusive finance provides a foundation for sustainable and equitable economic development, offering vast opportunities for the development of digital finance. This symbiosis implies that with proper guidance and utilization, we can harness digital finance to bring greater prosperity to a broader spectrum of people.

Moreover, digital finance offers significant advantages in terms of efficiency improvement and cost reduction. By eliminating the need for physical infrastructure, digital finance lowers the cost of delivering financial services. This enables consumers to more easily afford financial service fees while also enhancing the profitability of financial institutions. Digital finance significantly reduces transaction costs by simplifying financial transactions and reducing reliance on physical infrastructure, leading to overall lower operational costs in the economy. It helps decrease the costs associated with search and bargaining, creating more efficient and competitive markets, and further reducing overall economic operating costs.

Lastly, digital finance also fosters innovation in new business models and products. It has the potential to create novel forms of financial intermediation, such as peer-to-peer lending and crowdfunding, and drive the development of new financial products, such as virtual currencies and digital assets. This provides new opportunities for entrepreneurship and innovation in the financial sector.

In summary, digital finance is becoming increasingly important in the modern economy due to its potential to enhance financial inclusion, improve efficiency, lower costs, and enable new business models and products. These aspects are of significant importance for economic development and maintaining financial stability.

Part 4: Understanding Digital Finance from an Interdisciplinary Perspective

After understanding digital finance from an economic perspective, let's explore its value from other disciplinary fields. Digital finance is becoming increasingly important in the modern economy and influencing various domains, including economics, computer science, sociology, and philosophy, among others.

Firstly, digital finance has the potential to transform companies' operational methods and customer interactions, making it of significant value for research in business schools.

Here are three examples from globally renowned companies, along with insights from three distinguished scholars that shed light on the importance of digital finance.

Alibaba is a Chinese e-commerce giant that ventured into the digital finance sector through its payment system Alipay. According to research by Erik Brynjolfsson and Andrew McAfee (2014), Alipay had already become a major force in the Chinese financial market at that time, boasting over 700 million users and holding more than half of the market share in China's mobile payment sector. These scholars believed that Alipay represented a significant disruption to the traditional financial system, democratizing access to financial services and reducing the reliance on physical banks.

PayPal, as a global online payment system, enjoys widespread recognition in the digital finance sector. According to Clayton Christensen (2013), PayPal disrupted the traditional payment industry by providing faster, more convenient, and secure online transaction methods. He believed that PayPal's success demonstrated the importance of disruptive innovation in the digital finance field, as companies that offer superior customer experiences can rapidly gain market share and change the industry landscape.

Square is a US-based financial technology company that provides payment and financial services to businesses. According to Clayton Christensen (2013), Square disrupted the traditional payment industry by enabling small businesses to accept credit card payments through mobile devices. He believed that Square's success highlighted the importance of understanding and meeting the needs of small businesses, as traditional financial institutions often fail to provide adequate services to them.

These examples highlight the importance of digital finance research in business schools. The perspectives of these three prominent scholars emphasize the significance of disruptive innovation and customer-centric design in the digital finance domain.

Research conducted in business schools not only helps us better understand the impact and opportunities of digital finance but also provides guidance and strategic direction for businesses and financial institutions to address the challenges posed by the digital economy.

In addition to business schools, scholars in the field of artificial intelligence (AI) have also begun to pay attention to digital finance and realize its significance in relation to the development of AI. The application of AI in digital finance holds the potential to fundamentally transform the financial industry, a point that has been acknowledged by Turing Award laureates such as computer scientist Yoshua Bengio.

One of the key applications of artificial intelligence (AI) in digital finance is risk management. According to Bengio (2020), AI can be utilized to analyze vast amounts of financial data and identify patterns and anomalies that may indicate potential risks. For instance, AI can be employed to detect fraudulent transactions, predict credit risks, and identify market trends. This enhances the efficiency and accuracy of risk management, leading to better financial outcomes. AI is also used to automate financial processes, such as customer service and investment management. AI-powered chatbots and virtual assistants can provide personalized financial advice and support to customers, improving their overall experience and reducing costs for financial institutions. Furthermore, AI can optimize investment portfolios by analyzing market trends and making data-driven investment decisions. This can lead to better investment performance and outcomes.

However, the use of digital finance has raised concerns about privacy and security as financial institutions and third-party vendors have easier access to personal financial data. From the perspective of information philosophy, this has triggered important questions about fairness, justice, and privacy. Several renowned contemporary philosophers, including Luciano Floridi, Helen Nissenbaum, and Daniel Solove, have expressed their opinions on these issues. Let's take a look at the different directions they are concerned about:

First and foremost, philosophers are deeply concerned about privacy protection.

Floridi is a leading global philosopher of information, and his research in information ethics is extensive. He believes that digital finance is reshaping our understanding of money, trust, and value. He emphasizes the significant potential of digital finance in promoting inclusive finance and reducing economic inequality. However, he also warns that digital finance brings significant moral and social challenges, including issues related to privacy, security, and the concentration of power in a few large digital finance companies.

Floridi's research aids our understanding of the complex societal and ethical implications of digital finance and emphasizes the need for a robust ethical framework to guide the development and use of digital finance technology.

According to Floridi's (2015) perspective, digital finance must be designed as a tool that promotes information justice and information privacy. Information justice means that information should be distributed fairly, avoiding situations of discrimination. Information privacy, on the other hand, refers to protecting personal information and avoiding unreasonable surveillance.

In addition, philosophers also focus on the domain of data rights.

Helen Nissenbaum is a technology philosopher and a privacy expert who emphasizes the importance of transparency and accountability in digital finance, particularly concerning the collection and use of personal data.

She believes that digital finance platforms should provide clear privacy policies and explicit data usage regulations, enabling users to understand and control the ways in which their personal data is used. Moreover, digital finance institutions and platforms should establish effective oversight and accountability mechanisms to ensure the lawful and transparent use of personal data.

Daniel Solove is a privacy law expert who has conducted extensive research on the importance of privacy in the digital age. He believes that digital finance must be designed with the principles of promoting fairness and avoiding discrimination based on personal information. He points out that digital finance platforms generate and process a large amount of sensitive financial information, which poses significant privacy risks. Solove advocates for robust security measures to prevent cyber threats and data breaches.

Additionally, Solove emphasizes the importance of regulatory oversight to ensure that digital finance companies are accountable for their privacy and security practices. He calls for increased transparency in data collection and usage practices of digital finance platforms.

From the perspective of information philosophers, digital finance raises important questions about fairness, justice, and privacy, which also involve research in digital jurisprudence.

Lastly, let's discuss the impact of digital finance development from the perspective of international political science. We will briefly explore the significance of digital finance from an international political viewpoint and cite the views of three renowned scholars.

Joseph Stiglitz, a globally acclaimed Nobel laureate in economics, offers profound insights into the impact and role of digital finance. He believes that digital finance can promote financial inclusion by providing financial services to those who are excluded from the traditional financial system, particularly in developing countries, where this effect is more pronounced. He also points out that the widespread adoption and application of digital finance have the potential to promote economic growth by increasing financial inclusion, thus contributing to poverty reduction and improving social welfare.

However, Stiglitz also reminds us that digital finance is not a panacea, and its development and application need to be carried out under careful regulation. The misuse of digital finance can lead to a range of issues, including infringement of consumer rights and violations of personal privacy. Therefore, Stiglitz emphasizes the importance of transparency and accountability, particularly in the areas of consumer protection and data privacy.

Furthermore, Stiglitz highlights some potential issues that digital finance may bring, such as the possibility of excessive concentration of financial power in the hands of a few large digital finance companies, which could pose a threat to the healthy development of financial markets. Hence, effective measures need to be taken to address these potential negative impacts brought about by digital finance.

In conclusion, Stiglitz's research provides valuable perspectives for understanding the potential benefits and risks of digital finance. He emphasizes the need for a balanced approach in developing and utilizing digital finance technology, harnessing its advantages while effectively managing and controlling the potential risks it may bring.

Dani Rodrik is a political economist who has conducted in-depth research in the fields of globalization and economic development.

Rodrik's views first recognize the potential of digital finance in advancing financial inclusion and reducing income inequality, especially for those marginalized in the traditional financial system. Digital finance can provide more convenient and efficient financial services. He also highlights the disruptive nature of digital finance, which has, to some extent, changed traditional economic activities, particularly evident in developing countries.

However, Rodrik also points out potential issues that digital finance may bring. He believes that with the application and widespread adoption of digital finance, there may be new winners and losers in the global economy, with some individuals and countries benefiting while others may lose out in the process.

Additionally, he highlights that digital finance can be used for tax evasion and regulatory avoidance, which could threaten the legitimacy of fair democratic systems. If not properly regulated, digital finance may exacerbate economic inequality and even lead to financial instability.

Therefore, Rodrik emphasizes the need to establish appropriate regulatory frameworks to promote the positive impact of digital finance while mitigating its potential negative consequences.

Overall, Rodrik's research helps us gain a deeper understanding of the opportunities and challenges of digital finance and underscores the importance of establishing and improving regulatory mechanisms for digital finance.

Parag Khanna is a renowned global strategist who has conducted in-depth research and offered unique insights into how digital finance is transforming our economic activities and even the global economic landscape.

Khanna points out that digital finance is fundamentally changing our economic activities. Traditional banks and financial services are being replaced by new digital commerce and peer-to-peer lending. This transformation is not only changing the way we conduct financial transactions but also how we understand and utilize financial services.

Khanna sees the tremendous potential of digital finance in promoting economic development, especially in emerging markets. He emphasizes that digital finance, by increasing access to financial services and facilitating cross-border trade, provides a powerful impetus for economic growth and development in emerging markets. Additionally, he believes that establishing robust digital infrastructure is crucial to support the development of digital finance and ensure its security and stability.

However, his insights go beyond this. Khanna believes that digital finance has the potential to reshape the global economic landscape. He points out that digital finance could weaken the influence of traditional financial centers like New York and London while promoting the rise of new financial centers, particularly in Asia. This shift not only has the potential to alter the distribution of global financial power but also brings unprecedented development opportunities for emerging markets.

Nevertheless, Khanna also warns that digital finance may bring about new forms of economic and political instability, especially in the absence of proper regulation.

Therefore, he emphasizes the need for a strategic approach when developing and utilizing digital finance technologies in the global economy.

Overall, Khanna's research provides valuable insights into the transformative potential of digital finance and how to strategically harness it in the global economy.

Through the discussions above, we deeply appreciate the importance and influence of digital finance in the modern global economy. The research conducted by Joseph Stiglitz, Dani Rodrik, and Parag Khanna provides us with comprehensive frameworks to understand and assess the impact of digital finance, enabling us to view its benefits and risks from multiple perspectives. Stiglitz emphasizes the potential of digital finance in promoting inclusive finance and reducing poverty, while Rodrik focuses on the risks of inequality and the potential harm to fair democracy that it may bring. Khanna explores how digital finance is transforming the nature of economic activities and global economic patterns.

These perspectives remind us that the development of digital finance requires appropriate regulation and guidance to ensure that it can contribute to social welfare and enhance fair democracy. We hope that these viewpoints and discussions will inspire readers to think more deeply about digital finance, foster a better understanding of its influence, and provide navigational guidance in our increasingly digitized world.

Part 5: Digital Finance and Capitalism

The interaction between digital finance and capitalism constitutes a complex relationship. This article will quote the views and insights of renowned scholars such as Karl Marx, David Harvey, and Nick Srnicek to explore the potential negative effects brought about by the development of digital finance. This is the primary focus of our research framework.

Marxist theory regards the core features of capitalism as labor exploitation and capital accumulation. The capitalist class increases profits and accumulates capital by extracting surplus value from laborers. In the perspective of Marxism, digital finance can be understood as a modern tool that extracts surplus value from consumers through the commodification of information and innovation of new financial products.

In the digital finance environment, this exploitation is manifested through the commodification of information and the creation of new financial products, through which surplus value is extracted from consumers. Companies reliant on digital finance can design new financial products, often sold to consumers at high prices, by collecting and analyzing data on consumer behavior and preferences.

However, Marx pointed out that capitalism has a tendency toward crises, stemming from contradictions between productive forces and relations of production. In the context of digital finance, these contradictions may be seen in the tense relationship between financial market expansion and the real economy. While digital finance drives the expansion of financial markets and the creation of new financial products, it may also exacerbate the decoupling of financial markets from the real economy, potentially threatening financial stability and leading to economic crises. Therefore, we must remain vigilant and continue monitoring the impacts of these developments.

Furthermore, Marx's analysis emphasizes a key characteristic of capitalism: the high concentration of wealth and power. In the backdrop of digital finance, this concentration is evident in the phenomenon of "platform capitalism," where a few dominant companies control key digital infrastructure for financial transactions. These companies wield immeasurable power, not only shaping the financial system but also exerting far-reaching effects on the broader economy and society.

Clearly, Marx's theories provide us with an insightful framework to deeply analyze the complex relationship between digital finance and capitalism. This framework allows us to view the commodification of information and the creation of new financial products as new forms of exploitation. It also reveals the appearance of crises and the concentration of wealth and power as widespread trends within capitalism.

However, for such an intricate subject, further in-depth research is necessary. For instance, we need to explore the characteristics of platform capitalism and its impact on the socio-economic landscape. We also need to study how the creation of new financial products and the commodification of information change consumer behavior and how these changes, in turn, affect the development of capitalism. The answers to these questions will enable us to better understand the relationship between digital finance and capitalism and how this relationship influences our society and economy.

David Harvey, as a renowned Marxist scholar, has conducted in-depth and extensive research on the interactive relationship between digital technology and capitalism. His theories provide a profound perspective for understanding the connection between digital finance and capitalism. Harvey reveals how the development of digital finance accelerates financialization, exacerbates social inequality, and profoundly impacts the global economic system.

Nick Srnicek, as a political theorist and a philosopher, has deeply studied how digital technology shapes the future of capitalism. Srnicek's contribution lies in his analysis of the relationship between digital finance and capitalism. He believes that digital finance plays a crucial role in the transformation of capitalism, driving new forms of economic activity and accumulation. Srnicek points out that digital finance stimulates the innovation of new financial products and services, while also expanding the financial market, giving rise to a new form of capitalism he refers to as "platform capitalism." In this new model, a few large digital platforms like Amazon, Google, and Facebook control the infrastructure and data that support digital finance.

In summary, the relationship between digital finance and capitalism is indeed complex and multifaceted. In the new digital era, Marxist theories, particularly those concerning labor exploitation and capital accumulation, remain highly relevant. The rise of digital finance has given rise to new forms of commodification and financialization, intensifying the dynamism of capitalism. Digital finance presents both opportunities and risks. The emergence of new automated technologies and platform capitalism is transforming the nature of work and production, potentially leading to profound social and economic impacts. For example, the rise of digital platforms has fueled the gig economy, resulting in labor market fragmentation and erosion of workers' rights.

Shanghai, China Zhiyi Liu
Edinburgh, UK Wenxuan Hou

Contents

Chapter 1
Opportunities and Challenges of Digital Financial Development

Abstract The historical process of financial technology is complex and diverse, tracing back to the origins of early computerized trading and evolving with the rise of the internet, mobile payments, and blockchain technology.

1.1 History and Theories Influencing the Development of Digital Finance

The historical process of financial technology is complex and diverse, tracing back to the origins of early computerized trading and evolving with the rise of the internet, mobile payments, and blockchain technology. In this article, we will analyze the history of digital finance, dividing it into the stages of automation, the internet, and mobile payments and blockchain technology, to better understand the development of financial technology.

The first phase is the Automation Phase, which represents the initial stage of the development of digital finance and has had a significant impact on the advancement of financial technology. Starting from the 1960s, automation technology began to be applied in the financial sector, ushering in a new era for the financial industry. The introduction of automated systems notably enhanced the processing speed of financial transactions and significantly improved transaction efficiency. Moreover, automation technology enabled the implementation of more sophisticated transaction risk controls and market analysis, providing robust technical support for the rapid development of financial operations.

During this stage, the emergence of large-scale computers was a key technological innovation. Large-scale computers refer to powerful machines capable of handling substantial volumes of data and swiftly processing transactions. Financial institutions widely adopted large-scale computers to automate many processes that were previously performed manually. Additionally, another significant technological advancement was the development of new programming languages specifically designed for financial applications, such as COBOL and FORTRAN. These languages allowed

Z. Liu and W. Hou, *Digital Finance*, https://doi.org/10.1007/978-981-99-7305-7_1

financial institutions to create customized software programs, automating specific financial processes.

Next is the Internet Phase, which began in the 1990s with the rise and popularization of the internet, marking the digitization of finance. The development of internet technology has driven the process of online transformation in the financial industry, providing people with more convenient financial services. The emergence of online banks and securities companies has made the financial market more open and transparent, enabling financial transactions to transcend national borders and achieve globalization. During this stage, the financial industry shifted towards a customer-centric service model, offering online trading and banking services that cover a broader audience, reduce costs, and provide personalized services.

At the same time, the Internet Phase witnessed the rise of new online financial trading platforms. Platforms like E-TRADE and Ameritrade allowed investors to buy and sell stocks and other securities online. Additionally, the emergence of online banking platforms enabled customers to access their accounts and conduct transactions anytime, anywhere. Furthermore, computer scientists developed new financial analysis and risk management algorithms and models. For instance, the Black–Scholes model, originally developed by two computer scientists in the 1970s, was used for pricing options contracts. With the growth of online trading in the 1990s, this model became widely applied.

Finally, we have the Mobile Payment Zhou and Lu (2016) and Blockchain Technology Werbach (2018) Phase, which is characterized by the rise of mobile payments and blockchain technology in the development of digital finance. With the widespread adoption of mobile devices, mobile technology has been extensively applied in the financial sector. Mobile applications enable functions such as fund transfers, payments, transactions, and wealth management, greatly enhancing user experience. At the same time, the application of blockchain technology injects new momentum into the development of digital finance. The distributed nature of blockchain technology improves transaction security and credibility while reducing transaction costs. The application of these emerging technologies brings new opportunities and challenges to digital finance, driving innovation and transformation in financial services.

This stage marks the transformation of financial services. Mobile payments are revolutionizing the way people interact with financial institutions, while blockchain technology is changing the way financial transactions are processed and verified. Clearly, the 21st-century phase of digital finance with mobile technology and blockchain is a significant milestone in the history of financial technology development.

During this period, computer scientists continue to play a critical role in the development of digital finance. The new technologies and software programs they develop enable financial institutions to conduct transactions and manage accounts using mobile devices. One of the key technologies in this stage is biometric authentication, which enhances the security of mobile transactions. Biometric authentication uses unique physical characteristics such as fingerprints, facial recognition, or voice recognition to verify the user's identity and prevent fraudulent activities.

Furthermore, the establishment of new mobile payment platforms is another important advancement in this stage. For example, the introduction of Apple Pay and Google Pay allows users to make payments using their mobile devices. These platforms use Near Field Communication (NFC) technology to securely transmit payment information between the user's mobile device and the merchant's payment terminal.

In conclusion, the history of digital finance demonstrates the transformative power of technology in the financial industry. From the early era of computerized transactions to the current era of mobile payments and blockchain technology, digital finance enables financial institutions to process transactions faster, reach a wider audience, and provide personalized services to customers. This technology-driven transformation not only enhances the efficiency of financial institutions but also delivers a superior service experience to consumers, indicating the greater possibilities of future financial technology.

To understand the development of digital finance, it is important to examine the influential theories and ideas that have shaped its progress, in addition to tracing its technological evolution. Several key theories have impacted the development of digital finance, among which the following are crucial:

First, Disruptive Innovation Theory. This theory explains how new technologies can disrupt existing markets and create new ones. In the realm of digital finance World Bank (2017), the introduction of digital technologies has disrupted the traditional business models of financial institutions and created new opportunities for individuals and businesses. Digital finance, as a disruptive innovation, has the potential to transform the entire financial industry.

Traditional financial institutions often fail to meet the needs of individuals without credit histories or sufficient assets. However, digital finance, through the use of new technologies and data analysis, better understands the needs and risks of these customers, providing personalized financial services. It adopts simple and convenient solutions such as mobile payments, online lending platforms, and investment platforms, which are not only more convenient but also generally more cost-effective than services offered by traditional financial institutions.

Based on this theory, we can understand the development of digital finance from the following perspectives:

(1) Disruptive Potential: Digital finance has the potential to disrupt traditional financial institutions. It does so by offering simple, inexpensive, and convenient solutions that challenge the traditional financial institutions. For example, the advent of mobile payment systems and online banking platforms enables people to manage their finances more easily without the need to visit physical bank branches.
(2) Business Model Transformation: Digital finance is transforming the traditional business models within the financial industry. It is creating new business models, such as peer-to-peer lending and crowdfunding, based on the principles of the sharing economy and financial democratization. These new models provide

more direct and efficient financial services and create new opportunities for individuals and businesses.

(3) Financial Democratization: Digital finance promotes financial democratization by making financial services more accessible to a broader population. It fosters the sharing of financial resources through peer-to-peer lending and crowdfunding, providing new opportunities for people to finance and invest in emerging enterprises and advancing financial democratization.

(4) Disintermediation: Digital finance is also disrupting the role of financial intermediaries. It establishes direct connections between borrowers and lenders, investors and issuers, and buyers and sellers, weakening the traditional role of intermediaries like banks and investment companies. This trend towards disintermediation makes financial transactions more efficient, transparent, and reduces transaction costs.

Secondly, the Network Effect Theory. This theory explains how the value of a network increases with the growing number of users. Digital finance relies heavily on network effects, as the value of digital finance platforms increases with more users joining the network. This creates a positive growth cycle that can lead to the dominance of a few major companies in the market. Specifically, based on this theory, we can understand the development of digital finance from the following perspectives:

(1) Dominance of Major Players: Network effects cause the value of digital finance platforms to be directly proportional to the number of users. As more users join the platform, its value continuously increases. This leads to a few major players dominating the market because they can leverage their large user base to gain a greater advantage from network effects.

(2) Lock-in Effect: Digital finance platforms can create a lock-in effect by attracting users and building user investment. Users' time, effort, and monetary investment in a particular platform make them less willing to switch to other platforms. This sets up barriers for existing major players, making it difficult for new entrants to compete with them.

(3) Viral Marketing: Digital finance platforms can utilize viral marketing strategies to expand their networks. By using social media, word-of-mouth marketing, and referral programs, platforms encourage users to share the platform within their social circles. This social spread can lead to exponential network growth, accelerating the platform's development.

(4) Network Externality: Digital finance platforms create positive network externalities, meaning that the value of the network increases with the addition of more users. This externality makes the platform more attractive to new users. Platforms can create tipping points by introducing new services, features, or incentive measures to further stimulate the influx of more users.

(5) Winner-Takes-All Market: Digital finance markets with strong network effects often exhibit a winner-takes-all trend. A few major companies establish higher entry barriers through investments in infrastructure, technology, and marketing, making it difficult for small companies to compete. The characteristics of high

fixed costs and low marginal costs allow these major companies to fully leverage network effects and monopolize the market.

The third theory is the theory of platform economics. This theory explains how digital platforms create value by connecting buyers and sellers and facilitating transactions. Digital financial platforms such as mobile payment systems, peer-to-peer lending platforms, and crowdfunding platforms create value by connecting borrowers and lenders, investors and issuers, and buyers and sellers. Based on this theory, we can understand the development of digital finance in the following aspects:

(1) Two-sided market: Digital financial platforms facilitate financial transactions by connecting different user groups. This two-sided market model enables the platform to provide a wider range of transaction opportunities for borrowers and lenders, investors and issuers, and buyers and sellers.
(2) Multi-homing effects: Digital financial platforms exhibit multi-homing effects, where users can simultaneously use multiple platforms. This creates competition between platforms and reduces the bargaining power of individual platforms. Users can choose to use multiple platforms to obtain better services and more favorable transaction conditions.
(3) Platform competition: There is fierce competition among digital financial platforms, and they attract users by offering different services, features, and incentive measures. This platform competition drives innovation and efficiency improvement, benefiting users.
(4) Platform regulation: Operating digital financial platforms involves regulatory challenges that require balancing the interests of various stakeholders. Regulatory authorities should ensure the safety, reliability, and transparency of digital financial platforms to prevent market abuse and systemic risks.

The fourth theory is the theory of the sharing economy. This theory explains how digital platforms enable individuals to share goods and services. Digital finance promotes the sharing economy by sharing financial resources, such as peer-to-peer lending and crowdfunding, which creates new opportunities for individuals to obtain financing and invest in new enterprises. Based on this theory, we can understand the development of digital finance in the following aspects:

(1) Financial democratization: Digital finance enables a broader population to access financial services and opportunities by sharing financial resources, such as peer-to-peer lending and crowdfunding. This promotes financial democratization, providing new opportunities for individuals and businesses that previously had limited access to financial support.
(2) Establishing trust: The success of sharing economy platforms relies on trust among users. Digital finance uses technologies like blockchain and smart contracts to establish trust, providing transparency and security in financial transactions. This trust mechanism helps strengthen cooperation and mutual trust among users.
(3) Collaborative consumption: The sharing economy emphasizes the principle of collaborative consumption, reducing waste, improving efficiency, and

promoting community development through resource sharing. Digital financial platforms enable people to share financial resources, invest in new enterprises, and support social initiatives, thereby fostering collaborative consumption and community development.

(4) Regulatory challenges: The sharing economy faces regulatory challenges during its operation, and digital financial platforms are no exception. To ensure the safety, reliability, and transparency of sharing economy platforms and prevent market abuses and systemic risks, regulatory agencies need to formulate appropriate standards and regulatory policies.

The fifth theory is the theory of digital transformation. This theory explains how businesses utilize digital technology to create new business models, products, and services. Digital finance serves as a typical example of the digital transformation in the financial industry, as it is creating new business models such as mobile banking and robo-advisory services, as well as introducing new products like cryptocurrencies and digital wallets. Based on this theory, we can understand the development of digital finance in the following aspects:

(1) Customer-centric approach: Digital transformation places customers at the core, and businesses use digital technology and platforms to provide personalized and convenient financial products and services that cater to customer needs and enhance customer experience. Digital financial platforms, such as mobile payment systems and online banking platforms, achieve this customer-centric transformation by offering features like real-time notifications, personalized offers, and seamless transactions.

(2) Data-driven decision-making: Digital transformation empowers businesses with more data sources and analytical capabilities. Companies leverage data analysis and artificial intelligence technologies to make more accurate decisions. Digital financial platforms analyze customer behavior, detect fraud, and improve risk management through data analysis, thereby enhancing decision-making accuracy and efficiency.

(3) Platform ecosystems: Digital transformation drives collaboration and innovation between businesses and other stakeholders. Digital financial platforms collaborate with retailers, e-commerce platforms, and social media, among others, to create platform ecosystems that result in mutual benefits and comprehensive financial services.

(4) Agile innovation mechanisms: Digital transformation enables businesses to rapidly develop and test new products and services. Digital financial platforms adopt agile methodologies, enabling them to respond quickly to market demands and develop innovative products and services like mobile payment systems, digital wallets, and robo-advisory services, enhancing the speed and effectiveness of innovation.

In conclusion, the development of digital finance is driven by the ever-changing technological environment and supported by theories in the field of the digital economy. The application of emerging technologies such as mobile payments, blockchain, and artificial intelligence, as well as the development of disruptive innovation, platform economics, the sharing economy, and digital transformation theories, all contribute as vital drivers and guides to the innovation and development of digital finance.

1.2 The Key Factors Influencing the Development of Digital Finance

Technology is the crucial driving force behind financial development, especially in the realm of digital finance. With the continuous progress and innovation of technology, financial technology (FinTech) has become a key element driving digital financial innovation. The innovations in financial technology encompass the application of technologies such as mobile payments, blockchain, artificial intelligence, and big data analytics.

Through digital transformation and the impetus of financial technology, financial institutions can offer more diverse products and services, enhance efficiency, reduce costs, and establish collaborative ecosystems with other industries for mutual benefits. At the same time, the rise of the digital finance industry has given birth to new financial instruments and services. Among them, digital currencies like Bitcoin and Ethereum present a challenge to traditional banking systems and offer people an alternative means of payment and investment. These digital currencies, based on blockchain technology, facilitate secure and transparent transactions in a decentralized manner, providing users with greater financial autonomy and privacy protection. Additionally, peer-to-peer lending platforms represent a significant innovation in the digital finance industry, enabling individuals to engage in direct lending on the platform without the need for traditional banks as intermediaries. This model provides another source of financing for small businesses and individuals, lowering the barriers and costs of obtaining funds.

By leveraging advanced technology and innovative business models, digital finance Pew Research Center (2019) not only offers more diversified choices but also transforms the power structure within the traditional financial system. It provides individuals and small businesses with more opportunities and convenience, promoting financial inclusion and sustainable economic development.

However, people are concerned about the impact of digital finance on traditional financial institutions, as many companies are striving to keep up with technological changes. We believe that the key factors influencing the development of digital finance mainly include:

Firstly, mobile technology GSMA (2019). Mobile technology has always been a crucial driving force behind the development of digital finance. It has changed the economic model of financial services, reduced the cost of financial services, and enabled those who previously lacked bank accounts to access financial services.

From the perspective of information philosophy, digital finance relies on the ability to create, store, and transmit information. In this process, mobile technology plays a crucial role as it enables people to access and transmit financial information anytime and anywhere. Additionally, mobile technology is a key driver of social change. Smartphones have created entirely new forms of social interaction, enabling people to connect with each other in innovative ways. In the realm of digital finance, mobile technology presents new opportunities for inclusive finance, especially in developing countries lacking traditional banking infrastructure.

Secondly, the regulatory environment is a critical factor in the operation of digital finance. The regulatory landscape for digital finance is complex and constantly evolving due to its operation in a rapidly developing technological environment. Let's summarize and review relevant viewpoints based on regulatory policies in important countries in the European and American markets.

In the European market, countries like the UK, Germany, and France adopt regulatory policies aimed at balancing innovation and consumer protection. The UK's Financial Conduct Authority (FCA) has established a regulatory sandbox Nana and Peng (2018), allowing digital finance companies to test new products and services in a controlled environment. Germany's Federal Financial Supervisory Authority (BaFin) implements regulations that require digital finance companies to obtain licenses before operating in the country. The French Financial Markets Authority (AMF) has set up a financial technology laboratory to provide regulatory compliance guidance to digital finance companies.

In the US market, countries like the US and Canada also implement regulatory policies aimed at balancing innovation and consumer protection. The US Consumer Financial Protection Bureau (CFPB) develops regulations that require digital finance companies to disclose fees and service terms to consumers. The Canadian Financial Consumer Agency (FCA) implements regulations that require digital finance companies to provide transparent and clear information to consumers.

Thirdly, consumer behavior plays a crucial role in the development of digital finance. Consumer behavior is often irrational, and companies that understand and respond to such behavior are more likely to succeed in the digital finance industry.

Furthermore, trust and security are key factors that influence consumer behavior in the digital finance domain. If digital finance applications are supported by reputable financial institutions, have clear privacy policies, and employ advanced security measures such as biometric authentication, consumers are more likely to trust them. The case of the leading online payment platform, PayPal, illustrates how the company's focus on security and fraud prevention has helped it gain the trust of millions of users worldwide.

Personalization and customization are another key factor influencing consumer behavior in the digital finance domain. Consumers are more likely to use digital financial services that offer personalized recommendations and advice based on their individual financial goals and preferences. The case of the digital investment platform, Betterment, illustrates how the company uses algorithms and data analysis to provide personalized investment advice to its users, thereby increasing customer satisfaction and loyalty.

Fourthly, partnerships play a crucial role in the development of digital finance. Successful digital finance companies often establish strategic partnerships with other companies to expand their business scope and offer new services.

In the digital finance domain, successful partnerships enable companies to leverage each other's strengths and provide new services that neither company could offer alone. Successful digital finance partnership cases include collaborations between PayPal and Mastercard, as well as Ant Group and Standard Chartered Bank. The partnership between PayPal and Mastercard allows customers to make purchases through PayPal using Mastercard's digital wallet, while the collaboration between Ant Group and Standard Chartered Bank enables Ant Group to offer mobile payment services to Standard Chartered Bank's customers.

Fifthly, globalization. The relationship between digital finance and globalization is complex and multidimensional. As a global industry, successful digital finance companies are often those that can explore new markets and adapt to the challenges of globalization. Globalization brings new opportunities to digital finance companies, but also new challenges, especially in dealing with different regulatory frameworks and cultural norms.

Globalization creates a more interconnected and interdependent world. In the context of digital finance, successful companies are those that can leverage this interconnectedness to expand their reach and offer new services to global customers. As digital finance continues to grow and develop, globalization is likely to remain a major driving force for the industry's development.

In conclusion, the key factors driving the development of digital finance include technological innovation and digital transformation, robust legal frameworks and regulatory environments, user demands and experiences, data privacy and security, reliable financial infrastructure and interoperability, education, and outreach. These factors collectively drive the rapid development of digital finance and bring about new financial tools and services. However, the digital finance industry also faces challenges such as the risks of cyber-attacks and data breaches, as well as the impact on traditional financial institutions. Therefore, establishing sound regulatory policies, enhancing consumer trust and security, building partnerships, and adapting to the trend of globalization are key to driving the sustainable development of digital finance. With ongoing technological advancements and market evolution, digital finance will continue to play a vital role globally, providing people with more diverse, convenient, and reliable financial services.

1.3 Challenges and Opportunities Brought by Digital Finance

As a rapidly developing industry, digital finance is full of challenges and opportunities. As of 2021, the global investment in the digital finance sector has exceeded 90 billion USD and has been continuously growing over the past few years. This trend reflects the immense potential of the digital finance market and optimistic expectations for future development. The growth of digital finance has brought lucrative investment opportunities to investors and also driven innovation and upgrades in financial services. However, the digital finance sector also faces several challenges. The rapid development and emergence of new technologies, business models, and constantly changing regulatory environments pose risks and uncertainties to investors.

A cross-disciplinary perspective on the development of digital finance can cover multiple fields, such as finance, computer science, data science, economics, law, etc. From the viewpoints of these different disciplines, the development of digital finance faces the following challenges:

Firstly, technological innovation Anderson and Moore (2006)challenges are crucial issues in the digital finance sector. Although technological advancements bring tremendous opportunities to digital finance, the introduction and application of new technologies also face a series of challenges. These include security issues, such as network security and data privacy protection, as well as requirements for stability and reliability. Digital finance companies need to invest significant resources and efforts to address these technological challenges and ensure the security and stability of their systems.

Secondly, financial regulatory Zohar (2015) challenges are another significant issue in the digital finance sector. Due to the rapid development of digital finance, regulatory mechanisms and policies need to be timely updated and improved. Some activities in the digital finance sector may pose risks, such as data privacy breaches, cyber-attacks, fraud, etc. Therefore, establishing sound regulatory frameworks, strengthening compliance, and protecting the interests of investors and users are essential tasks in the development of digital finance.

Additionally, data governance Rubinstein (2013) challenges are another aspect that the digital finance sector faces. Digital finance relies on technologies such as big data and artificial intelligence, which also bring issues related to data privacy and data security. Digital finance companies need to ensure proper governance and management of data, safeguarding the security and privacy of user data while fully utilizing the value of data for business innovation and targeted marketing.

Finally, talent development challenges are a significant issue in the digital finance sector. Digital finance requires comprehensive talents with knowledge and skills in various aspects, such as finance, technology, data, etc. However, such comprehensive talents are currently relatively scarce, and the industry needs to cultivate and attract more professionals to meet the demands of industry development. This involves exploration and innovation in higher education, training, talent introduction policies, etc., to improve the supply and quality of talents in the digital finance field.

Furthermore, from a macro perspective, digital finance faces challenges related to consumer trust, regulatory frameworks, and cross-border operations.

Firstly, consumer trust is a crucial factor in the development of digital finance. Consumer trust and confidence in digital financial services are influenced by risk perception and fair treatment, among other factors. Digital finance companies need to invest in security measures and effective communication strategies to build consumer trust and confidence. Transparent fee and pricing policies, as well as clear and concise information disclosure, can increase consumers' trust in digital financial services.

Secondly, digital finance faces complex regulatory frameworks. Different countries and regions have varying regulatory policies, presenting challenges for digital finance companies operating across borders. Digital finance companies need to understand the regulatory environment in each market and develop effective compliance strategies. Close cooperation with regulatory authorities is essential to ensuring the safety, reliability, and protection of consumers' interests in digital financial services.

Additionally, cross-border operations bring regulatory framework issues in different jurisdictions. Digital finance companies must comply with constraints from different laws and regulatory frameworks, especially concerning data protection and privacy. Transparent data collection and sharing practices and compliance with relevant laws and regulations are crucial aspects that digital finance companies must prioritize.

Furthermore, another challenge that digital finance faces is addressing issues related to financial knowledge and education, including lack of awareness and understanding, security concerns, limited access, and complexity.

Digital financial tools and services can often be too complex for individuals with limited financial knowledge or experience, making it difficult for them to understand how to use these tools and services effectively. Digital finance companies need to design user-friendly interfaces, provide simplified and easy-to-understand operational processes to ensure that ordinary users can fully utilize the functionality and advantages of digital finance.

Certainly, despite these challenges, digital finance also brings forth many opportunities.

Firstly, the application of artificial intelligence (AI) in the digital finance sector can provide personalized financial advice and services. By analyzing vast amounts of data and individual characteristics, AI can offer customized financial recommendations and solutions based on users' needs and preferences. Such personalized services contribute to increased customer satisfaction and loyalty, providing digital finance companies with a competitive advantage.

Secondly, AI can enhance fraud detection and risk management. By analyzing user behavior patterns and transaction data, AI can identify abnormal and suspicious activities, promptly detecting and preventing fraudulent behavior. This helps protect users' financial security and enhances the reputation and reliability of digital finance companies.

Additionally, blockchain Gang (2018) technology also holds potential for application in the digital finance sector. The decentralized, tamper-resistant, and traceable nature of blockchain can improve the security and transparency of transactions. Through blockchain technology, digital finance companies can offer more secure, efficient, and cost-effective transaction and settlement services.

Overall, the development of digital finance, with the application of new technologies like AI and blockchain, is expected to enhance transaction efficiency, improve risk management and fraud prevention, and provide consumers with more cost-effective and personalized financial services. For digital finance companies, investing in technological innovation and research and development is essential to maintain competitiveness and seize these opportunities.

As an AI professional, I am eager to explore its profound impact on the digital finance field from a unique perspective. Artificial Intelligence is no longer a foreign term in the tech world; its power, especially in the FinTech domain, is shaping a brand-new future. Here are some of my thoughts on how AI technology influences digital finance.

Firstly, we need to recognize the development of large-scale general models, which has become a significant advancement in AI and has also triggered transformative changes in digital finance. These powerful models can handle massive financial data and, with their insight, identify patterns and trends hidden within the data, making accurate predictions about future market conditions.

Taking econometric models as an example, they employ complex statistical techniques to analyze economic data and forecast future economic trends. These models have made remarkable achievements in analyzing relationships between economic variables such as interest rates, inflation rates, and stock prices. They provide us with a deeper understanding of the rules governing economic operations.

Another noteworthy large-scale model is time-series models. They utilize sophisticated statistical techniques to analyze time-series data, such as stock prices or exchange rates, and predict future trends. These models have played a crucial role in the financial sector by providing in-depth analyses of financial data and enabling highly accurate market trend predictions.

Furthermore, we should explore the impact of AI technology on risk management in digital finance. AI models have the ability to analyze customer data in real-time and identify potential risks, such as fraud or credit defaults. This capability not only helps financial institutions make more precise decisions but also effectively reduces the risk of financial losses.

In recent years, computer scientists and finance experts have collaborated to develop a range of AI-based financial risk management tools and technologies. These tools harness the power of algorithms to analyze vast amounts of financial data, thereby identifying patterns and trends that may indicate potential risks. One noteworthy application area is fraud detection. AI algorithms can analyze financial transaction data in real-time and identify abnormal patterns or situations that may indicate fraudulent activities. Over time, these algorithms can continuously learn and adapt, making them more efficient in responding to emerging types of fraud.

Another critical application area is credit risk assessment. AI algorithms can analyze individuals' financial history, credit scores, and other relevant data to assess their creditworthiness and potential default risks. This helps financial institutions make wiser lending decisions, thereby reducing the risk of loan defaults.

Furthermore, AI plays a crucial role in market risk management. It can analyze market data and identify potential risks associated with specific investments or portfolios. AI algorithms can also be used to optimize investment portfolios by identifying and selecting investments with lower correlations to reduce risk. In this age of information explosion, the application of AI technology in risk management demonstrates its immense potential and value, bringing revolutionary changes to risk management in the digital finance field.

Lastly, AI technology has numerous applications in customer service in the digital finance domain. AI models can provide personalized recommendations and services based on customers' individual preferences and financial history. This not only enhances customer satisfaction and loyalty but also generates more revenue and profits for financial institutions.

Of particular significance is the advent of Artificial Intelligence technologies represented by Generative Pre-trained Transformers (GPT) models. This technology marks a new era of generative AI and has a tremendous impact on our understanding of digital finance.

Regarding GPT technology, we can conduct an in-depth analysis from the following perspectives:

Intelligent Customer Service: In the digital finance industry, there is a huge demand for customer service, and human resources costs can be high. Using GPT models for intelligent customer service can provide financial institutions with 24/7 online support, reducing customer service costs, and increasing customer satisfaction.

Sentiment Analysis: GPT models can be used to analyze large amounts of text data, such as user comments and social media content in the digital finance industry. Through sentiment analysis, financial institutions can better understand user needs and emotional states, thereby improving marketing and service effectiveness.

Investment Decision-making: Investment decisions require analysis of a large amount of economic and financial data. GPT models can help financial institutions achieve semantic understanding and natural language descriptions of financial data, improving the accuracy and efficiency of investment decision-making.

Risk Control: In the digital finance domain, risk control involves identifying and classifying a large number of risk events. GPT models can assist financial institutions in automatically classifying and identifying risk events, thereby improving the efficiency and accuracy of risk control.

Text Generation: In digital finance, there is a need for natural language generation of contracts, reports, announcements, and other text information. GPT models can help financial institutions automatically generate text information, improving efficiency and accuracy.

The opportunities brought about by the digital finance field are diverse and can have many positive impacts on financial service providers and consumers. For example:

Financial Inclusion: Digital finance helps bring financial services to those who are not accessible by traditional financial systems, especially in remote areas and low-income groups. This helps improve financial inclusion, promote economic growth, and development.

Improved Access: Digital finance makes financial services more accessible, allowing more people to conveniently and efficiently use banking, insurance, and investment products.

Cost Savings: Digital finance helps reduce costs for financial service providers, enabling them to offer lower fees to customers and higher profit margins for financial institutions.

Enhanced Customer Experience: Digital finance provides better customer experiences through personalized and user-friendly services, increasing customer loyalty and satisfaction.

Financial Innovation: Digital finance drives innovation in the financial industry, creating new products and services, such as peer-to-peer lending, crowdfunding, and mobile payments. The application of artificial intelligence technology allows financial institutions to develop new products and services that meet customer demands and improve overall performance.

In this analysis, we will focus on the relevant theories related to innovation in the digital finance domain, mainly including the following aspects:

Financial Innovation Theory: This theory focuses on the innovation of financial products, services, and business models, especially in combination with the characteristics of digital technology, to explore how to promote the innovative development of digital finance. This includes innovations such as digital currencies based on blockchain technology, P2P online lending, and robo-advisors.

Financial Technology (FinTech) Theory: FinTech theory focuses on the application of technologies such as artificial intelligence, big data, cloud computing, and blockchain in the financial domain. By combining these technologies with financial business, it can drive the development of digital finance, improve financial service efficiency, and enhance user experience.

Financial Regulatory Theory: This theory focuses on the goals, institutions, regulations, and other aspects of financial regulation, emphasizing that the innovation in the digital finance domain requires close collaboration with regulatory authorities. By formulating appropriate regulatory policies and systems for digital financial businesses, it can promote the healthy development of digital finance.

Digital Economy Theory: Digital economy theory focuses on aspects such as digital technology, digital platforms, and digital markets, viewing digital finance as an important component of the digital economy. It explores how to integrate digital economy theory with the digital finance domain to promote innovation and development in the digital finance field.

From an economic perspective, the relationship between digital finance and innovation can be further analyzed from the following aspects:

Theory of Information Asymmetry: The development of digital finance helps to eliminate information asymmetry, improve market transaction efficiency, promote market competition, and maximize social welfare. By utilizing technologies like big data and artificial intelligence, financial institutions can better acquire and analyze information, reducing information gaps between buyers and sellers.

Innovation-Driven Theory: Innovations and technological advancements in the digital finance domain can bring new growth points and momentum to the economy, driving high-quality economic development. The application of financial technology, blockchain, and other technologies can stimulate financial industry innovations, providing more possibilities for socio-economic development.

Financial Deepening Theory: The development of digital finance can expand financial services and market depth, providing more financing channels and investment opportunities for the socio-economy, further promoting economic growth. For example, digital finance can offer more financing channels for small and medium-sized enterprises and expand the scope of financial institution business.

Digital Economy Theory: Digital finance is an integral part of the digital economy, and the application of digital technologies will bring more innovation and transformation to financial services. Digital finance can provide individuals and businesses with more convenient and personalized financial services, promoting the emergence of new markets and business models.

References

Anderson, R., & Moore, T. (2006). The economics of information security. Science, 314(5799)

Di Gang. Innovative Application of Blockchain Technology in Digital Bill Scenarios [J]. Chinese Financier, 2018 (05)

GSMA. (2019). State of the Industry Report on Mobile Money. GSMA Mobile Money Programme.

Meng Nana, Lin Peng. Research on the Adaptability of Regulatory Sandbox Mechanism and Financial Technology Innovation in China: From the Perspective of Inclusive Regulation [J]. Southern Finance, 2018 (01)

Pew Research Center. (2019). Mobile Connectivity in Emerging Economies

Rubinstein, I. S. (2013). Big data: The end of privacy or a new beginning?. International Data Privacy Law, 3(2)

Werbach, K. (2018). The Blockchain and the New Architecture of Trust. MIT Press

World Bank. (2017). The Global Findex Database 2017: Measuring Financial Inclusion and the Fintech Revolution. World Bank Publications.

Zhou, T., & Lu, Y. (2016). A Comparative Study of Mobile Payment Procedures. Journal of Electronic Commerce Research, 17(2)

Zohar, A. (2015). Bitcoin: under the hood. Communications of the ACM, 58(9)

Chapter 2
Research on Monetary Theory in Digital Finance

2.1 The Importance of Monetary Theory in Digital Finance

Monetary theory, as a core element of digital finance, provides us with a powerful framework to understand the role of money in the economic system and the impact of monetary policy on the financial markets. From an economic perspective, monetary theory plays a crucial role in analyzing the close relationship between money and economic activities. At a functional level, monetary theory offers a comprehensive theoretical structure for analyzing the impact of monetary policy on inflation, employment, and economic growth.

In this chapter, we will review and summarize the research approaches of scholars to construct a rigorous theoretical framework for the readers. Through this framework, we can gain a deeper and more systematic understanding of the essence of monetary theory in digital finance and better grasp its role in real economic activities.

Firstly, we will explore how digital currencies affect inflation.

First, digital currencies can influence inflation by adjusting the money supply Bordo and Levin (2017). For example, some central banks are considering using digital currencies as a policy tool to directly issue digital currencies to the public to adjust the money supply and control inflation rates. Additionally, digital currencies may alter the transmission mechanism of monetary policy, thus affecting the efficacy of monetary policy.

Secondly, digital currencies have the potential to enhance the transparency and predictability of monetary policy Meaning et al. (2018). For instance, the blockchain technology behind digital currencies can increase the transparency of transactions, enabling regulatory authorities to more easily monitor the money supply and inflation rates. Moreover, digital currencies can improve the predictability of monetary policy because their issuance and management can be more transparent and standardized.

Lastly, digital currencies could weaken the effectiveness of central bank's monetary policy. For instance, digital currencies may lead to capital outflows, making it challenging for central banks to implement their monetary policies. Furthermore,

Z. Liu and W. Hou, *Digital Finance*, https://doi.org/10.1007/978-981-99-7305-7_2

digital currencies may render monetary policies ineffective since the issuance and circulation of digital currencies are beyond the control of central banks, making it difficult to control the money supply and inflation rates.

Secondly, let's discuss how digital currencies impact the job market.

First, digital currencies are likely to have a positive impact on employment. They can stimulate innovation and entrepreneurial activities, thereby creating more job opportunities. For example, digital currencies can lower payment costs, promote cross-border payments, and boost e-commerce, leading to increased job opportunities.

However, digital currencies may also have negative effects on employment. For instance, the emergence of digital currencies might lead to a reduction in the size of traditional banks and financial institutions, thus affecting job opportunities.

Lastly, the impact of digital currencies on employment could be complex. Some studies suggest that the development of digital currencies could trigger a profound transformation of the financial system, which in turn affects the organizational structure and employment patterns within the financial industry. For example, the emergence of digital currencies may drive financial institutions towards more decentralized and distributed organizational forms, thereby altering employment patterns.

Thirdly, let's explore how digital currencies affect economic growth.

First, the emergence of digital currencies provides new financing channels for the capital market. Their technological features make capital market financing more convenient and efficient. The fast transaction speed and low transaction fees facilitate faster and more cost-effective financing, improving the efficiency of corporate financing and thus driving economic growth.

Second, the emergence of digital currencies can reduce the costs and time involved in payments and settlements Tapscott and Tapscott (2016). Compared to traditional payment and settlement methods that rely on banks and other financial institutions, digital currencies enable intermediary-free and decentralized payment and settlement.

Finally, the emergence of digital currencies promotes innovative Swan (2015) developments within the financial industry, further driving economic growth. For instance, the integration of digital currencies with smart contracts enables more complex financial products and services. Digital currencies can also be applied in fields such as the Internet of Things (IoT) and big data, creating more business opportunities.

Indeed, we can observe that the relationship between monetary policy and digital currencies mainly manifests in the following aspects:

Firstly, the issuance and management of digital currencies do not rely on traditional central banks Mersch (2017). This makes it challenging for central banks to control the quantity and value of digital currencies, thereby affecting their monetary policies. For example, an excessive supply of digital currencies may lead to inflation and economic instability.

Secondly, the emergence of digital currencies complicates the implementation of monetary policy. Traditional monetary policies primarily rely on adjusting interest rates and money supply to control economic growth and inflation. However, the advent of digital currencies introduces additional complexities in implementing monetary policies. For instance, digital currencies may affect factors like interest rates and money supply, thereby influencing the effectiveness of monetary policies.

Finally, the emergence of digital currencies enhances the transparency and openness of monetary policy. The blockchain technology used in digital currencies ensures transparent and public transaction records, thereby making the implementation of monetary policy more transparent and open. This can help central banks better monitor economic and market conditions, leading to more effective monetary policy implementation.

So, in what aspects does digital currency impact policies? We have summarized some representative viewpoints:

Firstly, digital currencies bring new challenges to the regulation of digital finance. Digital currencies threaten traditional monetary systems as they can bypass central banks and traditional financial institutions. Additionally, research indicates that the lack of regulation in the Initial Coin Offering (ICO) market results in fraudulent activities and mispricing of assets Zetzsche et al. (2017). Therefore, policymakers should establish new regulatory frameworks to protect investors and enhance market efficiency.

Secondly, the potential of digital currencies as a monetary system is often overlooked. Scholars call for attention to the potential of digital currencies as a more efficient and decentralized monetary system. However, they also point out challenges in using digital currencies as a medium of exchange, such as volatility in value and lack of widespread adoption.

Expanding and considering the relationship between monetary policy and digital currencies, with references to classical monetary theory analysis, we can draw the following conclusions:

Firstly, monetary policy can influence the demand for digital currencies, thereby impacting their value. According to the quantity theory of money, an increase in the money supply leads to rising prices. Similarly, for digital currencies, an increase in the money supply may increase demand and, consequently, raise their value. Hence, an expansionary monetary policy may boost demand for digital currencies, while a contractionary policy may decrease it.

Secondly, monetary policy also affects the stability of digital currencies. Digital currencies are subject to significant price fluctuations and are influenced by market volatility. Changes in monetary policy can impact the stability of digital currencies. For example, an interest rate hike by the central bank may reduce demand for digital currencies, leading to a decrease in their value. Conversely, a rate cut may increase demand and boost their value.

Lastly, monetary policy can shape the regulatory environment for digital currencies. The regulatory framework for digital currencies is still evolving, and monetary policy can play a vital role in developing these regulations. Central banks can enact regulations that restrict the use of digital currencies or provide incentives to promote their adoption. These measures may include limiting digital currency transactions or offering incentives to encourage their use.

Indeed, besides influencing monetary policy, we can observe that digital currencies also exert impacts on the monetary system in other ways:

Firstly, digital currencies have the potential to disrupt traditional monetary systems. They can provide a more efficient and decentralized monetary system, reducing transaction costs and promoting inclusive finance. Additionally, digital finance can lower financial transaction costs and enhance financial literacy. To address these impacts, policymakers need to establish new regulatory frameworks to support the development of digital finance and ensure its benefits reach the entire society.

Secondly, regulating digital finance presents a challenge. Digital currencies pose a threat to traditional monetary systems as they can bypass central banks and traditional financial institutions. Therefore, policymakers need to develop new regulatory frameworks to address the risks and opportunities brought about by digital currencies. Additionally, regulatory agencies need to engage in international cooperation to establish consistent regulatory standards.

Lastly, Central Bank Digital Currencies (CBDCs) have the potential to impact monetary policy. CBDCs have the potential to provide a more efficient and secure payment system, but they also pose risks to financial stability and privacy. Thus, central banks need to carefully consider the design and implementation of CBDCs to ensure they do not disrupt monetary policy or financial stability.

Next, let us understand the impact of digital currencies from an economic perspective. Based on classical monetary theory, we can further extend our analysis with the following three points:

Firstly, the Quantity Theory of Money suggests that an increase in the money supply leads to a rise in the price level. However, digital currencies may disrupt this relationship by providing a fixed money supply that central banks cannot manipulate. This could lead to higher price stability and a more predictable monetary system, resulting in positive effects on the economy.

Secondly, the Monetary Policy Transmission Theory indicates that changes in the money supply and interest rates impact the real economy through channels such as investment, consumption, and exports. Digital currencies may disrupt these channels by offering more direct means of transactions for individuals and businesses without intermediaries. Such innovations could enhance economic efficiency and establish a more direct link between monetary policy and economic outcomes.

Thirdly, the Optimal Currency Area Theory suggests that a single currency should be shared by a group of countries with similar economic characteristics to maximize efficiency and stability. However, digital currencies may disrupt this theory by providing a currency that is not tied to any specific country or region. This could foster greater global integration and a more interconnected global economy, leading to broader economic benefits.

In addition to that, we also see that the impact of Central Bank Digital Currencies (CBDCs) is a hot topic in the financial field. Clearly, the introduction of CBDCs can affect the transmission mechanism of monetary policy by changing how monetary policy influences the economy. According to the Monetary Policy Transmission Theory, changes in the money supply and interest rates affect the real economy through channels such as investment, consumption, and exports.

With the introduction of CBDCs, central banks may have more direct control over the money supply and interest rates, thus forming a more effective transmission mechanism. By referencing classical financial theories, we can expand our thinking in three aspects:

Firstly, the Seigniorage Theory points out that central banks profit by issuing currency at a cost below its face value. However, with the introduction of CBDCs, central banks may lose this revenue source as CBDCs do not incur printing costs like traditional currencies. This could affect the central bank's ability to implement monetary policy and lead to changes in how monetary policy is financed.

Secondly, the Quantity Theory of Money suggests that an increase in the money supply leads to a rise in the price level. With the introduction of CBDCs, central banks may have more direct control over the money supply, leading to a more predictable and stable monetary system. The launch of CBDCs also has the potential to improve the efficiency of monetary policy by reducing the time lag between policy changes and their impact on the economy.

Thirdly, the Currency Substitution Theory indicates that individuals and businesses may choose to use foreign currency instead of their domestic currency if they have more confidence in the stability of the foreign currency. With the introduction of CBDCs, individuals and businesses may be more inclined to use their own country's CBDC since it will be supported by the central bank and may be more stable than traditional currencies.

Finally, let's examine the thoughts of some renowned economists in this field. In this section, we will quote the viewpoints of several Nobel laureates in economics to see how their theories help us understand digital finance.

Milton Friedman: Friedman was a renowned American economist, a professor of economics at the University of Chicago, and a prominent figure in the second generation of the Chicago School of Economics. He was awarded the Nobel Prize in Economics in 1976 for his contributions to consumption analysis, monetary supply theory, history, and the complexity of stabilization policy. He is considered one of the most important and influential economists of the twentieth century.

In his monetary theory works, Friedman emphasized the importance of stable prices and the role of monetary policy in achieving this goal. In the context of digital finance, stable prices are crucial for the operation of cryptocurrencies and other digital assets. Therefore, monetary policy must adapt to the unique characteristics of digital finance to ensure price stability. Friedman highlighted the role of the money supply in determining inflation and the importance of central banks in controlling the money supply in his monetary theory works. However, the rise of cryptocurrencies and digital assets challenges the traditional view of money as a physical exchange medium.

Paul Krugman: Krugman is an American economist and a columnist for The New York Times. He was a professor in the economics department at Princeton University and is a representative of the New Keynesian economics. In 2008, Krugman was awarded the Nobel Prize in Economics for his analysis of trade patterns and location of economic activity.

Krugman's work in international trade and globalization is relevant to digital finance as it has led to the establishment of a global financial system. In this system, digital finance plays an increasingly important role in facilitating cross-border transactions and reducing transaction costs. However, risks associated with digital finance, such as cybersecurity and financial stability, must be addressed through international cooperation and coordination.

Joseph Stiglitz: Stiglitz is a Nobel laureate in Economics (2001) and a recipient of the John Bates Clark Medal (1979). He has previously served as the Chief Economist and Senior Vice President of the World Bank. Stiglitz made significant contributions in the field of information economics and is an important member of the New Keynesian economics.

His work in information economics emphasizes the importance of transparency and information sharing in digital finance. He believes that as digital finance becomes increasingly complex, obtaining reliable and accurate information is crucial for making wise decisions. Therefore, policymakers must ensure that digital finance is transparent and open to all stakeholders. Stiglitz's work highlights the necessity of transparency and information sharing in digital finance to ensure the efficient functioning of financial markets.

By analyzing these comprehensive and diverse perspectives, we can gain a broader understanding of various aspects of digital finance and have a more accurate understanding of its development trends and potential impacts.

2.2 Traditional Monetary Theory and Its Relevance to Digital Finance

After understanding the importance of monetary theory in digital finance, we return to the considerations of traditional monetary theory to expand upon the points mentioned earlier and help us form a framework for understanding digital finance. In fact, traditional monetary theory focuses on controlling the money supply to stabilize prices and promote economic growth and has been the basis of monetary policy for decades. However, the rise of digital finance challenges the traditional views of money and the role of central banks in the monetary system.

In financial capitalism, financial institutions profit by creating and managing assets, and the fluctuations in financial markets have a significant impact on the entire economy. Therefore, the supply and value of money are influenced not only by the regulation of central banks but also by the actions of financial institutions and the market. Commercial banks and investment banks increase the money supply through lending and financing, and the volatility of hedge funds and the stock market also affect the value of money.

The emergence of digital finance further changes the dynamics of money supply and value. Digital finance, based on the internet and blockchain technology, creates new financial instruments and technologies, such as digital currencies, blockchain, and smart contracts. These tools and technologies make the issuance and management of money no longer dependent on central banks but are achieved through decentralized mechanisms. For example, the issuance and management of certain digital currencies are collectively decided and supervised by participants in the blockchain network. This makes the supply and value of digital currencies influenced by different factors and mechanisms, not just central bank regulation.

Therefore, digital finance presents a challenge to traditional monetary theory, requiring us to rethink the nature of money, the supply–demand relationship, and the mechanisms of value formation. It also prompts researchers and policymakers to reassess the applicability of monetary policy and contemplate how to maintain financial stability and economic development goals in the digital finance era.

Next, we will cite the views of several renowned economists and financial experts on the traditional monetary theory and its relevance to digital finance, aiming to analyze the relationship between digital finance and traditional monetary theory.

Robert Mundell, the Nobel laureate in Economics in 1999 and known as the "Father of the Euro," laid the foundation for the Optimum Currency Area theory. His perspective is closely related to digital finance, emphasizing that the emergence of digital currencies has led to the establishment of a global financial system but has also brought challenges in global digital financial regulation.

Mundell believes that the traditional monetary theory still applies to the field of digital finance. He points out that monetary policy's management of money supply and interest rates has significant implications for the economy and financial markets, including digital finance. He emphasizes that policymakers need to focus on monetary stability and avoid excessive inflation that could undermine the value of digital currencies.

Mundell is concerned about the challenges faced in using digital currencies as exchange mediums. He calls for policymakers to establish new regulatory frameworks to address these challenges and ensure the stability of digital currencies.

Furthermore, Mundell discusses the potential of digital currencies in promoting economic growth Schär (2020). He believes that digital currencies can reduce transaction costs and facilitate inclusive finance, thus stimulating economic activities. He recommends that policymakers encourage the development of digital finance while ensuring monetary and financial stability.

Ben Bernanke: Ben Bernanke is an American economist and former chairman of the Federal Reserve Board. He was awarded the Nobel Prize in Economics in 2022. In his works on monetary policy, Bernanke emphasizes the importance of central banks in promoting financial stability and ensuring economic growth. He highlights that central banks need to adapt to the unique characteristics of digital finance to ensure their effectiveness in the monetary system. His main points are as follows:

Firstly, Clear Definition of Digital Currencies: Bernanke believes that traditional monetary theories can still be applied to digital currencies, but policymakers need to establish a clear definition of what constitutes a digital currency.

Secondly, Potential Benefits of Digital Currencies: Bernanke points out that digital currencies can provide financial services to individuals and businesses who are excluded from the traditional financial system, such as those without access to bank accounts or with limited banking services.

Thirdly, Regulatory Challenges of Digital Currencies: Bernanke highlights that digital currencies can be used for illegal activities, such as money laundering and financing terrorism, posing risks to financial stability and consumer protection.

In addition to the aforementioned economists who have conducted in-depth research on this topic, many scholars have also published different research findings. For example, economists Robert Kaufman and Önür İnèş, believe that traditional monetary theory is still relevant to digital finance. They argue that despite digital currencies operating outside the traditional banking system, they still adhere to the same economic principles as the traditional financial system, such as supply and demand dynamics and the impact of macroeconomic factors on currency value.

However, there are also viewpoints suggesting that digital finance requires a reevaluation of traditional monetary theory. Economists David Yermack and Michael Casey, in an article published in the "International Finance Analysis Review," argue that digital finance necessitates a rethinking of traditional monetary theory. They point out that digital currencies challenge traditional assumptions about the role of central banks, the nature of money, and the relationship between currency and nation-states.

Clearly, these divergent viewpoints indicate that economists have different interpretations of the relationship between traditional monetary theory and digital finance. Some believe that digital finance fundamentally disrupts traditional monetary theory, while others believe that traditional economic principles still apply in the current financial environment. Additionally, some economists propose reexamining traditional monetary theory to better understand the unique characteristics and impacts of digital finance. Our perspective is that while digital finance poses challenges to traditional monetary theory, we can still draw upon its underlying logic and framework. During this process, we need to reevaluate the role of digital finance to gain a deeper understanding of the effects it generates.

2.3 The Impact of Digital Finance on Monetary Theory

In the preceding discussion, we explored the challenges faced by traditional monetary theory in the advent of digital finance. This revolution has reshaped our understanding of the concept of currency and the role played by central banks in the monetary system. So, how will digital finance continue to impact monetary theory in the long term?

Financial capitalism, as an economic system based on the operation of financial capital, encounters the emergence of a novel concept in the financial domain—digital finance. Rooted in blockchain technology, digital finance encompasses various aspects, including digital currencies, cryptographic assets, and smart contracts. The development of digital finance has had profound effects on monetary theory.

This chapter takes financial capitalism as a starting point to investigate how digital finance influences monetary theory, with the aim of outlining future development trends in this field.

First, let's examine the wave of monetization brought about by digital finance.

Monetization Menger (1892), a transformation in modern economic systems, has increasingly emphasized the role of currency in economic life, gradually replacing the barter system of exchange.

The development of digital finance has sparked a wave of monetization, accelerating the transformation of the role of currency in modern economic systems. The rise of digital finance technologies has acted as a catalyst for the process of monetization, enhancing the significance and liquidity of currency in economic life.

Digital finance has facilitated the popularization and use of digital currencies. With the advancement of digital finance technologies, digital currencies have become one of the mainstream payment tools, significantly improving payment efficiency. Digital currencies, characterized by convenience, security, and efficiency, have made currency circulation more convenient and rapid. People can make instant payments through methods like mobile phones and e-wallets, no longer relying on traditional physical currency exchange, thereby expediting economic activities.

Digital finance has driven the digitization of assets Tapscott and Tapscott (2016). Through the development of blockchain technology and digital assets, assets in the financial market can be digitized, forming a market for digital assets. This enables various types of assets such as stocks, bonds, commodities, etc., to be traded and circulated in digital form, expanding the scale and liquidity of assets. The rise of digital assets has also spurred innovation and development in the financial market, enhancing the influence of currency in the financial market.

Next, let's examine the challenges that digital finance poses to monetary theory stability.

In traditional monetary theory, central banks manage the money supply and maintain stable currency value through monetary policies. However, the decentralized nature of digital finance means that currency issuance and management are no longer solely controlled by central banks, but are determined by market participants and technological protocols together.

Firstly, digital finance's reliance on blockchain technology and decentralized cryptocurrencies means they are not subject to control by specific institutions or governments. This decentralization implies that the determination of currency supply and value is dispersed among a wide range of participants, rather than centralized in a central bank. This decentralization may lead to currency supply and value being influenced by market fluctuations and speculative behavior, causing instability and volatility.

Secondly, cryptocurrencies in digital finance face technological and security challenges. The issuance and transactions of cryptocurrencies rely on blockchain technology, which itself has potential security vulnerabilities and technical flaws. Technical malfunctions, network attacks, or market manipulation could lead to significant fluctuations in the value of cryptocurrencies, introducing uncertainty to currency stability.

Thirdly, digital finance encounters challenges in regulation and compliance. In the traditional monetary system, central banks have the responsibility to regulate and supervise financial markets to ensure the stable operation of currency. However, the decentralized nature of digital finance makes regulation and compliance more complex. The lack of a unified regulatory framework and regulatory authorities may lead to market disorder and risks, further challenging the stability of monetary theory.

Next, let's explore the financial globalization process driven by digital finance.

Financial globalization is an ongoing process where financial capital transcends borders, creating a global financial market. The rise of digital finance acts as a powerful driver, accelerating the pace of financial globalization and bridging the global distance of currencies. It provides a pathway for financial capital to flow freely across borders, reaching every corner of the global market.

Through digital payments and blockchain technology, cross-border payments and transfers have become easy and efficient, creating a seamlessly connected global economic system. International trade and capital flows are no longer restricted by cumbersome procedures and expensive fees but are rapidly propelling global economic development.

Digital finance has also brought unprecedented opportunities for investors. Regardless of their location, investors can easily access opportunities for cross-border investments, directing capital into projects and assets in various countries. This globalized investment portfolio not only offers individuals and businesses more choices but also promotes global capital flows and optimized resource allocation.

Enterprises have undergone revolutionary changes due to digital finance. Through digital trading platforms and blockchain technology, they can more easily obtain financing support on a global scale, driving corporate internationalization and globalization. The global financial market fostered by digital finance provides a broader stage for enterprises, enabling their voice and value to spread worldwide.

The globalization trend brought about by digital finance may challenge traditional monetary theory's interpretation of currency circulation and value. This calls for a need to reevaluate and revise monetary theory to better understand and adapt to the impact of digital finance on the global financial landscape.

We strive to build a comprehensive and in-depth theoretical framework and perspectives for our readers regarding the relationship between digital finance and monetary theory. Additionally, we aim to shed light on the key issues arising from the development of digital finance, enhancing readers' understanding of its future prospects. We encourage readers to stand on the shoulders of giants and continue advancing research and development in the field of digital finance and monetary theory. We firmly believe that this will enable us to better navigate the uncertainties of the future economic landscape and provide theoretical support for building a more robust and innovative financial system.

References

Bordo, M. D., & Levin, A. T. (2017). Central bank digital currency and the future of monetary policy. National Bureau of Economic Research.
Meaning, J., Dyson, B., Barker, J., & Clayton, E. (2018). Broadening narrow money: Monetary policy with a central bank digital currency. International Journal of Central Banking, 14(1)
Menger, K. (1892). On the Origin of Money. Economic Journal, 2
Mersch, Y. (2017). Digital base money: an assessment from the ECB's perspective. European Central Bank.
Schär, F. (2020). Decentralized Finance: On blockchain- and smart contract-based financial markets. Federal Reserve Bank of St. Louis Review, 102(1)
Swan, M. (2015). Blockchain: Blueprint for a new economy. O'Reilly Media, Inc.
Tapscott, D., & Tapscott, A. (2016). Blockchain revolution: how the technology behind bitcoin is changing money, business, and the world. Penguin.
Zetzsche, D. A., Buckley, R. P., Arner, D. W., & Föhr, L. (2017). The ICO gold rush: It's a scam, it's a bubble, it's a super challenge for regulators. University of Luxembourg Law Working Paper No. 2017–011.

Chapter 3
Digital Financial Innovation and Regulation

3.1 Innovative Digital Financial Models

In recent years, digital finance has emerged as a significant trend in the financial industry Zohar (2015a). This innovative domain encompasses a wide range of practices, including Bitcoin mining, supply chain finance, algorithmic trading, and more. The objectives of these innovative models are to enhance the efficiency and security of the financial system while driving the globalization and accessibility of financial services. However, the influence of digital finance extends far beyond these well-known areas; it also leads to a series of other innovative forms, such as virtual banking, digital securities, and smart contracts.

Virtual banking Chiu and Koeppl (2017) is a novel banking service model based on internet and mobile technology. Leveraging digital processes and automation, it offers customers more convenient, flexible, and cost-effective banking services. On the other hand, digital securities are an innovative way of issuing and trading securities using blockchain technology. They enable asset digitization, equity decentralization, and anonymous trading, promoting the globalization and innovation of capital markets. Smart contracts, built on blockchain technology, are an automated form of contract execution. They offer features like automatic execution, decentralization, and security, driving the automation and intelligence of financial services.

This section will delve into these innovative digital financial models to provide a comprehensive understanding of the field of digital finance.

Bitcoin mining, as a unique method of generating digital currency, has garnered widespread attention due to its economic and environmental impacts. Researchers have found that while Bitcoin mining has a noticeable impact on energy consumption and carbon dioxide emissions, it is relatively lighter on the environment compared to traditional banking systems. Additionally, Bitcoin mining represents an innovative form of digital finance, utilizing distributed ledger technology to ensure transaction security and anonymity while promoting the widespread adoption of digital currencies.

Z. Liu and W. Hou, *Digital Finance*, https://doi.org/10.1007/978-981-99-7305-7_3

Supply chain finance is another innovative model emerging in the realm of digital finance. Scholars have extensively examined the application of distributed ledger technology in supply chain finance and found that it enables automation, trustlessness, and decentralization in the supply chain financial processes, significantly reducing costs and risks. By employing blockchain technology, supply chain finance can achieve more efficient and secure capital flow and settlement, driving the development and popularization of this field. In other words, the main advantage of supply chain finance innovation lies in providing more diversified and flexible financing options for small and medium-sized enterprises.

Algorithmic trading, as another innovative form in the field of digital finance, has drawn the attention of scholars. Research has shown that the impact of algorithmic trading on market quality depends on market liquidity and investors' trading strategies. In high liquidity markets, algorithmic trading contributes to improved market efficiency and cost-effectiveness of trading. However, in low liquidity markets, algorithmic trading may lead to market imbalances and instability. Furthermore, algorithmic trading can utilize technologies such as data mining and machine learning to provide investors with more precise trading strategies and decision support.

In recent years, innovative digital finance has gradually become a significant driving force in the development of the financial industry. Let's explore the main types of current digital finance innovations:

Firstly, let's take a look at Decentralized Finance (DeFi).

Decentralized Finance (DeFi) refers to financial services built on decentralized blockchain networks, such as Ethereum. It disrupts traditional financial markets by providing innovative financial services based on decentralized blockchain networks. DeFi is an emerging financial model that utilizes blockchain and smart contract technology, allowing users to engage in financial transactions and various financial activities on decentralized platforms.

Innovative financial services within DeFi include decentralized lending, decentralized exchanges, stablecoins, liquidity mining, and more. These services offer faster, cheaper, and more accessible financial products and services without relying on traditional financial institutions. Users can participate in lending and borrowing through smart contracts and engage in liquidity provision and trading, enabling more efficient capital utilization and transaction execution.

DeFi's development also contributes to financial democratization by offering financial services opportunities to those excluded by traditional financial systems. Due to its decentralized nature, DeFi platforms are open to individuals and businesses worldwide, regardless of their background, geographical location, or financial status. This fosters equal access to financial services for a broader audience, promoting financial inclusivity and accessibility.

Next, let's explore Non-Fungible Tokens (NFTs).

Non-Fungible Tokens (NFTs) are a new and innovative digital financial model. NFTs represent unique digital assets that are verified on a blockchain network, allowing them to be bought, sold, and traded like physical assets.

NFTs Tapscott and Tapscott (2016) are disrupting traditional markets and creating new opportunities for creators and investors. They are used to represent a wide range of assets, including art, music, and collectibles. NFTs provide a secure and transparent way to verify ownership and authenticity of digital assets, changing the rules in the art and collectibles markets.

NFTs are also bringing innovation to emerging industries, but their value needs careful evaluation. For example, NFTs have the potential to reshape the gaming industry by enabling players to own and trade in-game assets. However, valuing and assessing the liquidity of NFTs can be challenging, as they are unique and difficult to compare with other assets. Unlike fungible assets, NFTs are not easily traded on traditional exchanges and require specialized markets. This poses challenges for NFT liquidity and valuation, requiring new tools and methods to assess their worth.

Finally, let's take a look at digital currencies.

Digital currencies, including Central Bank Digital Currencies (CBDCs), are rapidly gaining popularity. They represent a digital form of traditional currencies and are validated through blockchain networks. CBDCs are digital currencies issued and supported by central banks. We will analyze the innovations of CBDCs from the following perspectives:

Firstly, the introduction of CBDCs is expected to improve the efficiency of the payment system. It provides central banks with a new tool to influence the money supply and interest rates, thereby enhancing the efficiency and effectiveness of monetary policy. Additionally, CBDCs can reduce the demand for physical cash, thereby increasing the efficiency of the payment system and lowering costs associated with cash handling and storage.

Secondly, CBDCs have the potential to become inclusive financial instruments, but careful consideration is needed in their design and implementation. CBDCs allow individuals without traditional bank accounts to access digital payment systems and participate in the digital economy. However, to achieve this goal, the design of CBDCs must balance the benefits of improving the efficiency and effectiveness of monetary policy with the risks of financial stability and privacy. The implementation of CBDCs must also be carefully managed to ensure their smooth integration into existing payment systems and financial infrastructure. This requires comprehensive consideration of technological, economic, legal, and regulatory factors and close collaboration with relevant stakeholders to ensure the smooth advancement and sustainable development of CBDCs.

In addition to the aforementioned digital financial innovations, there are other forms of innovation worthy of attention. Here are three examples that help further expand our understanding of digital financial innovation:

Firstly, mobile banking is rapidly transforming the financial industry, providing customers with a convenient and user-friendly way to manage their finances. By offering services to those who cannot access traditional banking, mobile banking improves financial inclusivity. Furthermore, mobile banking drives innovation in financial products and services, such as mobile payments and peer-to-peer lending. However, mobile banking also faces challenges in security and privacy, as it involves the transmission of sensitive financial information over mobile networks. There are risks of data breaches, cyberattacks, and other network threats related to mobile banking.

A typical example is the mobile banking service in Kenya called M-PESA. M-PESA was launched in Kenya in 2007 by the mobile network operator Safaricom, allowing users to deposit, withdraw, pay bills, and transfer money using their mobile phones. The service has achieved tremendous success, with over 40 million active users in Kenya and other countries. One of the key factors contributing to its success is the proactive regulatory approach taken by the Central Bank of Kenya, ensuring that mobile banking services are safe and reliable for consumers.

Clearly, mobile banking has the potential to completely change the way people access financial services, especially in countries where traditional banking services are limited. However, the success of mobile banking relies on establishing a supportive regulatory environment that ensures the safety of financial services. Therefore, in the continuously evolving field of digital finance, it is crucial to establish a secure and reliable regulatory framework.

Secondly, in the field of digital finance, the widespread application of blockchain technology in the banking industry is another important innovation scene. Due to its unique technical features, blockchain has the potential to revolutionize the banking sector by providing secure and transparent financial transactions. Blockchain technology helps to reduce financial transaction costs, improve efficiency, and reduce fraud and other financial crime risks. By automating processes and reducing reliance on intermediaries, it can enhance the efficiency and reduce the costs in the banking industry.

However, blockchain technology faces challenges in terms of regulation and risk management, as its operation goes beyond traditional regulatory frameworks. Regulatory agencies find it difficult to supervise and enforce compliance in decentralized and open systems.

In the banking industry, Ripple is an example of blockchain technology. It is a blockchain-based payment system that allows banks and other financial institutions to conduct fast and secure cross-border transactions. Over 300 financial institutions worldwide are already using Ripple's payment system.

Another example is JPMorgan's Quorum platform, which is based on the Ethereum blockchain. Quorum develops a range of financial services, including smart contracts, trade financing, and supply chain finance. This demonstrates the potential of blockchain technology to change the banking industry by providing secure and transparent financial transactions.

However, the application of blockchain technology Schär (2021) in the banking industry will depend on the acceptance of new technology by financial institutions and the formulation of supportive regulatory policies. Additionally, blockchain technology needs to collaborate and integrate with existing banking systems and technologies. Financial institutions must work together to establish standardized protocols and systems to ensure interoperability and compatibility.

The last case is the rise of robo-advisory services in the financial industry. Robo-advisors provide a low-cost alternative to traditional financial advisors. We will analyze the impact of robo-advisors in this field from three perspectives:

(1) Improving access to financial advice: Robo-advisors improve access to financial advice by offering low-cost and convenient investment management services. They utilize algorithms and automation tools to provide personalized investment advice and portfolio management, democratizing access to financial advice and reducing investment costs for individual investors.
(2) Challenges in regulation and risk management: Robo-advisors present challenges in regulation and risk management as they operate in a rapidly changing and complex environment. There are risks associated with data breaches, hacking attacks, and other cyber threats related to robo-advisory services. Regulatory agencies must collaborate with industry stakeholders to develop frameworks that promote innovation while mitigating potential risks.
(3) Focus on performance and transparency: Robo-advisors need to focus on performance and transparency as they are typically evaluated based on investment returns and fees. Financial institutions must provide transparent information about their investment strategies, performance, and fees to build trust with their clients. They also need to continuously monitor and evaluate their investment strategies to ensure competitive returns and meet customer demands.

One example of robo-advisory service is Betterment Zheng (2017), which was launched in 2008 and currently manages over $20 billion in assets. Betterment utilizes algorithms to provide investment advice and portfolio management, charging as low as a 0.25% asset management fee. Another example of a robo-advisor is Wealthfront, which was launched in 2011 and currently manages over $11 billion in assets. Wealthfront also utilizes algorithms to provide investment advice and portfolio management, charging as low as a 0.25% asset management fee.

These robo-advisory services disrupt the traditional financial advisory industry by offering low-cost investment advice and portfolio management. However, their success will depend on their ability to provide high-quality investment advice, effective portfolio management, and their competitiveness against traditional financial advisors. In a competitive market, robo-advisors need to continuously improve their technology and algorithms to meet customer demands and gain trust.

It is essential to emphasize that whether it is traditional financial advisors or robo-advisory services, investment decisions should be made with caution as investments involve risks, and each individual's financial situation and goals are different. Before making any investment decisions, it is advisable to consult with a professional financial advisor and fully understand the associated risks and potential returns.

The innovation of digital financial models involves multiple aspects, including financial product innovation, technological innovation, business model innovation, and more. Here is a brief summary:

Firstly, digital financial product innovation serves as the cornerstone for driving innovation in digital financial models. It includes innovations in payments, lending, insurance, investments, and other areas. For example, smart contracts enabled by blockchain technology provide increased trust in internet finance, while decentralized credit assessment and asset management offer secure and reliable financial transactions. Digital currencies such as Bitcoin and Ethereum are becoming increasingly popular investment choices.

Secondly, digital financial technology innovation acts as a driving force behind the innovation of digital financial models. The applications of technologies such as blockchain, big data, and artificial intelligence have improved the efficiency and security of financial institutions. The use of big data enables financial institutions to assess and predict customer credit risks more accurately, providing more precise support for financial services.

Additionally, digital financial business model innovation is crucial for the development of digital financial models. Platform-based business models connect platforms and users, offering various financial services, enhancing user stickiness. Typical examples are Alipay and WeChat Pay. Sharing-based business models focus on the social attributes of digital finance, such as P2P online lending platforms, facilitating investment and borrowing through online social connections.

Lastly, the innovation of the digital financial ecosystem is at the core of digital financial model innovation. The digital financial ecosystem is a platform of digital financial services, constructed by digital financial enterprises through networking and social means. Cooperation among multiple parties, including governments, financial institutions, technology companies, and consumers, is critical for building the digital financial ecosystem. For instance, in China's digital financial ecosystem, the government encourages collaboration between fintech companies and traditional financial institutions to provide convenient and inclusive financial services.

3.2 Overview of Digital Financial Innovation and Regulation

Digital financial innovation and regulation Xiaoyan et al. (2016) are important topics in the current financial sector. The rapid development of digital finance and the emergence of innovative technologies bring new opportunities and challenges to the financial industry. Innovative digital financial products and services not only change the way people engage in financial activities but also impose new requirements on the operation and regulation of financial markets.

Firstly, let's discuss the challenges that digital financial innovation poses to the existing legal framework.

Digital financial innovation presents a series of challenges to the existing legal framework. Its speed and complexity may exceed the capacity of regulatory authorities. Particularly in the realm of virtual currencies, the current laws still lack clarity in terms of regulation. Virtual currencies possess characteristics such as anonymity, decentralization, and cross-border nature, making regulation more difficult. Additionally, in the field of internet finance, some platforms may engage in irregular issuance of wealth management products or use funds for illegal activities, which raises higher demands on regulatory authorities.

To address these challenges, it is necessary to establish regulatory policies that adapt to digital financial innovation. Regulatory authorities should strengthen supervision over digital financial institutions to ensure their compliance with regulatory requirements. In the case of virtual currencies, clear regulatory standards are required to strike a balance between regulation and innovation. Moreover, regulation in the internet finance sector should be strengthened to promote standardized industry development and prevent risks Hui'an (2018).

At the same time, digital financial innovation also needs to protect consumer interests. Regulatory authorities should establish clear regulatory standards and regulations to ensure the legality and transparency of digital financial products and services. Strengthening cooperation and communication between regulatory authorities and digital financial institutions is crucial in establishing sound regulatory compliance mechanisms and enhancing credibility and transparency.

Secondly, let's look at what kind of regulatory policies need to be formulated for digital financial innovation to protect the interests of consumers?

To protect consumer interests in the context of digital financial innovation, a series of regulatory policies need to be established:

Firstly, regulatory authorities should establish clear regulations and guidelines to ensure the legitimacy and transparency of digital financial products and services. This includes defining operational requirements, disclosure rules, and compliance procedures for digital financial institutions, ensuring that consumers have access to truthful and accurate information to make informed financial decisions.

Secondly, regulatory authorities should strengthen their oversight of digital financial institutions to ensure compliance with regulatory requirements and effective fulfillment of responsibilities. This can be achieved through strengthening audit mechanisms, regulatory reporting, and risk assessments. Comprehensive reviews of the operations of digital financial institutions should be conducted to ensure business compliance and risk management, while promptly identifying and addressing potential violations.

Thirdly, regulatory authorities should formulate appropriate regulatory policies to regulate the development of the digital financial industry and mitigate financial risks. In the case of virtual currencies, regulatory authorities can strengthen oversight, including compliance requirements, anti-money laundering measures, and investor protection, to ensure the security and legality of digital currency transactions. For internet financial platforms, regulatory authorities can provide guidance by defining business scope, fund management, and risk control requirements to prevent platform risks and protect the interests of investors.

Finally, let's discuss how digital financial innovation can maintain its vitality while complying with regulatory policies.

Digital financial innovation needs to maintain its vitality while adhering to regulatory policies. To achieve this goal, regulatory authorities should strive to formulate flexible policies that promote the development of digital financial innovation. When regulating the field of virtual currencies, regulatory agencies should balance the relationship between regulation and innovation and fully consider the characteristics and trends of digital financial innovation to ensure the protection of consumer interests.

On the other hand, digital financial institutions should focus on self-discipline and compliance to enhance credibility and transparency, thereby gaining trust from regulatory authorities. They should strengthen internal controls and risk management to ensure compliance and actively cooperate with regulatory agencies by providing transparent information and data. Additionally, drawing on foreign regulatory experiences, understanding the rules and practices of regulatory agencies, and engaging in communication and cooperation with them, can contribute to the establishment of a more stable and healthy digital financial ecosystem.

Going further, we can see that digital financial innovation has transformed the financial industry, creating new opportunities for financial institutions and consumers. However, these new technologies also bring new risks that require new regulatory frameworks.

From the perspective of digital financial regulation in various countries around the world, we can observe some characteristics:

Firstly, the challenge of digital financial innovation to existing legal frameworks lies in the lack of uniformity in digital financial regulation among different countries and regions, leading to regulatory arbitrage. Regulatory arbitrage allows companies to conduct business in countries with more lenient regulations to gain greater benefits. This phenomenon has resulted in the fragmentation of the global financial system, with different countries and regions adopting varying regulatory frameworks. As countries compete to provide lenient regulatory environments, a phenomenon of regulatory competition has emerged. To address this challenge, international cooperation is crucial. It is necessary to enhance cross-border collaboration and promote the establishment of a unified and coordinated global digital financial regulatory framework to prevent regulatory arbitrage.

Secondly, the rapid development of digital financial innovation has surpassed the pace of regulatory framework development, making traditional regulation inadequate to effectively address the rapidly changing digital financial landscape. Regulatory authorities are striving to keep up with the rapid changes in the digital financial industry, but this has also led to problems such as regulatory gaps, overlaps, and inconsistencies. Digital financial innovation brings about new risks, such as the emergence of decentralized finance (DeFi) and non-fungible tokens (NFTs), which present new challenges for regulatory authorities. The rise of DeFi and NFTs is testing the regulatory agencies' ability to keep pace with technological advancements. To keep up with the pace of digital financial innovation, regulatory sandboxes and other experimental measures are particularly important. Regulatory sandboxes allow companies to test new products and services in a controlled environment, enabling regulatory authorities to understand new risks and address regulatory loopholes. Therefore, regulatory authorities need to strengthen the regulation of technological innovation and adopt flexible regulatory approaches to ensure that regulatory frameworks remain consistent with the pace of digital financial innovation and can respond timely to emerging risks and challenges.

Lastly, to effectively manage risks related to digital finance, cross-border regulatory cooperation and coordination among regulatory authorities are essential. The cross-border nature of digital finance means that risks can spread rapidly across multiple jurisdictions, making cross-border regulatory collaboration critical. International standards and norms are necessary to promote regulatory coherence and consistency, ensuring that regulatory frameworks remain consistent and coherent across different countries and regions. Strengthening cross-border regulatory cooperation and developing unified international standards can effectively address the cross-border risks brought about by digital finance and ensure the stability and security of the global financial system.

From the above analysis, it is evident that regulatory policies for digital financial innovation face complex and ever-changing challenges. Regulatory authorities need to promote innovation while protecting consumers from risks such as fraud, cyber-attacks, and data breaches. Additionally, regulatory authorities must ensure that regulatory policies have cross-border adaptability to ensure financial technology companies maintain transparency when interacting with consumers and fully protect consumers from risks associated with digital financial innovation.

So, how should the digital financial regulatory framework be constructed? We believe that a feasible regulatory framework for digital financial innovation should include the following key elements:

(1) Risk-based approach: Regulatory authorities should adopt a risk-based regulatory approach, focusing on high-risk areas in the digital financial domain and allowing experimentation with new technologies in a controlled environment. Digital finance brings unique risks, and a risk-based regulatory approach enables tailored regulatory measures to address these risks.

    Moreover, a risk-based regulatory approach can promote innovation and competition in the digital financial domain. Companies can develop customized new products and services targeting specific risk scenarios under this framework, thereby driving innovation and competition.

    Additionally, the risk-based approach helps allocate regulatory resources effectively. By concentrating regulatory resources on the areas with the highest risks, this approach ensures the efficient utilization of regulatory resources.

(2) Regulatory sandbox: Regulatory authorities should establish regulatory sandboxes to allow controlled experimentation, testing new technologies, and ensuring consumers are adequately protected from risks. The introduction of regulatory sandboxes is crucial for promoting digital financial innovation and risk management. By permitting companies to test new products and services in a controlled environment, regulatory sandboxes facilitate innovation in the digital financial domain while ensuring effective management of related risks.

    Furthermore, regulatory sandboxes help regulatory authorities better understand newly emerging risks in digital finance. They also contribute to promoting regulatory coherence and consistency. By providing a common framework for testing new products and services, regulatory sandboxes can help enhance regulatory coherence and consistency across different countries and regions.

(3) Harmonized regulatory standards: Regulatory authorities should establish harmonized regulatory standards to facilitate cross-border cooperation and ensure the effectiveness of regulatory policies on a cross-border scale. As financial institutions conduct business across multiple jurisdictions, digital financial innovation poses new challenges for cross-border cooperation.

To address these challenges, regulatory authorities can collaborate by formulating common regulatory standards, sharing information and best practices, and cooperating in regulatory enforcement.

By establishing common regulatory standards, regulatory authorities can achieve consistency and coordination on a cross-border scale, ensuring financial institutions face similar regulatory requirements in different jurisdictions. Sharing information and best practices can help regulatory authorities in each country better understand the regulatory approaches of other nations and learn from each other's experiences. This cooperation can reduce opportunities for regulatory arbitrage and enhance the effectiveness and consistency of regulation.

Furthermore, collaboration in regulatory enforcement is also crucial. Regulatory authorities can strengthen information exchange and cooperation to jointly address cross-border financial crimes, fraud, and misconduct. By working together to combat cross-border violations, regulatory agencies can enhance the stability and transparency of financial markets.

(4) Consumer Protection: Regulatory authorities should establish a consumer protection framework tailored to the unique risks and opportunities brought about by digital financial innovation to ensure full protection of consumer rights. Balancing the demands of innovation with consumer protection is an important challenge faced by regulatory authorities, requiring proactive regulatory approaches and close collaboration with financial institutions to identify and mitigate risks through controlled experiments, such as regulatory sandboxes.

Through proactive regulatory approaches, regulatory authorities can identify and address potential risks in the field of digital financial innovation in advance. Collaborating with financial institutions, regulatory authorities can jointly develop regulatory standards and best practices to ensure that digital financial products and services meet consumer protection requirements. Additionally, enhancing communication and cooperation between regulatory authorities and financial institutions helps promptly understand the characteristics and risks of innovative products and services and take appropriate measures to protect consumer rights.

Furthermore, regulatory authorities should focus on consumer protection in terms of cybersecurity, data privacy, and financial literacy. They can develop relevant policies and regulations to require financial institutions to strengthen cybersecurity measures, safeguarding consumers' personal information and financial security. Simultaneously, through educational and promotional activities, consumer financial literacy and awareness can be raised, enabling consumers to better understand and respond to the risks brought about by digital financial innovation.

(5) Regulating Tech Companies Petralia et al. (2019): The entry of technology companies such as Google, Facebook, and Amazon into the financial industry and their provision of new products and services have posed new challenges for regulatory authorities. Their entry may give rise to unique risks and opportunities, necessitating the formulation of new regulatory frameworks to address these challenges.

Close collaboration with tech companies is also crucial. Regulatory authorities should establish strong partnerships with tech companies to facilitate information sharing and dialogue, ensuring that these companies fully understand and comply with regulatory requirements. This collaboration may involve regular communication and negotiation to jointly address challenges arising from the interplay of regulation and innovation.

In summary, the regulatory policy for digital financial innovation is a complex issue that requires careful consideration of the risks and rewards of new technologies. Regulatory authorities must balance innovation and consumer protection, address cross-border challenges, and develop new regulatory frameworks to adapt to the unique risks and opportunities brought about by tech companies.

3.3 The Challenges and Opportunities of Digital Financial Innovation and Regulation

Digital financial innovation is disrupting traditional financial services and having a profound impact on the entire financial industry. Emerging digital financial products and services, such as mobile payments, peer-to-peer lending, and digital currencies, are changing the way we perceive and use financial services. This provides financial institutions with opportunities to enhance efficiency, reduce costs, and expand financial service channels.

However, digital financial innovation also brings some challenges. Regulatory uncertainty is one of them, as regulatory authorities need to adapt to emerging technologies and business models and develop adaptable regulatory frameworks.

Moreover, cybersecurity risks are also a significant concern, as digital financial platforms and users face the risk of hacker attacks and data breaches. Additionally, consumer protection issues need attention to ensure that users' rights are protected in the digital financial environment.

To fully harness the potential of digital financial innovation, regulatory authorities and financial institutions need to work together to address these challenges. Regulatory authorities should create an environment that promotes innovation while protecting consumer rights and maintaining financial stability. Financial institutions need to invest in new technologies and talent and collaborate with other stakeholders to build infrastructure that supports the vibrant development of digital financial innovation. This includes establishing secure digital financial networks and payment systems, enhancing data privacy and security measures, and providing relevant training and education to increase public awareness and understanding of digital finance.

So, what are the main areas where these opportunities and challenges of digital financial innovation and regulation arise? In the final part of this chapter, we will expand and explore this topic, as well as supplement some aspects that were not emphasized in the previous sections.

Firstly, the improvement in efficiency and cost reduction in digital finance is indeed an obvious advantage. By digitizing financial transactions, reliance on physical infrastructure and intermediary institutions can be reduced, thereby lowering transaction costs and increasing transaction speed. Additionally, digital financial innovation provides financial institutions with better data and analysis tools, helping to improve risk management and mitigate the impact of risks. The application of advanced identity authentication and encryption technologies in digital finance can also enhance the security of financial transactions and reduce occurrences of fraudulent activities.

However, digital financial innovation also faces some challenges, with cybersecurity risk being one of the most critical. As more financial activities shift to online platforms, the risk of cyber attacks and data breaches increases.

Cyber attacks are considered the third-ranked global risk and pose a severe threat to the stability and integrity of the financial system. Specifically, we can analyze the challenges from three perspectives:

(1) Increase in frequency and complexity of cyber attacks: With the development of digital finance, the frequency and complexity of cyber attacks are also increasing. Forms of cyber attacks such as phishing, hacking, and ransomware attacks pose serious threats to digital financial institutions, potentially leading to financial losses and reputational damage. To address these risks, financial institutions need to implement robust cybersecurity measures, including strengthening defense mechanisms, using advanced encryption technologies, and implementing multi-layered security controls.
(2) Blockchain technology enhances security: The use of blockchain technology can enhance the security of digital finance. Through the decentralized and tamper-resistant nature of blockchain, a more secure ledger system can be provided, preventing fraud, errors, and data breaches while increasing transparency and accountability. However, the implementation of blockchain technology also needs to consider its potential limitations and challenges, such as performance constraints, privacy protection, and standardization issues.
(3) Human factors as critical vulnerabilities: Human factors remain a key vulnerability in cybersecurity. Human errors and deception techniques, such as weak passwords, failure to timely update software, and social engineering, pose risks to cybersecurity. Therefore, educating and training to improve cybersecurity awareness and best practices are crucial for mitigating these risks. Financial institutions should enhance employee training, promote password management and cybersecurity awareness education, and establish internal controls and audit mechanisms to reduce security vulnerabilities caused by human factors.

Clearly, regulatory authorities need to strike a balance between promoting innovation and protecting consumers from cybersecurity risks. They must ensure that financial institutions implement robust cybersecurity measures and comply with relevant regulations and guidelines. At the same time, they must support innovation and ensure that regulations do not stifle innovation.

Digital financial innovation also presents an opportunity to improve financial inclusion. Firstly, through innovations such as mobile payments and digital banking, people in remote and underserved areas can access banking services. Additionally, digital financial services have lower costs, making it easier for low-income households to access financial services. Moreover, digital financial innovation helps to promote financial literacy, providing access to financial information and resources, thus aiding users in making informed financial decisions.

While digital financial services have the potential to extend financial services to underserved populations, such as those without bank accounts or with limited access, they also pose challenges to those who cannot use digital infrastructure or have limited digital literacy. We can analyze these challenges from three perspectives:

(1) Access to formal financial services is a necessary condition for financial inclusion but not sufficient: While digital financial innovation can expand the accessibility of financial services, simply providing financial services is not enough to achieve financial inclusion. Many individuals may have access to financial services, but due to factors such as lack of financial knowledge, trust issues, or cultural barriers, they may not actively use these services. Therefore, in addition to providing financial services, there is a need to enhance financial education and training, raising people's financial literacy and awareness so that they can better utilize digital financial services.
(2) Financial inclusion can bring positive economic and social benefits: Achieving financial inclusion has positive effects on economic and social development. By providing financial services to those previously excluded from the formal financial sector, financial inclusion can promote increased savings, investments, entrepreneurship, and improve financial stability, driving social inclusion and poverty reduction. The specific economic and social benefits of financial inclusion may vary depending on different regions and types of services.
(3) Challenges in achieving financial inclusion persist: While digital financial innovation offers opportunities for financial inclusion, there are still challenges to be addressed. These include the lack of digital infrastructure, particularly in remote areas and developing countries; regulatory barriers and cultural norms; and issues related to financial education and literacy. Addressing these challenges requires collaborative efforts from governments, financial institutions, and other stakeholders. Regulatory authorities, while ensuring digital financial innovation, also need to focus on promoting financial inclusion by supporting digital infrastructure development, providing financial education and training, and implementing appropriate regulatory policies to ensure that everyone can access and afford digital financial services.

Digital financial innovation also presents opportunities for international coordination. Due to the global nature of digital finance, international coordination becomes crucial in regulation and policy-making. The following are several opportunities that digital financial innovation brings for international coordination:

(1) Digital financial innovation also presents opportunities for international coordination. Due to the global nature of digital finance, international coordination becomes crucial in regulation and policy-making. The following are several opportunities that digital financial innovation brings for international coordination.
(2) Establishing common regulatory standards and guidelines Zohar (2015b): Digital financial innovation transcends borders, necessitating the establishment of common regulatory standards and guidelines to ensure financial market stability and consumer protection. International coordination can encourage mutual consultations among regulatory authorities from different countries, leading to the formulation of common rules applicable to the digital financial domain.
(3) Addressing regulatory arbitrage and cross-border risks: The global nature of digital finance makes regulatory arbitrage and cross-border risks a reality. International coordination can help address regulatory loopholes in cross-border financial activities, reduce regulatory arbitrage, and enhance cooperation between countries to tackle cross-border risks and challenges.
(4) Promoting financial innovation and market competition Arner et al. (2017): International coordination can foster financial innovation and market competition, providing broader development opportunities for digital finance. By harmonizing regulatory requirements and policies across different countries and regions, barriers to entry for innovators can be lowered, thereby promoting global financial innovation.
(5) Supporting cross-border businesses and collaboration: Digital finance offers financial institutions opportunities to engage in cross-border businesses. International coordination can provide support and facilitation for cross-border financial activities, promoting cooperation and mutual benefits among different countries and regions.

However, at the same time, digital financial innovation also faces challenges brought about by regulatory fragmentation. Due to the cross-border nature of digital financial services, different countries and regions may have distinct regulatory systems and requirements, leading to confusion and uncertainty for financial institutions and consumers. We can analyze this issue from the following three perspectives:

(1) Regulatory fragmentation may lead to regulatory arbitrage and increased risks. Financial transactions can cross borders and jurisdictions, creating differences between regulatory authorities. Financial institutions may exploit these regulatory differences for arbitrage opportunities. This can be confusing for consumers and increase risks related to digital finance. Regulatory fragmentation can also

lead to inadequate supervision and enforcement, posing challenges to financial stability and consumer protection.

(2) Effective regulation of digital finance requires coordination among regulatory authorities. Cooperation and information sharing between regulatory agencies are crucial to ensuring that digital finance is used for legitimate purposes and that associated risks are appropriately managed. Moreover, the development of international standards and best practices is necessary to promote regulatory consistency and effectiveness.

(3) Regulatory authorities must strike a balance between promoting innovation and protecting consumers and the market. The digitization of currencies has brought about numerous innovative financial products and services but also introduced new risks. Regulatory agencies need to establish flexible and adaptive regulatory frameworks to ensure the responsible development of digital financial services. At the same time, they must ensure that regulations do not unnecessarily hinder innovation but instead foster its development while strengthening consumer protection measures.

References

Arner, D. W., Barberis, J. N., & Buckley, R. P. (2017). FinTech, RegTech, and the Reconceptualization of Financial Regulation. Northwestern Journal of International Law & Business.

Chiu, J., & Koeppl, T. (2017). The Economics of Cryptocurrencies – Bitcoin and Beyond. Queen's Economics Department Working Paper.

Zhong Hui'an. Research on Financial Technology Development and Risk Prevention [J]. Financial Development Research, 2018 (03)

Petralia, K., Philippon, T., Rice, T., & Véron, N. (2019). Banking Disrupted? Financial Intermediation in an Era of Transformational Technology. Geneva Reports on the World Economy.

Schär, F. (2021). Decentralized Finance: On Blockchain- and Smart Contract-Based Financial Markets. Federal Reserve Bank of St. Louis Review.

Tapscott, D., & Tapscott, A. (2016). Blockchain Revolution: How the Technology Behind Bitcoin is Changing Money, Business, and the World. Penguin.

Zhang Xiaoyan, Wang Xiaoting, Shen Peilong. Research on China's Bank Regulation under the Concept of Financial Inclusion [J]. Economic Issues, 2016 (5)

Zhou Zheng. Comparison of Domestic and Foreign Intelligent Investment Advisory Business Models [J]. Banker, 2017, (12)

Zohar, A. (2015). Bitcoin: The Decentralized Trust. Oxford Business Law Blog.

Zohar, A. (2015). Bitcoin: Under the Hood. Communications of the ACM.

Chapter 4
Digitalization of Commercial Banks

4.1 Commercial Bank Digitalization Overview

Commercial bank digitalization is the process in which commercial banks optimize and innovate their internal business processes and external service models using digital technologies. Its purpose is to enhance the bank's operational efficiency, service quality, and customer experience. Commercial bank digitalization is a transformation driven by information technology and digital technology, leveraging internet, big data, artificial intelligence, blockchain, and other technologies to integrate bank's business processes and provide intelligent, automated, and personalized services to better meet customer needs.

The development of commercial bank digitalization can be traced back to the widespread adoption and advancement of the internet in the 1990s. With the rise of mobile internet and big data technology, commercial bank digitalization has shown rapid growth momentum. It is driven by three main factors:

(1) Technological Drivers: The rapid development of digital technologies, especially emerging technologies such as cloud computing, artificial intelligence, and blockchain, provides strong technical support for commercial bank digitalization. The application of these technologies enables commercial banks to better cope with market competition, improve operational efficiency, and drive innovation.
(2) Market Demand Drivers: Modern consumers have increasingly urgent demands for financial services, expecting more convenient, fast, and personalized services. Commercial bank digitalization can meet this market demand by providing more efficient financial service models through digital means, enhancing customer experience.
(3) Policy Environment Drivers: Governments have formulated a series of policies and measures to encourage and guide the development of commercial bank digitalization, providing a favorable policy environment and support. Government encouragement of financial technology innovation, promotion of digital

Z. Liu and W. Hou, *Digital Finance*, https://doi.org/10.1007/978-981-99-7305-7_4

economy development, strengthening data protection, and privacy security policies have driven the process of commercial bank digitalization and promoted innovation and development in the financial industry.

So, how to understand the digitalization of commercial banks? We believe that there are four key aspects of digitalization for commercial banks, namely strategy, technology, organization, and culture.

Firstly, strategy is the foundation of the digital transformation of commercial banks. Digital banks need to formulate practical and feasible digital strategies, clarifying the goals and directions of digital transformation. This includes a clear understanding of the positioning of the bank itself and the competitive environment of the market, as well as in-depth knowledge of customer demands and industry trends, in order to develop a digital strategy that aligns with the market. The strategy of a digital bank should clearly define the objectives of the digital transformation, such as improving efficiency, optimizing user experience, and innovating products and services.

Secondly, technology Jia et al. (2018) is a crucial support for the digital transformation of commercial banks. Digital banks need to possess certain technological capabilities, including information technology and digital technology, such as cloud computing, big data analytics, artificial intelligence, and mobile payments, among others. Digital banks need to keep up with the development trends of new technologies and actively adopt them to improve efficiency and innovate services. Additionally, digital banks should pay attention to technology security and risk control, strengthen data management and privacy protection, and enhance the safety and reliability of digital banks.

Thirdly, organization is a crucial element in the digital transformation of commercial banks. Digital banks need to optimize their organizational structure, improve business processes, enhance internal collaboration and communication, and drive digital transformation. To better respond to market changes and customer demands, digital banks should adopt agile organizational structures and management approaches. Additionally, digital banks need to make adjustments in their organizational culture and processes, cultivate digital competencies and capabilities, and promote a cultural transformation and management innovation in the digital banking realm.

Lastly, culture is a vital element in the digital transformation of commercial banks. Digital banks need to establish a digital culture, encompassing digital thinking, digital collaboration, and digital innovation, among others. To achieve this, digital banks should nurture their employees' digital competencies and capabilities, encourage their active participation in digital transformation practices and innovations, and drive a cultural transformation within the digital banking environment. Additionally, digital banks should also pay attention to changes in customer culture and demands, promptly adjust their own culture and services, and enhance customer experience and satisfaction.

After understanding the elements of digital transformation in commercial banks, let's take a closer look at three different approaches that can be explored in the practice of digital transformation in commercial banks:

Firstly, starting with internal process optimization. Commercial banks can utilize digital technology to optimize and restructure internal business processes, improve work efficiency and service quality, and reduce operational costs and risks. This approach emphasizes comprehensive digitization of the bank's overall processes, achieving comprehensive optimization of business, processes, and services through digital transformation. Commercial banks need to possess advanced digital and information technology capabilities, while comprehensively optimizing and restructuring their business processes to achieve the goals of digital transformation.

Secondly, starting with innovative financial services. Commercial banks can leverage digital technology to innovate and upgrade financial service products and models, providing more convenient, fast, and personalized financial services to enhance customer loyalty and competitiveness. This approach emphasizes rapid iteration, where commercial banks continuously launch innovative products and services through rapid trial-and-error and iterations to meet ever-changing customer demands. Additionally, banks need to strengthen interaction and feedback with customers to promptly adjust and optimize products and services.

Thirdly, starting with ecological cooperation. Commercial banks can use digital technology to establish an open financial ecosystem and establish cooperative relationships with other financial institutions, technology companies, and platform enterprises to achieve resource sharing, business complementarity, and mutual advantages, jointly advancing the digitalization of the financial industry. This approach emphasizes ecosystem construction, where commercial banks need to establish digital ecosystems with external partners to achieve resource sharing and complementarity, enhancing the bank's competitiveness and innovation capabilities. Choosing suitable partners is crucial to achieving a win–win situation for successful digital transformation.

It is important to note that these three approaches can be combined in practice to form multiple digital transformation schemes. For example, commercial banks can improve efficiency and service quality through internal process optimization while engaging in innovative financial services with external partners, achieving comprehensive progress in digital transformation. Each bank should choose a digital transformation approach that suits its own circumstances and strategic positioning, and flexibly apply the elements and methods to achieve successful digital transformation.

After understanding these three different approaches, let's examine the methodology for the practical implementation of digital transformation in commercial banks. The following is a suggested process to follow:

Firstly, assess the current level of digitization. This assessment will help the commercial bank understand its starting point for digital transformation, enabling the formulation of more targeted strategic plans Chakravorti (2017). The assessment of the current level of digitization can be carried out in the following aspects:

(a) Assess the use of digital technology: This includes evaluating the scope, application areas, and effectiveness of digital technology. It means that the commercial bank needs to understand its investments and applications of digital technology and the actual impact of these technologies on its business processes.
(b) Assess customer needs and experiences: The commercial bank should assess customer demands and experiences regarding digital technology, understanding customer usage patterns, needs, and preferences for digital channels. Such assessment helps the bank understand customer expectations of digital services, thereby determining the focus and direction of digital transformation.
(c) Assess the level of competitors Kapoor and Adner (2012): This includes an analysis of the technology and platforms used by competitors, their digital services and experiences, as well as their digital strategies and investments. By comparing and analyzing with competitors, the commercial bank can identify its strengths and weaknesses in digital transformation and develop corresponding strategies to enhance competitiveness.

Secondly, formulate a digital transformation strategy. The commercial bank should develop a digital transformation strategy to ensure alignment with its strategic objectives. Key elements in formulating the digital transformation strategy include:

(a) Define objectives and scope: This involves establishing key objectives for digital transformation, such as improving customer experience, enhancing operational efficiency, and innovating products and services, and determining the timeline and resource allocation for digital transformation.
(b) Optimize digital experiences and efficiency: This includes enhancing the design and functionality of digital channels, providing personalized digital services, optimizing digital processes and systems, and leveraging data and analytics to support digital transformation. Improving digital experiences and efficiency helps increase customer satisfaction and competitiveness.
(c) Drive digital innovation and change: This involves identifying opportunities for digital innovation and change, establishing relevant processes and mechanisms, and fostering a culture and capability for digital innovation and change. Commercial banks can also drive digital innovation and change through open innovation, establishing partnerships, and investments.

Thirdly, invest in digital technology and platforms. The commercial bank should invest in digital technology and platforms to improve its business processes and services. Key aspects of investing in digital technology and platforms during the digital transformation process include:

(a) Invest in digital infrastructure and technology: This includes investments in digital technologies such as cloud computing, big data analytics, artificial intelligence, blockchain, and digital platforms and tools such as digital payments, mobile banking, and social media. By investing in digital infrastructure and technology, the commercial bank can enhance business process efficiency, data analysis capabilities, and customer experiences.

(b) Invest in the digital ecosystem: This involves designing, building, opening up, and cooperating in the digital ecosystem, as well as managing and optimizing it. By establishing cooperative relationships with other financial institutions, technology companies, and platform enterprises, the commercial bank can achieve resource sharing, business complementarity, and mutual advantages, jointly advancing the digital transformation process.
(c) Invest in digital talent and culture: This includes recruiting and nurturing talents with digital skills and capabilities, fostering and implementing a digital culture, and developing and enhancing digital leadership. The commercial bank can cultivate employees' digital qualities through training programs, collaboration projects, and innovative practices, promoting a culture of innovation and change.

Fourthly, establish a digital culture and organization. The commercial bank should establish a digital culture and organization to facilitate the success of digital transformation. Key aspects of establishing a digital culture and organization during the digital transformation process include:

(a) Establish digital leadership: This includes establishing mechanisms and processes for digital leadership, cultivating leadership capabilities with digital competencies at the leadership level, and incentivizing behaviors and performances that demonstrate digital leadership. Digital leadership needs to guide the bank's digital vision and strategy, actively supporting and driving various initiatives for digital transformation.
(b) Establish a digital culture: This includes defining the concepts and values of digital culture, implementing behaviors and practices of digital culture, and promoting the dissemination and publicity of digital culture. Digital culture should emphasize core values of innovation, agility, collaboration, and learning, encouraging employees' participation in digital transformation and innovation, to foster the rootedness and continuity of digital culture.
(c) Adjust organizational structure and processes: This includes adjusting the division of labor and responsibilities within the organization, optimizing process efficiency and collaboration, and establishing mechanisms and processes for a digital organization. Digital transformation requires flexible organizational structure and processes to facilitate cross-departmental collaboration and information sharing, to adapt to rapidly changing market demands and technological advancements.

After understanding the path of digital transformation in commercial banks, let's analyze the benefits brought by digitalization. These benefits are not necessarily solely financial gains but encompass various aspects such as user experience, data security, and technological innovation:

Improved Customer Experience and Engagement: Through digital transformation, commercial banks can offer more personalized and convenient services, enhancing customer experience and engagement. Innovations such as mobile banking applications and online banking platforms provide customers with access to more account and financial information, increasing satisfaction and loyalty.

Data Security and Privacy Protection: Digital transformation in commercial banks poses challenges related to security and privacy protection, as it involves the transmission of sensitive financial information through digital networks. Therefore, banks must implement robust security measures and privacy policies to safeguard consumers' financial information, thereby enhancing customer trust and ensuring data security.

Technological Innovation and Competitiveness: Digital transformation requires a focus on technological innovation and adoption to maintain competitiveness. Banks need to invest in new technologies and digital platforms to improve operational efficiency, reduce costs, and enhance the quality of customer service. Collaboration with financial technology companies and startups to develop new technologies and products and fostering an innovative culture that adapts to changing customer demands and preferences are crucial.

We have observed that different countries have varying approaches and theories regarding digital transformation in commercial banks due to their unique national and industry characteristics.

In China, digital transformation in commercial banks primarily starts with internal process optimization, with the goal of improving efficiency and reducing costs. This is due to the highly competitive financial market in China, where banks need to enhance their operational efficiency and cost-effectiveness to maintain a competitive edge. In the United States, digital transformation in commercial banks primarily begins with innovation in financial services, aiming to enhance customer experience and increase competitiveness. This approach is driven by the maturity of the U.S. financial market and the high expectations of consumers for high-quality financial services. To meet the demands of younger generations of consumers, digital banks in the U.S. widely offer mobile and online banking services. In Europe, digital transformation in commercial banks primarily starts with ecosystem cooperation, aiming to establish digital ecosystems as the main objective. This approach is influenced by the characteristic of Europe's financial market, which involves cross-border operations and diversification. Banks in Europe collaborate with technology companies and startups to create digital banking ecosystems, achieving resource sharing and mutual development.

In terms of theoretical considerations, the theoretical foundations and viewpoints of digital transformation in commercial banks vary among different countries, mainly influenced by their financial development stages, market demands, and policy environments.

In China, digital banking is regarded as the "new normal" in the financial industry. The widespread adoption of mobile payments, especially among the younger population, has greatly propelled the development of digital banking, making digital banking services an integral part of daily life. The government also pays high attention to this trend, promoting financial technology innovation and actively driving the transformation and upgrading of the financial industry to achieve high-quality development. In the United States, digital banking is seen as the "new direction" in the financial industry. With a mature financial market and diverse consumer demands, there is a higher expectation for the quality of financial services. Therefore, U.S.

commercial banks focus more on service innovation and enhancing customer experience during their digital transformation. In Europe, digital banking is considered the "new opportunity" in the financial industry. Although Europe's digital banking development lags behind the U.S. and China, the market potential is significant, and the region actively fosters developments in the digital economy and financial technology. Hence, European banks emphasize cooperation with technology companies and startups to jointly build digital banking ecosystems, achieving resource sharing and mutual development.

With technological advancements and changing consumer demands, banks worldwide are undergoing digital transformation. Let's delve deeper into the strategic and tactical differences in the digital transformation of banks in three different countries (regions): the United States, China, and Europe.

Let's begin with the United States, where banks focus on three core aspects in their digital transformation strategy: investing in digital technology and platforms, creating a digital ecosystem, and optimizing digital customer experience.

Investing in Digital Technology and Platforms: U.S. banks recognize that successful digital transformation requires significant investment, particularly in digital technology and platforms. They invest mainly in technologies such as cloud computing, big data, artificial intelligence, and blockchain to better serve customers, enhance efficiency and security, and drive business innovation.

Creating a Digital Ecosystem: During digital transformation, U.S. banks not only concentrate on individual digital technologies or platforms but also strive to create a comprehensive digital ecosystem encompassing digital channels, products, services, marketing, and operations. Through collaboration with technology companies and fintech startups, utilizing open APIs, and connecting various services and platforms, they provide more comprehensive and integrated services, enhancing user experience and loyalty.

Optimizing Digital Customer Experience: U.S. banks prioritize optimizing digital customer experience from a customer-centric perspective, a crucial component of their digital transformation strategy. They achieve this by offering personalized services, simplifying processes, providing diverse interaction channels, etc., to increase customer satisfaction and retention, thereby driving business growth and profitability.

Next, let's focus on China, where banks emphasize cooperation with fintech companies, building a digital ecosystem, and driving innovation in digital products and services.

Cooperation with Fintech Companies: In China's digital transformation, banks actively collaborate with fintech companies to leverage their advanced technology and platforms, enhancing their own digital service levels. This collaboration enables banks to adapt and respond more rapidly to the challenges of the digital age while providing better service experiences for customers. Additionally, through such partnerships, Chinese banks jointly develop and launch new digital products and services to meet evolving customer needs, enhancing their competitiveness and profitability.

Building a Digital Ecosystem: In their digital transformation, Chinese banks do not focus solely on singular technologies or products but rather aim to construct a comprehensive digital ecosystem comprising digital channels, products, services, marketing, and operations. Such an all-encompassing ecosystem allows banks to elevate customer experience from multiple angles, improve service efficiency and quality, and expand their market share and revenue.

Driving Innovation in Digital Products and Services: Chinese banks vigorously promote innovation in digital products and services during their digital transformation. They deeply understand and explore customer demands, customizing and developing various new digital products and services to enhance customer satisfaction and loyalty. Simultaneously, these innovative products and services also boost banks' market competitiveness, further increasing their revenue and profitability.

Lastly, let's consider Europe, where banks focus on investing in digital technology and innovation, optimizing digital customer experience, and building a digital ecosystem.

Investing in Digital Technology and Innovation: In Europe's digital transformation, banks heavily invest in digital technology and innovation. They recognize that digitalization involves not only technological changes but also business model innovation. Consequently, they actively introduce and utilize new technologies such as artificial intelligence, big data, blockchain, etc., to improve service efficiency, optimize customer experience, and develop new products and services. Moreover, they emphasize research and development in digital technology and innovation to maintain their technological advantage.

Optimizing Digital Customer Experience: European banks highly prioritize optimizing customer experience during their digital transformation. They believe that enhancing customer experience not only increases customer satisfaction and loyalty but also elevates the bank's brand value and reputation. Thus, they strive to improve service levels in various aspects, including optimizing online service processes, enhancing service speed, providing personalized products and services, etc., to enhance customers' digital experience.

Building a Digital Ecosystem: In their digital transformation, European banks also focus on constructing a comprehensive digital ecosystem. They endeavor to digitize various elements, including service channels, products, services, marketing, and operations, to build a holistic digital ecosystem that caters to diverse customer needs.

Next, we present three different cases to illustrate the above points.

4.1.1 Industrial and Commercial Bank of China (ICBC) Digital Transformation

ICBC, as one of the largest commercial banks in China and globally, embarked on its digital transformation journey as early as 2015. The bank's digital strategy primarily revolves around enhancing customer experience by leveraging advanced technologies to optimize business processes and improve service quality.

ICBC provides a diverse range of digital services, including but not limited to mobile banking, online banking, telephone banking, and WeChat banking. These channels not only greatly convenience customers and offer efficient service experiences but also help ICBC enhance customer satisfaction and loyalty.

It is worth noting that the Chinese government has shown great attention to the development of digital banking and provided active policy support. This precisely reflects the viewpoint of the Chinese government that regards digital transformation as the "new normal" in the financial industry. ICBC's digital transformation is not merely about the application of new technologies; it also represents the overturning and innovation of traditional financial business models, showcasing its profound understanding and unique insights into the future of the financial industry.

4.1.2 Citibank (Citigroup) Digital Transformation

Citibank, as one of the largest banks in the United States and globally, has been committed to digital transformation and achieved significant success in the process. Their digital strategy focuses on enhancing customer experience and innovating financial services.

They offer digital services through various means, including mobile banking, online banking, voice recognition, etc., aiming to provide more convenient and efficient services. Additionally, in terms of innovating financial services, Citibank actively invests in research and application of digital currencies and blockchain technology.

In the United States, the development of digital banking has gained widespread recognition, indicating that digital banking has been viewed as a new trend in the U.S. financial industry. Citibank's successful digital transformation has not only brought higher efficiency and improved customer experience but also set a positive example for the entire financial industry, demonstrating potential new directions for future financial services.

4.1.3 N26 Bank's Digital Transformation in Europe

N26 Bank, a fully digital bank headquartered in Germany, is renowned for providing convenient, secure, and efficient services. Its digital strategy revolves around innovative financial services and expanding ecological cooperation.

The bank is committed to offering a comprehensive range of digital banking services, including mobile banking, online banking, payment services, fund transfers, etc., to meet customers' financial needs in various scenarios. Additionally, N26 Bank actively seeks and establishes various cooperative relationships, such as partnering with online travel companies to provide travel insurance and payment services, further expanding its business scope and service capabilities.

In Europe, digital banking is seen as a new opportunity in the financial industry, reflecting the high attention given by investors and startups to digital banking. N26 Bank's successful practices fully demonstrate how digital banks can achieve comprehensive digitization of financial services, enhance customer experience, and offer new development perspectives for the entire financial industry through innovative services and ecological cooperation.

Analyzing the digital banking transformation from the perspectives of strategic goals, implementation measures, policy environment, and market situation, we can draw the following conclusions:

First, let's consider the strategic goals of digital banking transformation.

In terms of strategic goals, ICBC and Citibank focus primarily on improving customer experience and service quality, while N26 Bank emphasizes innovative financial services and ecological cooperation. This indicates that each bank formulates strategic goals based on its unique environment and market demands, aiming to maximize customer satisfaction and maintain its competitive advantage.

Next, let's examine the implementation measures of digital banking transformation.

Regarding implementation measures, all three banks offer various digital service channels, such as mobile banking, online banking, and voice recognition, enabling customers to conduct transactions and manage accounts more conveniently. Additionally, they all adopt innovative technologies and service measures, such as Citibank's research and application of digital currencies and blockchain technology and N26 Bank's ecological cooperation. This shows that during the digital transformation, banks need to actively implement innovative measures to meet evolving customer demands based on industry and market trends.

Lastly, let's assess the policy environment and market situation of digital banking transformation.

The policy environment and market situation significantly differ for these three banks. ICBC receives high attention and support from the Chinese government, reflecting the viewpoint of the Chinese government that regards digital transformation as the "new normal" in the financial industry. In contrast, Citibank and N26 Bank receive more attention from the market and investors, indicating that in the United States and Europe, digital banking is viewed as the "new direction" and "new opportunity" in the financial industry, respectively. This demonstrates that during digital transformation, banks need to adjust their strategies according to policy and market conditions to respond to various risks and challenges while leveraging their strengths and uniqueness.

These cases reveal the practices and theoretical considerations of commercial banks in different countries in digital transformation, influenced by various factors such as their respective governments, the financial industry, and investors.

Overall, during digital transformation, commercial banks need to consider various factors, including political, economic, and cultural elements, as they will profoundly impact the transformation process. Therefore, banks need to formulate and execute digital transformation strategies that align with their national or regional characteristics to achieve optimal transformation results.

4.2 Digital Banking Services and Products

Digital banking is a financial institution that provides various banking services and products through digital technologies such as the internet and mobile devices. Its development can be divided into three stages, reflecting the technological innovation and changes in customer demands in the financial services industry.

The first stage was the launch of online banking services. This phase primarily focused on the onlineization of traditional banking services, such as account inquiries, fund transfers, and credit card applications. Online banking allowed users to conduct banking transactions from the comfort of their homes or offices, significantly increasing convenience.

The second stage witnessed the rise of mobile banking services. Based on mobile devices, this stage brought banking services and products to users' fingertips, allowing them to conduct transactions and manage their accounts anytime and anywhere. Mobile banking services further enhanced the convenience and immediacy of banking services.

The third stage marked a comprehensive upgrade of digital banking services and products. During this phase, emerging services and products such as internet finance, smart investments, and intelligent wealth management were introduced. These offerings not only provided more choices for financial products but also offered more personalized and intelligent services.

Next, let's delve into the development overview of digital banking services and products.

The rise of digital banking originated from the development of internet finance and has gradually become a critical direction for commercial banks' strategic transformation and upgrades, driven by the following three factors:

(1) Changes in consumer demand and technological innovation: Customers' behavior patterns and demands have been continuously changing, with a growing preference for more convenient, fast, and personalized financial services. Simultaneously, advancements in cloud computing, big data, artificial intelligence, and other technologies enable banks to provide higher quality and more efficient services, meeting consumers' personalized needs.
(2) Regulatory policy promotion and support: Many countries and regions are encouraging and pushing for the digital transformation of the banking industry through measures such as open banking and regulatory sandboxes, accelerating the pace of digitalization.
(3) Competition and development needs of commercial banks: Faced with competition pressure from fintech companies, commercial banks need to enhance their competitiveness by undergoing digital transformation to improve service efficiency, reduce operational costs, and enhance customer experience.

In the process of practicing digital transformation, banks can adopt various strategies:

"Comprehensive digitalization" approach: Achieving digitalization in various aspects, such as business, processes, and services, to improve efficiency and optimize user experience.

"Fast iteration" approach: Continuously launching innovative products and services through rapid trial and error and iteration to adapt to market changes and customer demands.

"Ecological construction" approach: Establishing a digital ecosystem in collaboration with external partners, such as e-commerce platforms and technology companies, to achieve resource sharing and collaborative innovation, promoting the development of both the bank and the entire financial ecosystem.

Additionally, the characteristics of digital banking services and products include:

Efficiency and convenience: Leveraging modern technology, digital banking provides 24/7 services to users, enabling them to conduct transactions and manage their accounts at any time and place. This approach eliminates the need for users to wait in queues at physical banks, providing quicker and more convenient services.

Personalized customization: Utilizing big data analysis and artificial intelligence, digital banking can offer personalized products and services based on customer behavior patterns, financial status, and risk tolerance, enhancing customer satisfaction and loyalty.

Risk control Agrawal et al. (2018): Through advanced risk management technologies and tools, such as big data analysis and artificial intelligence, digital banks can monitor and assess customer credit risk and market risk in real-time, effectively reducing the possibilities of credit defaults and market risks.

Innovation capacity: Digital banks demonstrate greater innovation capacity, enabling them to respond quickly to market changes and customer demands by launching new products and services, such as digital currencies and blockchain applications.

Ecological system construction Chiu (2017): Digital banks are no longer isolated financial service providers; they build ecosystems by collaborating with various partners (e.g., e-commerce platforms and technology companies) to achieve resource sharing, enhancing their competitiveness.

Digital transformation allows banks to provide a broader range of services and products through new technologies and platforms, primarily manifested in:

Service innovation: Digital transformation enables banks to offer more intelligent, personalized, and integrated services. For instance, by using big data and artificial intelligence algorithms, banks can better understand customer needs and behaviors and provide more precise and personalized services. Digital transformation also facilitates providing more convenient and efficient services, such as mobile banking and online customer support, meeting customers' demands anytime and anywhere.

Product diversification: Digital transformation empowers banks to conveniently introduce new products and rapidly update and improve existing ones. Banks can utilize digital technologies and platforms to design more innovative and competitive financial products, such as digital currencies, mobile payments, and virtual credit cards. Additionally, digital transformation allows banks to provide more finely segmented products to meet diverse customer needs and preferences.

Industry structure reform: Digital transformation will significantly impact the entire financial industry's structure and competitive landscape. The emergence and development of digital banks have placed traditional banks under greater competition pressure and transformation challenges. The operating models and business models of digital banks will also have profound effects on the development of traditional banks. Meanwhile, digital transformation also promotes the rise and development of fintech companies, which will play a crucial role in driving innovation and transformation across the financial industry.

Improved customer experience: By leveraging digital technologies, banks can provide more efficient and flexible services, enabling customers to enjoy banking services anytime and anywhere. Additionally, through big data and artificial intelligence technologies, banks can better understand customer needs and provide personalized services, significantly enhancing customer experiences.

Cost reduction: As digital banks can reduce the number of physical branches, lower labor costs, and automate a significant portion of their operations through algorithms, they can greatly decrease operational expenses. This not only enhances bank profits but also allows more profit to be returned to customers, such as offering lower interest rates and reduced fees.

Enhanced risk management: Through technologies like big data and artificial intelligence, digital banks can conduct real-time analysis and processing of extensive data, improving the efficiency and accuracy of risk identification, assessment, and control, which helps prevent and mitigate financial risks.

Advancing financial inclusion: Due to lower costs, digital banks can provide financial services for smaller amounts, making it possible for underserved populations, such as low-income groups and rural populations, to access financial services, thereby promoting financial inclusion.

The impact of digital banking services and products is multifaceted, encompassing innovations in services, product diversity, and industry structural changes, which will have far-reaching effects on the financial industry and customers. Therefore, banks should actively promote digital transformation to enhance the innovation and competitiveness of digital services and products.

However, digital banking services and products still face some challenges during the digital transformation process.

Firstly, risk management is a crucial concern for digital banks Sullivan (2017). As digital banking rapidly advances, information security and privacy protection become critical issues. Banks need to increase technology investments and security measures to guard against risks such as hacking attacks and data breaches, enhancing system security and reliability.

Secondly, service quality is a key challenge in the development of digital banking. The goal of digital banks is to provide high-quality and convenient services, but service quality can be influenced by technology capabilities, management levels, and the diversity of customer needs. Banks need to enhance service quality, meet customer demands, and strengthen customer education and training to alleviate concerns about technology and security.

Moreover, regulation Arner et al. (2016a) is a challenge that digital banks must face. To ensure operational compliance and stability, digital banks must comply with relevant laws and regulations and establish cooperation with regulatory authorities. Strengthening the construction of internal control systems ensures service and product compliance and meets regulatory requirements.

Additionally, digital banks also encounter challenges in market competition and promotion. Product innovation and market promotion are crucial to the success of digital banks. Banks need to continuously innovate products with the support of technology, data, and talent, and develop effective marketing strategies to increase the popularity and competitiveness of digital banking.

To understand the development of digital banking products, we will discuss a few case studies:

4.2.1 Revolut, a Digital Bank in the UK

Revolut is a UK-based digital bank founded in 2015. The bank provides various currency exchange, trading, and payment services through its mobile application, primarily targeting frequent international travelers and those engaging in cross-border transactions. Over the years, Revolut has become one of the leading digital banks in the UK, serving over 10 million customers and generating over £100 million in annual revenue. Furthermore, Revolut has expanded its operations to countries in Europe and the United States.

Revolut, as a digital bank and fintech company, has several advantages:

Cost Advantage: As a digital bank, Revolut doesn't have the high operational costs of traditional banks, avoiding expenses related to physical branches, and high personnel salaries. Consequently, it can offer more competitive pricing, attracting a larger consumer base.

Technological Innovation: Leveraging artificial intelligence and machine learning, Revolut can process customer transactions and payments quickly and accurately, improving customer experience. Additionally, Revolut offers intelligent savings and investment services, meeting customers' demand for diverse financial solutions.

Convenience and Flexibility: Revolut provides convenient and fast services through its mobile application, enabling customers to conduct banking transactions at any time and place. It also offers various currency exchange, trading, and payment services, assisting customers in handling cross-border transactions effortlessly. Revolut supports multiple payment methods such as peer-to-peer payments and scan-to-pay, enhancing ease of use and flexibility for customers.

However, Revolut also faces some unavoidable challenges. As a digital bank, Revolut must comply with financial regulations and compliance requirements in different countries. It needs to ensure that its operations adhere to the laws and regulations of each country and maintain good communication and cooperation with regulatory authorities to avoid violations and penalties.

Moreover, Revolut needs to implement strict security measures, including data encryption, protection against data breaches, and network attacks, to ensure the security and privacy of customer data.

Revolut also faces competition from traditional banks and other digital banks, requiring continuous improvement of its service and product innovation capabilities to maintain a competitive advantage and expand market share.

4.2.2 *Chime, a Digital Bank in the US*

Chime is a US digital bank established in 2013 and is one of the most popular digital banks for US customers. Chime stands out as it allows users to utilize its services without needing to open a traditional bank account, enabling direct transactions and payments through the Chime platform. The bank operates through its mobile application and primarily targets young users. Chime adopts unique marketing strategies, using social media and other channels to attract a large number of young users. Additionally, Chime offers various rewards and incentives to attract more users. Chime prioritizes customer experience and service quality, streamlining processes and providing convenient features to improve customer satisfaction and loyalty.

Chime, as a digital bank and fintech company, has several advantages:

Fee-Free and Low Costs: Compared to traditional banks, Chime does not charge common bank fees such as monthly fees, minimum balance fees, or overdraft fees. This makes Chime particularly attractive to users who wish to avoid high fees.

Simple and User-Friendly Mobile App: Chime offers an intuitive, concise, and user-friendly mobile banking application. This app enables users to easily manage their accounts, conduct transactions, set up savings, and other features, providing a convenient banking experience.

Quick and Instant Transaction Processing: Chime collaborates with major payment networks to provide fast and instant transaction processing. This means users can view and access their funds immediately, without waiting for lengthy processing times.

Automated Savings and Financial Management Tools: Chime provides a range of automated savings and financial management tools to help users better manage their finances. For example, Chime's "Automatic Savings" feature automatically saves spare change from each transaction into a designated savings account, helping users accumulate savings.

High-quality customer support: Chime is committed to providing high-quality customer support. Users can contact the customer support team through the application, online chat, or phone and receive timely assistance and answers.

At the same time, Chime also faces some challenges:

Lack of physical branches: Chime is a fully digital bank without physical branch locations. While this provides convenience and flexibility for users, some customers may still prefer face-to-face customer service and support, especially when dealing with complex issues.

Limited products and services: Compared to traditional banks, Chime offers a relatively limited range of products and services. Although its core offerings include savings and checking accounts, the choices in areas such as credit cards, loans, and investments are relatively limited. This may restrict some users in meeting specific financial needs.

Dependence on partnerships: Chime relies on relationships with partner banks and payment networks to process user transactions and handle funds. This reliance may subject Chime to the policies and limitations of its partners, such as transaction processing times or service disruptions.

Intense competition: Chime faces competition from other digital banks and financial technology companies that also offer similar no-fee or low-cost banking services. In this highly competitive market, Chime needs to continuously innovate and enhance user experience to maintain its competitiveness.

Profitability and sustainability: Despite Chime's success in user growth, achieving profitability and sustainability remains a challenge. Digital banks typically rely on low fees, value-added services, and leveraging user data for revenue generation. Chime needs to find a sustainable revenue model while balancing user needs and profitability to ensure long-term business development.

4.2.3 Bank of China

The Bank of China Lu and Li (2018) is one of China's four major state-owned banks, established in 1912 and headquartered in Beijing. With the advent of the digital era, Bank of China began its digital transformation, combining traditional banking services with technological innovation to introduce a series of digital banking services. The digital transformation of Bank of China aims to enhance service quality, expand business scope, improve operational efficiency, and meet diverse customer needs. Through the introduction of advanced technology and innovative service models, Bank of China strives to build an efficient, intelligent, and secure financial service system.

The advantages of Bank of China's digital transformation mainly include:

Brand Influence and Customer Base: As one of China's largest commercial banks, Bank of China has a large customer base and wide brand recognition. This provides strong support for its digital transformation, enabling it to better attract and serve customers.

Diverse Financial Products and Services: Bank of China has introduced a range of financial products and services through digital transformation, including mobile banking, online banking, third-party payment, and mobile payment, among others. These services cater to different customer needs, offering convenient and efficient financial service experiences.

Technological Strength and Innovation Capability: By adopting technologies such as cloud computing, big data, artificial intelligence, and blockchain, Bank of China can enhance service efficiency, improve risk management, and provide personalized financial solutions.

Multi-Channel Service and User Experience: Bank of China offers convenient financial services through multiple digital channels, such as mobile applications and online banking, providing customers with a user-friendly banking experience. Customers can conduct banking transactions anytime and anywhere, enjoying efficient services

Compliance and Sound Operations: Bank of China's digital transformation emphasizes compliance and sound operations, actively addressing regulatory requirements and risk management challenges. The bank is dedicated to establishing a robust internal control system to ensure the security and reliability of digital services.

At the same time, Bank of China's digital transformation also faces some challenges:

Security and Privacy Concerns: With the advancement of digital transformation, Bank of China faces challenges in terms of cybersecurity and customer privacy. Protecting customers' personal information and financial security is a crucial task in the digital transformation process, necessitating enhanced cybersecurity measures and data privacy protection to mitigate the increasing complexity of cybersecurity threats and data breaches.

Technological Innovation and Application Capabilities: Digital transformation requires Bank of China to continuously innovate in technology and adopt new applications to enhance service quality and user experience. This demands a bank with an innovative mindset, quick responsiveness to market changes, and a highly skilled technology team capable of flexibly applying new technologies to drive the deepening of digital transformation.

Cross-Department and Cross-Industry Collaboration: Bank of China's digital transformation requires close collaboration with other departments and industries. For example, collaboration with technology companies, internet enterprises, and innovative companies is necessary to jointly explore the construction of a digital financial ecosystem. This requires the bank to have an open-minded and collaborative approach, building strong cooperative relationships to drive the progress of digital transformation.

User Acceptance and Education: Digital transformation also presents challenges in terms of user acceptance and education. Some customers may have doubts or difficulties adapting to digital banking services, necessitating the bank to actively engage in user education and promotion to increase user awareness and trust in digital services, encouraging broader usage of digital banking services.

In conclusion, banks across the board are actively tackling challenges during digital transformation, continuously enhancing their digital service capabilities and competitiveness, and driving innovation and development in financial services. Banks must remain attentive to market changes and customer needs, continuously optimizing digital services to provide customers with a more convenient, efficient, and secure financial experience.

4.3 Challenges and Opportunities of Digital Transformation in Commercial Banks

With the advent of the digital age, commercial banks are facing unprecedented challenges and opportunities. The development of digital technology has completely transformed the way banks operate and interact with customers, and commercial banks need to actively address these challenges and seize opportunities to maintain their position in the competitive market.

Let's first explore the opportunities brought about by digital transformation in commercial banks:

Market Expansion and Customer Base: Digital banks can reach a wider geographical area and customer base through technologies such as the internet and mobile devices. Unlike traditional banks limited by physical branch locations and operating hours, digital banks can provide services anytime and anywhere, catering to customer needs. This enables banks to expand their market share, attract more customers, and further increase business scale and revenue.

Enhanced Service Quality and Customer Experience: Digital banks can offer more efficient, convenient, and personalized services through technological innovation and optimized processes. Customers can easily conduct various banking transactions, such as transfers, payments, savings, and investments, through mobile applications or online platforms. Through big data analysis and artificial intelligence algorithms, digital banks can understand customer preferences and needs, providing customized products and services to enhance customer satisfaction and experience.

Cost Reduction and Increased Efficiency: Digital banks can lower labor and physical costs through automated processes and online transactions. Traditional banks often require a significant amount of human resources to handle manual operations and document processing, while digital banks can achieve automation and high efficiency through technological tools. This not only reduces the bank's operational costs but also speeds up business processing, improving efficiency and responsiveness.

Driving Innovation and New Business Models: Digital transformation provides banks with a broader space for innovation. Through digital technology and platforms, banks can introduce more innovative products and services, such as mobile payments, virtual credit cards, robo-advisory, etc. Digital banks can also collaborate with technology companies and startups to jointly develop new business models and cooperation mechanisms, driving the development of financial technology.

Now, let's discuss the challenges that digital transformation in commercial banks may bring:

Data Security and Privacy Protection: As digital banking services develop, a large amount of customer sensitive information is collected and processed, such as personal identification information and financial data. Therefore, banks need to implement effective security measures to ensure the security and privacy protection of customer data, preventing data leaks and cyber-attacks.

Technology and Infrastructure: Digital banking business relies on advanced technology and robust infrastructure to support its operations and service delivery. Banks need continuous investment in technology platforms, networks, and communication equipment, ensuring the stability, security, and reliability of the systems.

User Acceptance and Education: Although digital banking services are popular among the younger generation of users, some customers may still be unfamiliar with or distrustful of mobile applications and online transactions. Banks need to strengthen user education and training, provide user-friendly interfaces and functionalities to increase user acceptance and usability.

Competitive Pressure and Innovation Capabilities Eichengreen and Gupta (2018): Digital technology has lowered market entry barriers, leading to increased competition in the banking industry. Banks need to continuously innovate and improve business models, providing personalized products and services to maintain competitiveness and meet customer demands.

Regulatory and Compliance Environment Arner et al (2016b): Digital banking operations need to comply with the laws, regulations, and regulatory requirements of different countries, such as anti-money laundering, counter-terrorism financing, customer identity verification, etc. Banks need to closely monitor regulatory changes and establish a robust compliance system to ensure the legitimacy and compliance of their operations.

In summary, digital technology provides commercial banks with a wider customer base, more sales channels, higher efficiency, and lower costs. However, it also requires banks to strengthen data security and privacy protection, invest in digital transformation and infrastructure development, continuously innovate and improve business models, and closely monitor regulatory and regulatory changes.

References

Agrawal, A., Gans, J., & Goldfarb, A. (2018). Prediction Machines: The Simple Economics of Artificial Intelligence. Harvard Business Review Press.

Arner, D. W., Barberis, J., & Buckley, R. P. (2016). The evolution of fintech: A new post-crisis paradigm? Georgetown Journal of International Law, 47, 1271.

Arner, D. W., Barberis, J., & Buckley, R. P. (2016). The evolution of fintech: A new post-crisis paradigm? Georgetown Journal of International Law, 47(4)

Chakravorti, B. (2017). Digital Planet 2017: How Competitiveness and Trust in Digital Economies Vary Across the World. The Fletcher School, Tufts University.

Chiu, I. (2017). FinTech and RegTech in a Nutshell, and the Future in a Sandbox. CREATe Working Paper 2017/01.

Eichengreen, B., & Gupta, P. (2018). Digital banking and market competition. Journal of Financial Services Research, 53(1)

Li Jia, Qian Chen, Huang Zhihao. The Era of Big Data: Artificial Intelligence and Commercial Bank Innovation [J]. New Finance, 2018 (12)

Kapoor, R., & Adner, R. (2012). What Firms Make vs. What They Know: How Firms' Production and Knowledge Boundaries Affect Competitive Advantage in the Face of Technological Change. Organization Science.

Lu, Q., & Li, S. (2018). Digital Banking in China: Innovation and Challenges. Palgrave Macmillan.

Sullivan, C. (2017). Digital banking: Challenges, opportunities, and future prospects. Journal of Internet Banking and Commerce, 22(3)

Chapter 5
Digital Wealth Management

5.1 Overview of Digital Wealth Management

As an emerging form of wealth management, digital wealth management is gradually gaining attention. In recent years, the rapid development of digital technology and the internet has driven the rise of digital wealth management. With its efficiency, intelligence, and convenience, digital wealth management has attracted numerous investors and wealth management institutions.

First, let's clarify the concept of "digital wealth management." Digital wealth management refers to the effective management of assets for individuals and institutions using digital technology and platforms to achieve asset appreciation and preservation. It encompasses various aspects such as investment, risk control, asset allocation, and tax planning, providing investors with comprehensive wealth management services.

Correspondingly, the technological architecture is crucial during the construction of a digital wealth management platform. The platform needs to establish a secure, stable, and efficient technological architecture to ensure its reliability and security. It should adopt advanced information technology and data processing systems, possess high availability and scalability, and handle a large volume of data and transaction requests.

In addition, a digital wealth management platform should offer diversified investment products and services to meet investors' different needs. It should provide various investment options such as stocks, bonds, funds, insurance, etc., along with corresponding tools and functionalities like trade execution, asset allocation, risk management, etc. This enables investors to achieve diversified and well-distributed investments and receive personalized investment advice and solutions based on their risk preferences and goals.

User experience is a key consideration factor in designing a digital wealth management platform. The platform should focus on user-friendly interfaces, convenient operations, and information transparency, enabling investors to use the platform

Z. Liu and W. Hou, *Digital Finance*, https://doi.org/10.1007/978-981-99-7305-7_5

easily for investment and asset management. Additionally, the platform should provide real-time market data and portfolio performance information to help investors stay informed about their asset status and make timely decisions and adjustments.

Risk control and compliance are also vital aspects that a digital wealth management platform needs to consider. The platform should establish risk assessment and monitoring mechanisms to help investors understand and evaluate investment risks and take appropriate risk control measures promptly. Simultaneously, the platform needs to comply with relevant laws and regulations to ensure its compliance and protect investors' legitimate rights and interests.

Now, let's analyze the risk control in digital wealth management. Risk control is an essential part of digital wealth management. The platform needs to adopt multiple risk control measures to protect investors' assets and interests.

First and foremost, risk assessment forms the foundation of digital wealth management. The platform needs to understand investors' risk tolerance and preferences through customer risk assessment to provide them with suitable investment solutions. By leveraging big data and artificial intelligence technologies, the platform can more accurately assess investors' risk preferences and tailor risk-controlled investment portfolios for them.

Secondly, asset allocation and portfolio diversification are crucial means of risk control. By diversifying the investment portfolio into different asset classes, industries, and regions, overall portfolio risk can be reduced. A digital wealth management platform should offer diversified investment products and asset allocation plans, allowing investors to achieve reasonable asset allocation based on their needs and risk tolerance.

Furthermore, a digital wealth management platform needs to provide transparent investment information and risk alerts.

The platform should offer clear explanations of investment products, risk disclosures, and related fee information to enable investors to fully understand the risk and return characteristics of the investment products. Regular risk reports and alerts can also be provided to remind investors of market risks and investment fluctuations.

Lastly, the platform needs to establish a risk monitoring and management system. It should have a professional risk management team to conduct real-time risk monitoring and analysis, and take timely actions against potential risks in investment portfolios. The platform should also establish compliance controls to ensure that investment products and services comply with relevant laws and regulatory requirements, safeguarding investors' legitimate rights and interests.

Now, let's analyze the characteristics of digital wealth management. Compared to traditional wealth management, digital wealth management has several distinctive features:

(1) Data-driven decision-making Zeng et al. (2019): Digital wealth management utilizes big data technology to accurately understand clients' risk preferences, income status, and investment needs, thereby providing personalized investment portfolio solutions. Through data analysis and scientific modeling, digital wealth

management can more precisely assess investment risks and returns, providing more competitive investment solutions.

(2) Intelligent robo-advisory services Clarke et al. (2019): Digital wealth management leverages artificial intelligence technology to offer clients intelligent robo-advisory services. By using machine learning algorithms, digital wealth management can automatically analyze market trends, industry changes, macroeconomic environments, etc., to timely provide effective investment advice. Compared to traditional wealth management, digital wealth management is more intelligent and automated, providing efficient and low-cost investment services.
(3) Low barriers and low costs Baker et al. (2017): Digital wealth management offers low barriers and relatively lower costs. Clients can conduct transactions and consultations through internet platforms, avoiding the need to visit bank branches, thus lowering the threshold for investment and making investment services more inclusive. Additionally, digital wealth management typically adopts lower management and transaction fees, helping clients reduce investment costs and increase investment returns.
(4) Scientific risk control Fabozzi et al. (2018): Digital wealth management utilizes scientific risk control models to dynamically adjust investment portfolios and manage risks, helping clients better manage investment risks. Compared to traditional wealth management, digital wealth management's risk control is more scientific and systematic, better equipped to deal with market fluctuations and risk events.

Despite the many advantages of digital wealth management, there are also numerous challenges and risks:

(1) Technological and talent aspects: Digital wealth management requires the adoption of advanced technology and algorithms to support data analysis and intelligent robo-advisory services. This demands wealth management institutions to possess corresponding technological capabilities and talent reserves, capable of responding to rapidly changing technology environments and continuously enhancing technical proficiency.
(2) Data security and privacy protection: Digital wealth management involves a vast amount of customer data and sensitive information, making data security and privacy protection critically important. Wealth management institutions need to establish robust security systems, using encryption technology and security measures to protect customer data's security and privacy.
(3) Market competition: The digital wealth management market is highly competitive, with numerous wealth management institutions and platforms. To stand out in the competition, institutions need to constantly innovate and improve service levels, providing clients with unique value and high-quality experiences. Additionally, establishing a good brand reputation and customer trust is essential for gaining market share.
(4) Legal and regulatory aspects: Digital wealth management needs to comply with relevant laws and regulatory requirements, including data protection, investor

protection, compliance, etc. Wealth management institutions need to closely cooperate with regulatory authorities to ensure business compliance and adhere to relevant laws and guidelines.

It is worth mentioning that the rise and development of digital wealth management can be explained from the perspectives of information economics and financial technology.

Firstly, digital wealth management aligns with the fundamental principles of information economics. Information plays a significant role in the economy, enhancing market efficiency and resource allocation. Through digital data analysis, wealth management institutions can better assess risks and returns, providing optimized investment portfolios, thus improving market efficiency and resource allocation efficiency.

Secondly, the emergence of digital wealth management is a product of financial technology. FinTech involves the use of technology to improve financial services and business models. Digital wealth management, as one of the applications of FinTech, demonstrates the profound impact and transformation of technology on the financial industry. Digital platforms and intelligent robo-advisory services offer more efficient and cost-effective investment solutions, with higher social and economic benefits.

We can see that the development of digital wealth management is facilitated by the continuous advancement of technology and people's pursuit of wealth management. Modern individuals have a growing demand for personalized services and efficient investment returns, and digital wealth management perfectly meets these needs. The development of digital technology and the internet has made wealth management more convenient, cost-effective, and efficient, attracting an increasing number of clients to choose digital wealth management as their preferred method of managing wealth.

In addition to the aforementioned advantages, digital wealth management also possesses the advantage of sustainable investing. Sustainable investing involves considering social, environmental, and governance factors in investment decisions to achieve long-term financial returns and sustainable development of society and the environment. More and more investors recognize that focusing on sustainability factors can lower corporate risks, increase corporate brand value and reputation, thus enhancing long-term investment returns. The development of sustainable investing is not only driven by investor demand but also promoted by governments and regulatory bodies.

Through research, we find that digital wealth management not only changes the traditional wealth management business model but also drives the digital transformation of the financial industry. More and more financial institutions are joining the competition in digital wealth management, promoting industry innovation and improving service quality. However, this development also brings some risks and challenges, such as intensified market competition and insufficient regulation.

Firstly, the impact and challenges of digital wealth management on traditional financial institutions cannot be ignored. Traditional financial institutions such as banks and brokerage firms have long dominated the wealth management sector, and the rise of digital wealth management has placed significant pressure on these institutions. The market size of digital wealth management reached $3.26 trillion globally in 2019 and is expected to grow to $7.61 trillion by 2023, posing a serious challenge to traditional financial institutions.

Secondly, the development of digital wealth management drives the digitalization and intelligence process of the financial industry. The technologies and applications involved in digital wealth management include big data, artificial intelligence, blockchain, etc., which make wealth management business processes more efficient, convenient, and intelligent. For instance, digital wealth management can utilize artificial intelligence to provide customers with more personalized and accurate investment portfolios while automating the analysis of market data to offer real-time investment advice.

The emergence of digital wealth management has propelled the digitalization and intelligence of the financial industry, providing investors with more choices and convenience. However, the competition in the digital wealth management market is becoming increasingly fierce, and investors need to carefully choose digital wealth management platforms to ensure their safety and sustainable investment returns.

Next, let's analyze innovative digital wealth management models.

With the rapid development of digital technology, digital wealth management has become an emerging field in the financial industry. In this chapter, we will analyze the impact of digital wealth management on banks.

The rise of digital wealth management has had a significant impact on traditional banking institutions. Traditional banks are facing competition from digital wealth management platforms, which offer efficient, cost-effective, and personalized wealth management services, attracting many investors. To maintain a competitive advantage in the field of digital wealth management, traditional banks need to undergo digital transformation, strengthen customer relationship management, and improve service quality.

The emergence of digital wealth management has also brought about a transformation in the banking industry's business model. Traditional banks typically adopt a vertically integrated model, providing various financial services, from savings and loans to investment management. However, the development of digital wealth management has made financial services more modular and diversified. Digital wealth management platforms break down financial services into smaller modules, no longer relying on a single institution to provide all services. Instead, they can provide more comprehensive wealth management services by collaborating and integrating resources and expertise from multiple institutions. Such a more flexible financial service supply chain can meet the diverse needs of investors.

Therefore, traditional banking institutions need to actively address the challenges posed by digital wealth management. They should strengthen digital transformation, improve technological infrastructure, enhance customer experience, and service quality. Banks can draw on advanced technologies and innovative concepts from digital wealth management platforms to provide more convenient and personalized wealth management services through digital channels. Additionally, banks can collaborate with digital wealth management platforms to jointly develop and provide high-quality wealth management products and services, achieving mutual benefits.

Next, let's discuss strategic-related topics. Faced with the challenges and changes brought by digital wealth management, traditional banking institutions need to adopt corresponding strategies to maintain competitiveness and adapt to market demands.

Firstly, banks should focus on digital transformation and invest in advanced technology and infrastructure to enhance digital capabilities and efficiency. This involves organizational restructuring, cultural changes, and process reforms. Banks need to establish dedicated digital teams to drive digital transformation and ensure close integration of digital technology with business objectives.

Secondly, banks should prioritize improving customer relationship management and service quality. By gaining in-depth understanding of customer needs and risk preferences, banks can provide personalized wealth management solutions and enhance interaction and communication with customers. At the same time, banks should offer convenient digital channels and tools to enhance customer experience and satisfaction.

Thirdly, banks can consider cooperating with digital wealth management platforms to provide more comprehensive financial services. Such collaboration can expand the service scope and improve efficiency, while achieving better customer satisfaction through sharing technology and data resources. Simultaneously, banks can explore partnerships with other financial technology companies to jointly innovate and develop solutions in the digital wealth management field.

Finally, banks need to prioritize data security and privacy protection. Digital wealth management involves a large amount of customer data and sensitive information, so banks should establish robust information security management systems, strengthen data protection, and comply with privacy regulations to ensure the safety and confidentiality of customer data.

We can see that digital wealth management, utilizing information technology and data analytics, provides personalized wealth management services, representing an innovative wealth management model. Next, we will analyze several innovative management models related to digital wealth.

5.1.1 Robo-Advisor Model

The robo-advisor model, also known as intelligent advisory Miaomiao and Liang, 2017, is a typical innovation in the digital wealth management field. It utilizes artificial intelligence and machine learning technologies to provide investors with personalized investment portfolio recommendations and asset allocation services, being considered one of the innovations in the financial technology field.

Additionally, robo-advisors can adjust investment portfolios promptly based on market trends and customer demands, enhancing the flexibility and efficiency of asset allocation. Robo-advisors can also integrate with emerging technologies such as blockchain to offer more diversified asset allocation services, providing investors with more options. Robo-advisors have been widely applied and recognized, becoming a significant trend in the digital wealth management field.

The relationship between robo-advisors and traditional wealth management institutions has always been a matter of concern. While robo-advisors are extensively used in the digital wealth management field, traditional wealth management institutions still possess strong customer resources and capital strength, making them irreplaceable in the digital wealth management field. Therefore, the relationship between robo-advisors and traditional wealth management institutions should be one of cooperation and mutual benefit.

Robo-advisors can provide traditional wealth management institutions with more intelligent investment advice and asset allocation services, enhancing the industry's overall investment level and efficiency. Traditional wealth management institutions can leverage the technological advantages of robo-advisors to offer high-quality services to more investors, enhancing brand influence and market competitiveness.

Therefore, the relationship between robo-advisors and traditional wealth management institutions is interdependent, and both parties can jointly promote progress and development in the field of digital wealth management.

5.1.2 Social Investing Model

The social investing model is an innovative model in the digital wealth management field. It fully utilizes social media and internet platforms to connect clients and investors, providing investment advice and communication platforms based on social networks. Through social interaction, clients can obtain other investors' perspectives and experiences and engage in discussions and exchanges with them. Clients can also share their investment experiences and views, establishing connections and interactions with other investors.

The advantage of the social investing model lies in enhancing the interaction and trust between clients and investors. This interaction and information exchange help clients better understand the market and investment opportunities, enabling them to make wiser investment decisions.

However, the social investing model also faces some challenges and risks. For example, the authenticity and reliability of information may be questionable, and clients need to possess discerning capabilities. Additionally, privacy and data security are critical issues, and clients' personal information and transaction data need proper protection. To overcome these challenges, social investing platforms need to establish effective risk management mechanisms and security measures, ensuring the protection of clients' interests and privacy.

For example, eToro is a typical social investing platform, established in 2007, and headquartered in Israel. It provides social investing and trading services, allowing users to trade assets such as stocks, forex, and cryptocurrencies on the platform. eToro offers various social features, such as users can follow others, comment on their trades, and share their trading views. Such social interaction and engagement help users learn and improve their investment skills while enhancing their connections and loyalty to other users and investors.

5.1.3 Automated Trading Model

The automated trading model is another innovative model in the digital wealth management field. It utilizes algorithmic trading technology to monitor and analyze the market in real-time, automatically executing trading operations based on clients' investment objectives and risk preferences.

One of the advantages of the automated trading model is that it can leverage vast historical data and real-time market data, using machine learning algorithms to predict market trends and make trading decisions, resulting in better investment returns. Moreover, the automated trading model can lower transaction costs and risks, avoid human errors and emotional interference, achieving more precise trading decisions.

However, the automated trading model also faces some challenges and limitations. On one hand, the complexity and uncertainty of the market may affect the accuracy and performance of algorithms. On the other hand, the automated trading model may encounter technical risks and system failures, necessitating the assurance of system stability and security.

For instance, Nutmeg in the UK is an online investment platform that adopts the automated trading model. Nutmeg utilizes machine learning algorithms to provide personalized investment advice to clients and automatically executes trading operations. The company maximizes investment returns and controls investment risks through diversified asset allocation based on modern investment theories.

5.1.4 Smart Contract Model

The smart contract model is an emerging model in the field of digital wealth management. It utilizes blockchain technology to implement the automatic execution of smart contracts, providing customers with safer, more transparent, and efficient investment services. The advantages of the smart contract model lie in its decentralized and interference-free nature, which enhances customer trust and satisfaction. The application of smart contracts in the financial sector is increasing, especially in areas such as insurance, banking, and securities.

The advent of the smart contract model has made the investment process more transparent and traceable, allowing customers to view and verify transaction executions in real-time, thereby reducing potential risks. Additionally, the smart contract model provides higher security, as the decentralized nature of blockchain technology prevents data tampering and fraudulent activities.

Moreover, the application of smart contracts has expanded beyond the financial sector to other areas, such as real estate, energy, and supply chain management. In the real estate sector, smart contracts can be used for automated leasing and loan contracts, reducing human interference and errors. In the energy sector, smart contracts can help monitor and manage energy production and consumption, achieving more efficient energy management. In supply chain management, smart contracts can track the production, distribution, and sales of products and services, enhancing supply chain efficiency and transparency. Furthermore, smart contracts can also be applied in areas like cross-border transactions, inclusive finance, and digital identity verification.

However, the application of the smart contract model also faces some challenges, such as technological maturity, the formulation of legal regulations, and regulatory issues. With continuous technological advancements and improvements in the regulatory environment, the smart contract model is expected to play a more significant role in digital wealth management, providing safer and more efficient investment services.

In summary, these different digital wealth management models vary based on the technologies and service approaches they rely on. The robot advisory model and the automated trading model depend more on algorithmic trading and machine learning technologies, emphasizing the automation and intelligence of trading. The social investment model emphasizes customer interaction and trust with investors. The smart contract model achieves the automatic execution of smart contracts through blockchain technology, emphasizing the security and transparency of investment services. These innovative digital wealth management models are forward-thinking, presenting both opportunities and challenges for the future development of the financial industry.

Now, let's understand these innovative models from an economic perspective.

The digital wealth management models are innovative models centered around digital technology, holding significant theoretical and practical significance in the fields of economics and finance. These models utilize intelligent algorithms, artificial intelligence, blockchain, and other technologies, reshaping traditional wealth management methods, enhancing efficiency, and transparency, thereby creating more value for customers.

Firstly, let's analyze the strengths and weaknesses of these digital wealth management models from the perspective of transaction cost theory. Transaction costs refer to the various costs involved in conducting transactions, including information costs, search costs, negotiation costs, and monitoring costs. Traditional wealth management models have higher transaction costs since they require frequent communication and negotiation between customers and wealth management institutions, limiting the transparency and efficiency of transactions.

On the other hand, digital wealth management models utilize intelligent algorithms, data mining, artificial intelligence, and other technologies to achieve automated processing and intelligent analysis of information, significantly reducing transaction costs and enhancing transaction efficiency and transparency. Customers can quickly access information and execute decisions, minimizing unnecessary communication and negotiation costs, thereby creating more value for customers. For instance, robot advisory models and automated trading models utilize algorithmic trading and machine learning technologies to automate and intelligently conduct transactions, reducing human errors and emotional interference, improving transaction efficiency and returns.

Apart from transaction costs, digital wealth management models also demonstrate significant advantages in asset portfolio management and risk control. Traditional wealth management models primarily manage risk through diversification and asset allocation but face challenges of information asymmetry and limited stock selection capabilities. In contrast, digital wealth management models utilize intelligent algorithms and machine learning technologies to achieve automated data analysis and risk control, enhancing the capability of predicting portfolio returns and managing risks. Customers can more effectively conduct asset allocation and risk management, creating more value for them. The intelligent analysis and risk control capabilities of digital wealth management models make them innovative methods, contributing to improved portfolio returns and risk reduction.

Next, let's examine these models from the perspective of the Capital Asset Pricing Model (CAPM). The CAPM is a model used to assess the risk and return of financial assets such as stocks and securities, with its core being the relationship between asset portfolio risk and return. Traditional wealth management models primarily manage risks through diversification, asset allocation, and other means, but they face challenges of information asymmetry and limited stock selection capabilities, which limit their risk control and return prediction capabilities.

On the contrary, digital wealth management models utilize intelligent algorithms, machine learning, and other technologies to achieve automated data analysis and risk control, enhancing the capability of predicting portfolio returns and managing risks. Customers can more effectively conduct asset allocation and risk management, creating more value for them. The intelligent analysis and risk control capabilities of digital wealth management models make them innovative ways to improve portfolio returns and risk management.

Finally, let's analyze the digital wealth management models from the perspective of behavioral finance. Behavioral finance is a discipline that studies the relationship between human behavior and financial markets, emphasizing how behavioral decisions are influenced by psychological factors. Traditional wealth management models often overlook customer behavioral biases and emotional factors, such as overtrading and emotion-driven investment decisions, which may hinder investment returns. On the other hand, digital wealth management models leverage data analysis and artificial intelligence to better understand customer needs and behavioral preferences, providing personalized services and advice, which better satisfy customer requirements and achieve wealth growth.

In conclusion, digital wealth management models have many advantages in transaction costs, asset portfolio management, risk control, and customer satisfaction. Through intelligent algorithms, machine learning, and blockchain technology, digital wealth management models reduce transaction costs, enhance transaction efficiency and transparency, and achieve personalized asset management and risk control, creating more value for customers.

However, these models also face challenges, such as data privacy protection and addressing data biases. To drive the future development of digital wealth management models, continuous technological innovation and practical application are required under the guidance of economic theory, to better meet customer wealth growth needs and create social value.

5.2 Digital Wealth Management Platforms and Technologies

With the rapid development of digital technologies, the wealth management industry is undergoing significant transformation. Traditional wealth management businesses heavily relied on human services, but with the rise of digital technologies, the industry is accelerating its digital transformation. The impact of digital technologies on wealth management is multifaceted and comprehensive.

Firstly, digital technologies offer more efficient, convenient, and secure service methods. Through intelligent data analysis and processing, digital technologies can provide customers with more personalized and precise investment plans. Additionally, digital technologies enable round-the-clock online services, meeting customers' demands for real-time access to asset information and transactions.

Secondly, digital technologies expand the investment choices in wealth management. Investors can conveniently access investment information and market dynamics worldwide, enabling faster cross-border investments and asset allocations. The development of digital technologies also promotes diverse trading methods, such as mobile payments, cryptocurrencies, and other innovative trading options, providing investors with more flexibility and convenience.

Furthermore, digital technologies enhance the security and reliability of wealth management. Through intelligent risk control and data protection measures, digital technologies can reduce risks and losses during transactions, improving transaction security and reliability. Technologies like smart contracts enable automated and decentralized transactions, enhancing transaction transparency and trust.

In fact, digital wealth management platforms and technologies have been widely applied and developed. Based on different functions and services, digital wealth management platforms can be categorized as follows:

(1) Wealth Management Platforms Chaffey and Ellis-Chadwick (2019): These platforms primarily offer personalized asset management services to clients, including portfolio management, asset allocation, and risk control. Examples of typical digital wealth management platforms are Wealthfront and Betterment in the United States and Nutmeg in the United Kingdom. They use intelligent algorithms and data analysis to provide customized investment plans, helping clients manage their wealth more effectively.

(2) Investment Social Platforms Xie et al. (2016): These platforms promote investment and wealth management through social interactions and sharing, including investment blogs and social investment websites. Examples of representative investment social platforms are StockTwits in the United States and eToro in the United Kingdom. They provide platforms for clients to share investment experiences and exchange viewpoints, helping clients better understand the market and formulate investment strategies.
(3) Financial Technology Platforms Zhou and Lu (2018): These platforms improve traditional financial services through technological means, including payments, loans, and investments. Examples of representative financial technology platforms are Robinhood and Square in the United States and Ant Group in China. They utilize intelligent algorithms and blockchain technology to provide faster, more convenient, and more secure financial services, enabling clients to better manage and increase their wealth.

The technologies empowering digital wealth management platforms include blockchain, cryptocurrencies, virtual goods, distributed storage, and artificial intelligence (AI).

(1) Blockchain Technology Li and Shuo, 2018: As the core technology in digital wealth management, blockchain has multiple applications.

Firstly, the decentraliz ation feature of blockchain ensures the security and transparency of digital wealth, reducing the intervention and costs of intermediaries. This provides higher credibility and efficiency for wealth management. Secondly, blockchain technology supports the management and trading of digital wealth, such as cryptocurrency trading and digital art auctions, bringing new opportunities and challenges to wealth management.

One of the core applications of blockchain technology in wealth management is smart contracts. Smart contracts automatically execute contract terms, reducing reliance on intermediary institutions and increasing the efficiency and transparency of wealth management. Investors can have better protection through smart contracts, ensuring that wealth management institutions execute transactions according to agreed conditions, reducing human interference.

Another application of blockchain technology in wealth management includes decentralized investment platforms. These platforms, based on blockchain technology and smart contracts, enable transactions and asset management without the need for intermediary institutions. Investors can directly deposit assets into the platform and autonomously manage and control their investment portfolios.

(2) Cryptocurrency Technology: As a crucial component of digital wealth management, cryptocurrencies have diverse applications and roles.

Firstly, cryptocurrency technology enables peer-to-peer value transfer, enhancing transaction transparency and security, reducing intermediaries, and lowering costs. Cryptocurrencies like Bitcoin and Ethereum have been widely used in the digital wealth domain.

In terms of financial transactions, cryptocurrency technology facilitates faster, more convenient, and low-cost transactions. Bitcoin achieves peer-to-peer transactions in a decentralized manner, eliminating intermediaries and high transaction fees. Ethereum, on the other hand, supports smart contracts, which can automatically execute transactions, reducing the cost of human intervention.

Additionally, cryptocurrency technology provides decentralized digital identity authentication services, safeguarding user privacy and security. For example, the identity authentication system Civic uses blockchain technology to offer decentralized digital identity authentication, ensuring the security and trustworthiness of user identity information.

Cryptocurrency technology also supports the development and operation of decentralized applications. As a smart contract platform, Ethereum supports the development of decentralized applications, enabling applications to trade and operate without the need to trust third parties. This technology ensures application transparency, fairness, and decentralization.

(3) Virtual Goods Technology: As a significant part of the digital wealth management field, virtual goods have broad applications and important impacts.

Firstly, virtual goods technology is extensively applied in the gaming industry. Players can use virtual currency to purchase game items or engage in virtual currency exchanges, enhancing game playability and profitability. For example, popular online game Fortnite allows players to use virtual currency V-Bucks to buy game items or earn profits by providing services to other players.

Secondly, virtual goods technology drives the creation and trading of digital artworks. Through virtual goods technology, digital artworks can be authenticated and made non-replicable using blockchain technology, increasing their collectible value. Non-fungible tokens (NFTs), as blockchain-based digital assets, can represent various types of virtual goods, such as art, music, game items, and more.

Additionally, virtual goods tec0hnology is applied in the field of virtual real estate, where users can buy, sell, and trade virtual land and buildings. Virtual reality platform Decentraland, based on blockchain technology, provides such functionality, allowing users to own and operate virtual real estate.

Virtual goods technology also supports the creation and use of virtual currencies, which play a crucial role in the digital economy, improving the liquidity and convenience of the digital economy. For example, Facebook's virtual currency project called Libra aimed to improve the global financial system through blockchain technology and digital payment systems.

(4) Distributed Storage Technology: As one of the essential technologies in digital wealth management, distributed storage has extensive applications and a significant impact.

Firstly, distributed storage technology is used for cloud storage, where data is stored on multiple servers to enhance data security and reliability. Cloud storage solutions like Amazon S3 enable users to easily store and retrieve data while ensuring data backup and redundancy.

Secondly, distributed storage technology plays an important role in Content Delivery Networks (CDNs). CDNs use distributed storage to store content on multiple nodes, speeding up content transmission and improving content availability. CDN service providers like Akamai accelerate global user access to websites and applications by bringing content closer to users, providing a better user experience.

Furthermore, distributed storage technology is used for file sharing. By storing files on multiple nodes, distributed storage technology enhances file availability and reliability. File sharing protocols like BitTorrent allow users to share files and resources through distributed storage, achieving more efficient file transmission and sharing.

(5) Artificial Intelligence Technology: As a crucial technology in the digital wealth management field, artificial intelligence has wide-ranging applications and significant impacts.

Firstly, artificial intelligence can analyze financial market data, client investment preferences, and behavior patterns through its powerful algorithms and learning capabilities. This enables wealth management institutions to accurately predict market trends, risk levels, and investment returns, providing clients with precise investment portfolio advice and decision support.

Furthermore, artificial intelligence can provide personalized investment advice in wealth management. By gaining a deep understanding of clients' risk preferences, financial goals, and market conditions, artificial intelligence can tailor investment strategies for each client, meeting their individualized needs and objectives. Such personalized investment advice can enhance client satisfaction and investment performance.

Moreover, artificial intelligence can enable automated trading and execution. Through intelligent algorithms and automated execution, artificial intelligence can automatically execute trading instructions while meeting preset conditions and strategies, increasing the speed and accuracy of trades. This helps reduce human errors and emotional influences on trading decisions, improving trading efficiency and outcomes.

Additionally, artificial intelligence plays a crucial role in fraud detection and risk management. Through machine learning and pattern recognition techniques, artificial intelligence can analyze client behavior, trading patterns, and market dynamics, promptly identifying potential fraudulent activities and risk events. This allows wealth management institutions to implement corresponding risk control measures, safeguarding clients' wealth security.

Lastly, the natural language processing capability of artificial intelligence enables it to serve as an intelligent assistant for clients through voice and text interactions. By understanding and addressing clients' needs and inquiries, artificial intelligence can provide real-time market information, answer client questions, and execute trading instructions. This type of intelligent assistant service enhances clients' experience and satisfaction.

As technology continues to advance, digital wealth management platforms will become more intelligent, efficient, and secure. The application and development of these technologies will have a significant impact on the overall development and transformation of the digital economy.

5.3 The Challenges and Opportunities in Digital Wealth Management

Based on the above discussion, it is evident that the wealth management industry is undergoing a digital transformation, creating new opportunities and challenges for both institutions and investors in this historic change.

Digitization is at the core of this transformation. Digital technology can help wealth management institutions improve efficiency, reduce costs, enhance transparency, and security, while also providing investors with more personalized and high-quality services. This will usher in a new era based on data, algorithms, and artificial intelligence, where digital technology becomes the core competitive advantage in wealth management.

From an economic perspective, digital wealth management presents tremendous opportunities:

Firstly, the application of intelligent and automated digital technology will enhance the accuracy and efficiency of investment decisions. Through data analysis and predictive modeling, clients can receive more precise investment advice and asset allocation strategies. This will facilitate better investment returns for clients and drive economic growth.

Secondly, digital technology will promote the diversification and globalization of wealth management. Digital wealth management will offer more diverse investment choices, encouraging international investment and collaboration in asset allocation. Through digital platforms and intelligent algorithms, clients can access global investment opportunities, optimizing their asset allocation and risk control.

Moreover, digital technology places a strong focus on customer experience and service quality. Through intelligent data analysis and processing, digital wealth management can provide personalized and precise investment strategies and offer convenient and secure service experiences. This will enhance customer engagement and satisfaction, increase customer loyalty, and drive the development of the wealth management industry.

Finally, digital technology emphasizes social responsibility and sustainable development. The wealth management industry is increasingly concerned with social and environmental responsibility, and through Environmental, Social, and Governance (ESG) investment principles, digital wealth management can promote sustainable development in enterprises and projects, achieving a positive interaction between wealth growth and social responsibility.

At the same time, the digital wealth management industry faces various challenges, including data security and privacy protection, technological innovation, and digital transformation, as well as talent recruitment and development. To address these challenges, digital wealth management companies need to take corresponding measures.

Firstly, data security and privacy protection Smith et al. (2011) are the primary challenges facing digital wealth management. To safeguard customer data security and privacy, companies need to strengthen data encryption, establish secure management systems, and comply with relevant laws and regulations. For example, adopting data encryption technology, setting up firewalls and access control mechanisms, conducting regular security vulnerability scanning and risk assessments to ensure the security and privacy of customer data.

Secondly, technological innovation and digital transformation require significant investment and human resource support. Digital wealth management companies should actively promote technological innovation, employing advanced technology and digital platforms to improve the quality and efficiency of wealth management services. This includes utilizing technologies such as artificial intelligence and big data analysis to optimize investment decisions and customer services, and establishing digital platforms to offer more convenient services.

Additionally, talent recruitment and development are also challenges that digital wealth management companies need to address. Talent in the digital wealth management industry is relatively scarce, and companies need to actively recruit and develop high-quality professionals, including finance specialists, technology experts, and customer service personnel. This can be achieved through collaborations with universities, conducting internal training, and development programs to ensure the company has a skilled and knowledgeable workforce.

In conclusion, the opportunities in digital wealth management are substantial. Utilizing digital technology, it can provide personalized wealth management services to clients, positively impacting economic growth, financial market development, and financial inclusion.

References

Baker, H. K., Filbeck, G., & Ricciardi, V. (2017). How behavioral finance can inform financial advisors. Journal of Financial Service Professionals, 71(3)

Chaffey, D., & Ellis-Chadwick, F. (2019). Digital marketing. Pearson UK.

Clarke, R., Lee, D., & Ryu, H. (2019). Robo-advisors and wealth management. The Journal of Alternative Investments, 21(3)

Fabozzi, F. J., Focardi, S. M., & Jonas, C. (2018). High-tech and micropropagation VI. Handbook of Finance and Technology. Wiley.

Ma Li, Zhu Shuo. The Application and Risks of Blockchain Technology in the Field of Payment and Settlement [J]. Financial Review, 2018, 10 (04)

Li Miaomiao, Wang Liang. Intelligent Investment Advisors: Advantages, Obstacles, and Solutions [J]. Southern Finance, 2017 (12)

Smith, H. J., Dinev, T., & Xu, H. (2011). Information privacy research: An interdisciplinary review. MIS Quarterly, 35(4)

Xie, K., Chen, C., & Wu, S. (2016). Online social interactions: A natural experiment on word of mouth versus observational learning. Journal of Marketing Research, 53(2)

Zeng, Y., Zhang, L., & Liu, X. (2019). Big data-driven decision-making in financial services: A review and future prospects. Journal of Finance and Data Science, 5(2)

Zhou, T., & Lu, Y. (2018). A study of mobile payment (M-Payment) services adoption among university students using an extended Technology Acceptance Model (TAM). Technological Forecasting and Social Change, 128

Chapter 6
Central Bank Digital Currency

6.1 Overview of Central Bank Digital Currency (CBDC)

Central Bank Digital Currency (CBDC) is a type of digital currency issued and managed by a central bank. Unlike traditional cash, it does not rely on intermediaries for transactions but is based on a distributed ledger using blockchain technology. It has the potential for revolutionary impact and can serve as a bridge between traditional and digital currencies.

Let's explore the functions of digital currency Auer et al. (2020):

Firstly, the emergence of CBDC may promote financial decentralization. The traditional financial system has centralization issues, leading to excessive power in financial institutions, which can cause economic instability and financial crises. The decentralized design of the central bank digital currency is expected to reduce the power of financial institutions, making currency issuance more fair and transparent.

Secondly, widespread adoption of CBDC can enhance international financial cooperation and regulation. In the context of increasing globalization and cross-border transactions, CBDC provides new tools and mechanisms for international financial cooperation and regulation. The convenience of digital transactions and cross-border payments can improve the efficiency and security of international financial cooperation and regulation.

Thirdly, the development of CBDC will drive financial innovation and development. The introduction of CBDC will stimulate financial innovation and propel the development of financial technology. By incorporating smart contracts and blockchain technology, CBDC is expected to enhance the efficiency and quality of financial services, further promoting economic growth and development.

Fourthly, the widespread adoption of CBDC will facilitate broader and more convenient financial services for the poor and low-income groups. Many impoverished and low-income individuals often lack access to traditional financial services, but the emergence of central bank digital currency can lower the barriers to financial

Z. Liu and W. Hou, *Digital Finance*, https://doi.org/10.1007/978-981-99-7305-7_6

services, providing them with more accessible and convenient financial services and promoting social equity and development.

Finally, the development of CBDC can improve the flexibility and efficiency of monetary policy. CBDC provides central banks with more precise monetary policy tools, allowing better monitoring and regulation of currency circulation, thus enhancing the flexibility and effectiveness of monetary policy.

The issuance of central bank digital currency can be divided into account-based CBDC and token-based CBDC. Each approach has its advantages and disadvantages, with different characteristics and applicable scenarios.

Account-based CBDC refers to the central bank directly providing digital currency to the public, enabling users to conduct transactions by opening accounts with the central bank. This approach ensures the security and reliability of transactions since transaction records and funds are managed and monitored by the central bank. Additionally, account-based CBDC can achieve more precise monetary policy regulation, as the central bank can directly control the money supply and interest rates to stabilize the economy and financial system. However, account-based CBDC may require the establishment of complex technical infrastructure and regulatory mechanisms, involving issues such as user privacy and data security.

Token-based CBDC involves trading digital currency in the form of physical entities (tokens). This approach is similar to the use of traditional banknotes and coins, where users can directly hold and exchange tokens without relying on bank accounts. Token-based CBDC is characterized by convenience and speed, especially in scenarios where individuals lack bank accounts or stable internet connectivity. However, token-based CBDC may face challenges related to token circulation regulation and anti-counterfeiting measures to ensure the security and authenticity of tokens.

It is important to note that central banks can choose a combination of account-based and token-based approaches in the actual issuance of CBDC to balance security and convenience. For example, account-based CBDC can be used to provide secure savings and payment functions, while token-based CBDC can be utilized for daily small-value transactions.

Central bank digital currency serves multiple functions, including payment, store of value, and settlement:

Firstly, CBDC offers a faster and more convenient payment method. Users can use CBDC for instant electronic payments without relying on traditional payment channels such as bank transfers or credit card payments. Transactions with CBDC can be completed within seconds, providing a more efficient and immediate payment experience.

Secondly, CBDC can serve as a stable store of value. As CBDC is issued and endorsed by the central bank, its value stability is relatively high. Users can convert funds into CBDC for storage and asset preservation, mitigating risks such as inflation.

Additionally, CBDC plays an essential role in settlement. Particularly in cross-border payments, CBDC can provide faster, more transparent, and cost-effective settlement services, reducing transaction costs and exchange rate risks. It has the potential to improve existing cross-border payment systems, accelerating fund flows and trade settlements.

The development of central bank digital currency will have significant implications for monetary policy, financial stability, and the payment market, including the following aspects:

Firstly, CBDC will impact the execution of monetary policy. Central banks can provide liquidity directly to the public through CBDC, making the transmission mechanism of monetary policy more direct and efficient. With CBDC, central banks can better control the money supply, adjust interest rates, and implement other monetary policy tools to achieve economic stability and inflation targets. The introduction of CBDC may change the traditional execution of monetary policy, necessitating the formulation of corresponding regulatory policies and operational frameworks.

Secondly, CBDC is crucial to financial stability. CBDC can improve the efficiency and security of the financial system. By recording transactions through distributed ledger technology like blockchain, CBDC can increase transaction transparency and traceability, reducing fraud risks and financial crimes. Moreover, the introduction of CBDC can decrease reliance on cash, lowering systemic risks and providing better safeguards for financial stability.

Furthermore, the development of CBDC may significantly impact the payment market. CBDC offers a new payment tool, which may alter the roles and functions of traditional payment institutions. The convenience and immediacy of CBDC can promote the popularization and development of electronic payments, potentially putting pressure on traditional payment methods and intermediaries. This may lead traditional payment institutions to adjust their business models and service strategies to adapt to the new landscape of digital payments.

However, CBDC also faces various challenges. Firstly, its introduction may have an impact on traditional banking business since the public can directly transact with the central bank, resulting in changes to the role and profit model of traditional banks. Secondly, the development of CBDC may involve privacy concerns, as the central bank can track and record details of CBDC transactions, raising worries about individual privacy and data security. Additionally, CBDC's technological and regulatory challenges need to be addressed, including aspects like security, scalability, and compliance.

Therefore, in the process of advancing the development of central bank digital currency, it is essential to weigh its pros and cons. Relevant institutions should focus on resolving technological and regulatory challenges to ensure security and privacy protection. At the same time, active exploration of collaborative cooperation with traditional financial institutions is needed to balance the relationship between CBDC and the traditional financial system and mitigate the impact of CBDC on banking businesses.

In recent years, an increasing number of countries and regions worldwide have begun exploring and piloting central bank digital currencies, including 36 countries or regions such as the United States, Canada, Europe, Japan, Singapore, etc.

Next, we will share several typical cases and practices of central bank digital currencies (CBDCs):

(1) Swedish E-krona: Sweden is one of the earliest countries to explore CBDC and launched a pilot project for the digital currency E-krona in 2020. E-krona is a digital currency issued and managed by the Swedish central bank. Compared to existing payment methods, it offers faster transactions and lower costs, contributing to improved payment efficiency and security.
(2) Bahamian Sand Dollar: The Bahamas became the world's first country to officially launch a CBDC in 2020, known as the Sand Dollar. It is a blockchain-based digital currency aimed at providing convenient payment options for the unbanked population, promoting financial inclusion, and inclusive finance.
(3) Chinese Digital Yuan: China is one of the earliest countries to explore CBDC and started piloting the Digital Currency Electronic Payment (DCEP) in 2020. The digital yuan is issued and managed by the People's Bank of China (PBOC) and aims to improve payment efficiency and security, reduce cash usage, and combat illegal activities.
(4) Euro Digital Project: The European Central Bank (ECB) initiated the Euro Digital Project in 2020 to explore the possibility of digitalizing the Euro. While the project involves technologies and architectures related to CBDC, the ECB emphasized that it is not a CBDC pilot but a preparatory study for Euro digitalization.
(5) U.S. Digital Dollar: The Federal Reserve is conducting research on CBDC but has not publicly announced the issuance of a digital dollar. However, a report from the U.S. Congress suggested exploring the issuance of a digital dollar to improve payment system efficiency and security, and reduce cash usage. The report also emphasized considerations for privacy protection, anti-money laundering measures, and compatibility with existing payment systems.
(6) Singaporean Digital Singapore Dollar: The Monetary Authority of Singapore has been conducting CBDC research and trials for several years, and their digital currency is known as Project Ubin. The digital Singapore Dollar aims to enhance payment efficiency and security, promote financial inclusion and inclusive finance, while maintaining Singapore's competitiveness as an international financial center.

Regarding the design, functionality, and influencing factors of central bank digital currency issuance, we will analyze the following aspects:

First, attention should be given to how to design a central bank digital currency, as the design choices of CBDC have significant implications on its practical application and impact. This includes issuance methods, implementation approaches, and factors like security, privacy, and scalability.

Next, we will explore the various aspects of CBDC design choices and provide several different CBDC models to assist policymakers in selecting the most suitable model.

One important factor in CBDC design is the issuance method. Currently, there are three main issuance models: direct issuance model, indirect issuance model, and hybrid issuance model.

(1) Direct issuance model Bech and Garratt (2017): The central bank directly issues CBDC to the public or businesses, similar to the issuance of cash. This model can provide high availability and security since the central bank directly manages the issuance and transactions of CBDC. Users can hold and use CBDC directly without relying on third-party financial institutions. This model may be more suitable for countries that emphasize central bank control and supervision.
(2) Indirect issuance model Kumhof and Noone (2018): The central bank issues CBDC through commercial banks or other financial institutions, similar to the issuance of money market funds. In this model, the central bank delegates commercial banks or other financial institutions to issue and manage CBDC. Users can hold and use CBDC through accounts established with these financial institutions. This model can reduce the pressure on the central bank and is easier to implement as it leverages existing financial institution networks and systems. However, it may pose challenges in terms of regulation and risk management.
(3) Hybrid issuance model Auer and Boehme (2020): The central bank adopts both direct and indirect issuance methods to issue CBDC. This model can balance the advantages and disadvantages of both models. For example, the central bank can directly issue retail CBDC to the public while collaborating with commercial banks to issue wholesale CBDC to large businesses. This model offers a wide range of use cases and greater flexibility in choice.

Choosing the appropriate issuance model requires considering the specific circumstances of a country or region, the maturity of the regulatory and financial systems, and the impact on financial stability, payment system efficiency, user privacy, and data security, among other factors.

Second, another important factor in CBDC design is the implementation approach, which determines the storage and transmission methods of CBDC. There are currently four main implementation models: account model, token model, hybrid model, and layered model.

(1) Account model: CBDC is stored in central bank accounts, similar to how cash is stored in bank accounts. Users can conduct transactions and transfers through accounts established with the central bank. This model provides the highest level of security and traceability since the central bank has strong management and regulatory capabilities over the accounts. However, the account model requires more regulatory and management measures, including user authentication, anti-money laundering measures, and monitoring of fund flows.
2) Token model: CBDC is issued in the form of digital tokens, similar to cryptocurrencies. Users can hold and transfer these digital tokens, similar to using cash or cryptocurrencies for transactions. The token model can offer higher privacy and decentralization since transaction records do not need to be centrally stored in the central bank or other institutions. However, the token model may raise issues related to regulation and supervision, such as anti-money laundering and terrorist financing concerns.

3) Hybrid model: CBDC adopts a combination of the account model and token model, allowing users to choose between account-based transactions and token-based transactions. This model combines the advantages of both the account model and token model, providing greater flexibility and choice. However, the hybrid model requires more complex technical architecture and regulatory framework to support the conversion and management between accounts and tokens.
4) Layered model: CBDC is divided into two levels of management. One level interacts directly with the central bank and is responsible for CBDC issuance and management. The other level is managed by commercial banks or other financial institutions and is responsible for interactions with users and providing services. The layered model can separately manage the risks and security issues of the two levels while leveraging the distributed network and customer relationships of commercial banks. However, the layered model requires a more complex technical architecture and management framework to achieve coordination and interoperability between the levels.

Third, choosing the appropriate implementation approach requires comprehensive consideration of factors such as security, privacy, scalability, regulatory framework, and technical requirements.

In terms of security, the CBDC system needs to adopt robust encryption technologies and rigorous network security measures to protect users' funds and transaction information from hacker attacks and fraudulent activities. Security also encompasses the reliability and resilience of the system, ensuring that the CBDC system can maintain stable operation in the face of various potential risks and threats.

Privacy is another important factor to consider. The CBDC system should ensure the privacy of user transactions and personal information, adhering to appropriate privacy protection and data processing principles. Anonymous transaction mechanisms or de-identification technologies can be employed to balance user privacy and regulatory needs.

Scalability is crucial to ensuring that the CBDC system can handle increasing numbers of users and transaction volumes. The CBDC system needs to have high scalability and flexibility to process large-scale transactions and adapt to future demand growth. At the same time, system stability and performance are key to ensuring that the CBDC system can maintain excellent operation under high loads and high concurrency.

The regulatory framework is the foundation for the successful implementation and operation of Central Bank Digital Currencies (CBDCs). Central banks need to establish appropriate regulatory mechanisms and institutional frameworks to ensure compliance, transparency, and stability of CBDC systems. The regulatory framework should clearly define the legal status of CBDC, issuance and circulation rules, market access, and participation requirements to ensure the smooth operation of the CBDC system and protect user rights and financial stability.

Furthermore, we offer several different CBDC models to assist policymakers in choosing the most suitable one. These models are as follows:

Central Bank Account Model: This model is similar to cash, where users store CBDC in a central bank account and can directly transfer and make payments from the central bank. This model can provide the highest level of security and traceability but requires more regulatory and management measures.

Commercial Bank Account Model: This model is similar to traditional commercial bank accounts, where users store CBDC in commercial bank accounts and can transfer and make payments through commercial banks. This model can reduce the pressure on central banks and is easier to implement, but it may bring regulatory and risk management issues.

Digital Token Model: In this model, CBDC is issued as digital tokens similar to cryptocurrencies. Users can transfer and make payments through digital wallets, offering higher privacy and decentralization. However, it may raise concerns related to regulation and supervision.

Hybrid Model: This model combines the advantages of both account-based and token-based models, allowing users to choose their preferred storage and payment methods. However, it requires more complex technological architecture and regulatory frameworks.

Additionally, the competition between Central Bank Digital Currencies and the cryptocurrency market, as well as the potential impact of CBDC issuance on the cryptocurrency market, are worth noting.

Understanding this issue is crucial to avoid confusing the value of CBDCs with regular cryptocurrencies. Specifically, the competition between CBDCs and the cryptocurrency market can be seen in the following aspects:

(1) Transaction Speed: CBDCs will be a "centralized" digital currency issued and managed by central banks. In comparison, cryptocurrencies are based on decentralized blockchain technology, which may result in relatively slower transaction speeds. If CBDCs have an advantage in transaction speed, they may compete in the payment market with cryptocurrencies.
(2) Security: As CBDCs are issued and managed by central banks, they may be more reliable in terms of security. Cryptocurrencies, on the other hand, are susceptible to risks such as hacking, posing certain security concerns. If CBDCs have an advantage in security, they may compete in the digital asset market with cryptocurrencies.
(3) Legal Status: CBDCs will become a legal form of currency issued and managed by central banks, having a legal status. Most countries have not yet fully recognized cryptocurrencies. If CBDCs gain widespread legal recognition, they may compete in the currency market with cryptocurrencies.
(4) Price Volatility: Cryptocurrencies are known for their high price volatility, which may expose investors to greater risks. In contrast, CBDCs offer price stability and do not experience significant price fluctuations. If CBDCs can provide a more stable investment option, they may compete in the digital asset market with cryptocurrencies.

Understanding the differences between the two, we can consider the following thoughts regarding their relationship:

(1) The cryptocurrency market is relatively new, and with the rise of cryptocurrencies like Bitcoin, the market has gradually expanded. Due to the decentralized nature of the cryptocurrency market, there is fierce competition, rapid innovation, and ease of issuing new cryptocurrencies, as well as easy exchange between different cryptocurrencies.
(2) The development of Central Bank Digital Currencies may impact the cryptocurrency market. CBDCs have the backing of central bank credibility, stable value, and a reliable payment mechanism, which could exert greater competitive pressure on the cryptocurrency market. The issuance of CBDCs may also impose limitations on innovation and competition in the cryptocurrency market since the official digital currency of central banks may influence the circulation and issuance of other digital currencies.
(3) The relationship between Central Bank Digital Currencies and the cryptocurrency market is mutually influential. Innovations in technology and market patterns in the cryptocurrency market may affect the technology and implementation methods of CBDCs, thus influencing their development.

The impact of Central Bank Digital Currencies on financial stability is also a core issue that requires attention. Here, we can conduct some simple analysis:

(1) CBDC issuance may have an impact on deposit business and monetary policy. If CBDC coexists with cash and bank deposits, it may weaken the deposit business of banks and make the money supply more unstable. Additionally, CBDC issuance may affect the implementation of monetary policy by central banks since CBDC can be directly issued by the central bank and used for exchanges with other currencies and assets. If CBDC usage is substantial, the central bank may need to adjust its monetary policy framework to better control the money supply and interest rates.
(2) CBDC issuance may also impact payment systems and financial regulation. If CBDC is widely used, it may improve the efficiency and reliability of payment systems and promote cross-border payments and financial inclusion. However, CBDC issuance may also raise security and privacy issues, making regulation more challenging. Therefore, regulatory authorities need to formulate appropriate policies to ensure the safety, reliability, and transparency of CBDCs.
3) CBDC issuance may also affect the banking ecosystem and financial risks. If CBDC usage is widespread, it may impact the deposit and lending business of banks and potentially lead to adjustments in the banking industry's structure and risk transfer. Furthermore, if CBDC usage is significant, it may increase banks' operating costs and potentially alter their risk appetite for high-risk borrowers.

In reality, the future development trends of Central Bank Digital Currencies will be influenced by various factors. Technological advancements will drive the efficiency and security of CBDCs, particularly as blockchain technology continues to innovate and mature. Legal and policy support from governments and regulatory institutions will help promote the compliant issuance and stable operation of CBDCs. Additionally, market demand and user acceptance will play a crucial role in determining the market prospects and adoption level of CBDCs.

In conclusion, as an emerging form of currency, Central Bank Digital Currencies have the potential for revolutionary impacts. The development of CBDCs requires careful consideration of issuance methods, functionalities, effects, pros and cons, and future development trends. This requires collective efforts from central banks, governments, regulatory institutions, technology providers, and market participants.

6.2 Impact on Monetary Policy and Financial Stability

With the rapid development of the digital economy, Central Bank Digital Currency (CBDC) has become a hot topic of research for central banks worldwide. As a new type of digital currency, CBDC comes with various characteristics and functionalities that will have far-reaching effects on the traditional banking system, significantly influencing monetary policy and regulatory systems, and thereby affecting financial system stability. This chapter will focus on exploring the impact of digital currencies on monetary policy and financial stability.

The impact of CBDC on the banking system is mainly reflected in the following aspects:

Deposits and Loans: The introduction of Central Bank Digital Currency may affect bank deposit and loan operations. On one hand, if CBDC gains widespread usage, some individuals may transfer their assets into CBDC accounts, reducing the size of bank deposits. On the other hand, if CBDC can be directly provided to the public as loans, it may impact the loan operations of banks.

Interest Rates and Monetary Policy: The introduction of Central Bank Digital Currency may influence interest rates and the execution of monetary policy. On one hand, if CBDC can be directly provided to the public as liquidity, the central bank may find it easier to control the money supply and interest rate levels. On the other hand, if CBDC can coexist with traditional currencies, the central bank may need to formulate new monetary policy frameworks to manage the circulation of different currencies.

Payments and Settlements: Central Bank Digital Currency can be used for payments and settlements, potentially affecting traditional payment and settlement institutions. If CBDC enables faster and more convenient transactions, traditional payment and settlement institutions may lose market share.

Banking Business Models: The introduction of Central Bank Digital Currency may impact banking business models. Banks may need to adapt to the presence of CBDC, adjusting their business models to better suit the new financial environment. Additionally, banks may face increased competition, as CBDC may attract more users and funds.

In this scenario, banks can consider adopting the following strategies:

Collaboration with Central Banks: Establish partnerships with central banks to explore CBDC applications and technological support, enhancing payment and settlement efficiency and maintaining market competitiveness.

Improve Customer Relations and Service Quality: Strengthen customer relationship management and provide high-quality financial services to attract more users and enhance customer satisfaction. Tailor personalized services and customized products to meet diverse customer needs.

Investment in New Technologies and Platforms: Actively invest in and adopt new technologies and digital platforms to support the development and transformation of the digital economy. Utilize advanced technologies to improve the efficiency and security of the financial system, including artificial intelligence, blockchain, and big data analysis, among others.

Explore New Business Models: Actively seek innovation and explore new business models and revenue sources. Consider offering value-added services, collaborating with financial technology companies, and engaging in digital asset management to adapt to market changes and meet customer demands.

Establish Strategic Partnerships: Form partnerships with other financial institutions, technology companies, and payment service providers to expand service offerings and business capabilities, collectively addressing the challenges and opportunities brought by CBDC.

Next, let's discuss the impact of digital currencies on monetary policy:

Firstly, the introduction of CBDC may alter the transmission mechanism of central bank monetary policy Bindseil (2020). Currently, monetary policy relies mainly on the central bank injecting money into the economy through market purchases of government bonds and securities, thereby influencing interbank market rates. However, direct issuance of CBDC enables the central bank to have a more direct impact on the money supply and interest rate levels within the economy, potentially changing the transmission mechanism of monetary policy.

Secondly, the introduction of CBDC may lead to changes in asset allocation and currency demand, thereby affecting the stability of the entire currency market. In the traditional currency market, individuals mainly rely on cash and deposits for asset allocation. With the introduction of CBDC, individuals can directly hold CBDC for asset allocation, potentially reducing the demand for traditional currencies, thereby affecting the supply–demand relationship and stability of the currency market.

Additionally, CBDC issuance affects the transparency of monetary policy. The introduction of CBDC can enhance the transparency of monetary policy as the central bank can more directly track currency circulation and transactions, thereby better monitoring the economic situation. The digital nature of CBDC also makes it easier for the central bank to provide information on monetary policy and economic data to the public.

Finally, CBDC issuance may have an impact on central bank interest rate policies. The presence of CBDC may lead to a decline in market interest rates, thereby limiting the central bank's operating space for interest rate policies. Moreover, the introduction of CBDC may also lead to a liquidity trap, where the central bank is unable to stimulate economic growth by lowering interest rates.

After understanding the impact of Central Bank Digital Currencies on monetary policy, we need to delve deeper into its impact on financial stability, specifically in terms of its effects on financial intermediation and currency regulatory policies.

Firstly, Central Bank Digital Currency possesses characteristics such as traceability, security, and real time capability, which are expected to improve financial system stability. On one hand, the traceability of CBDC can assist the central bank in better monitoring money supply and circulation, facilitating more effective implementation of monetary policy. On the other hand, the security of CBDC can enhance the security of payment systems, reducing the occurrence of financial crimes. Additionally, the real-time capability of CBDC can enhance payment efficiency, reducing settlement and clearing risks, thus supporting financial stability.

However, the issuance of CBDC may also bring some challenges and risks. On one hand, the central bank needs to establish the appropriate technological and security systems to ensure the secure operation of CBDC. On the other hand, the central bank needs to strike a balance between the coordination and interaction of CBDC with the existing financial system to ensure cooperation and alignment with other financial institutions. Moreover, the central bank needs to strengthen regulation to guard against risks and improper behavior in the digital currency market, maintaining financial system stability and security.

In terms of the entire financial intermediary sector, the introduction of CBDC will intensify competition and directly compete with traditional banks, potentially impacting their businesses, especially in the areas of deposits and payments.

CBDC may also impact the payment market. Firstly, CBDC can serve as an alternative payment method, directly competing with existing payment instruments, such as cash, credit cards, and digital payment tools. Secondly, CBDC may influence payment networks and systems. For example, if CBDC can seamlessly transfer between different payment networks and systems, it may promote more cross-border payments, increasing international payment competition. However, if CBDC can only be used within a specific payment network or system, it may restrict competition and lead to monopolies.

CBDC may also impact competition policy in financial markets. Firstly, CBDC can act as an alternative savings method, directly competing with existing savings tools, such as savings accounts, bonds, and stocks. Secondly, CBDC may influence payment systems and settlement systems. For example, CBDC can facilitate faster, safer, and cheaper settlement methods, challenging existing settlement and clearing institutions. However, CBDC may lead to the monopoly of settlement and clearing institutions, as they may expand their market share through CBDC usage.

CBDC may also have an impact on financial regulation. For example, CBDC can make it easier for regulatory authorities to track currency circulation and transactions, thereby making financial crimes more difficult to conduct. However, CBDC may also raise privacy concerns as it can record transaction details, potentially affecting users' privacy.

In summary, the issuance of Central Bank Digital Currency will enhance the efficiency of central bank monetary policy and financial stability regulation. CBDC enables the central bank to better monitor the money supply and the operation of the payment system, allowing for quicker adjustments as needed.

Furthermore, CBDC can increase the transparency and predictability of monetary policy, enabling the public to have a clearer understanding of the direction and objectives of central bank monetary policy, thereby enhancing trust in monetary policy.

However, the issuance of CBDC may also pose risks to financial stability. It may lead the public to more readily abandon commercial bank deposits, increasing the fragility of the banking system. Additionally, CBDC issuance may cause instability in capital flows, potentially affecting exchange rates and the stability of capital markets.

6.3 Challenges and Opportunities for Central Bank Digital Currencies (CBDCs)

Central Bank Digital Currency (CBDC) is an emerging digital payment method aimed at providing the general public with a safer, more efficient, and convenient payment experience. The issuance of CBDCs can enable central banks to better regulate financial markets, enhance the flexibility and efficiency of monetary policy, and also aid in combating illegal activities and illicit trade. Additionally, CBDC issuance can reduce the dependency of banks on central banks, lower financial system risks, and strengthen financial stability.

Now, let's discuss the challenges and opportunities that CBDCs may face:

Firstly, CBDC issuance may lead to a flow of funds Kumhof and Noone (2018) from deposit accounts and other financial assets towards CBDCs, affecting the supply and demand of traditional currencies. Secondly, widespread usage of CBDCs may significantly impact the business models of banks, leading to a decrease in bank revenues and potential bank restructuring and mergers. Furthermore, the use of CBDCs may increase risks related to network and information security, such as fraud, money laundering, and cyber-attacks.

Clearly, the challenges for CBDCs encompass various aspects, including technology, security, privacy, and regulation:

Firstly, CBDC needs to address technical challenges, primarily focusing on security, reliability, scalability, privacy protection, and cross-border transactions.

(1) Security Challenge: CBDC must ensure the security of the digital transaction network, including safeguarding currency integrity, user privacy, and preventing fraud. Implementing advanced encryption technology, identity authentication, and digital signatures can effectively enhance CBDC's security.
(2) Reliability Challenge: CBDC requires the establishment of a stable transaction system to ensure high reliability and availability, guarding against technical failures that could lead to transaction system breakdowns. Creating a stable

digital infrastructure, including networks, data centers, data storage, and backup systems, can enhance CBDC's reliability.

(3) Scalability Challenge: CBDC needs to build a scalable technical architecture and an efficient transaction processing system to accommodate varying transaction demands and future digital currency requirements. Scalability is crucial to ensure that CBDC can meet future digital currency demands.

(4) Privacy Protection Challenge: CBDC needs to implement measures to protect user transaction data, prevent malicious attacks, and safeguard user privacy through techniques like anonymous transactions and user identity protection.

(5) Cross-border Transaction Challenge: CBDC faces technical challenges in cross-border transactions, including interoperability of cross-border payment systems, differences in legal frameworks, and inconsistent regulatory requirements. Establishing cross-border payment networks and collaboration mechanisms will ensure CBDC can smoothly facilitate global digital currency transactions.

Secondly, CBDC's security and privacy issues need significant attention, and its design should balance security stability with user privacy protection. It should aim to prevent illegal activities while preserving the confidentiality of user personal information.

To protect user privacy, various measures and schemes can be adopted. Firstly, data encryption and secure storage are crucial. By using advanced encryption technology, CBDC transaction data and user personal information can be protected from unauthorized access during transmission and storage.

Another aspect to address is the balance between anonymity and anti-money laundering regulation. One possible approach is adopting an anonymous transaction mechanism that allows users to conduct transactions without providing identity information. However, to meet anti-money laundering and counter-terrorism financing regulatory requirements, the central bank needs to ensure that regulatory agencies can track suspicious transactions and take appropriate regulatory measures.

Digital identity authentication technology is another essential aspect of protecting user privacy. The central bank can employ digital identity authentication technology to ensure the authenticity of transaction participants. This includes using digital signatures, multi-factor authentication, and other methods to enhance the security and credibility of transactions.

User control and consent should also be considered. The central bank can grant users more control and choices, such as allowing them to decide whether to share personal information and how their transaction data is used. Protecting user consent and informed decision-making is crucial to ensure privacy security.

Finally, CBDC's regulatory issues also require significant attention. As CBDC transactions are conducted through digital technology, the central bank needs to implement new regulatory measures to prevent CBDC from being used for illegal activities. Additionally, the central bank needs to develop new policy frameworks to address the relationship between CBDC and traditional financial institutions and the potential impact of CBDC on financial stability and monetary policy.

Different countries have adopted different measures in the regulatory policies concerning CBDC. For example, the People's Bank of China has implemented strict regulatory policies, such as limiting transaction amounts and preventing money laundering and illegal transactions, to ensure the safety and stability of CBDC. In Sweden, regulatory policies are developed based on existing regulations, and the issuance and regulation of CBDC are jointly managed by the central bank and financial regulatory authorities. The Federal Reserve in the United States is studying the regulatory framework for central bank digital currencies and coordinating with other regulatory agencies. Additionally, some countries are considering cooperating with others to develop CBDC regulations, aiming to share best practices and coordinate policies.

Next, let's explore the prospects and technical implementation of CBDC in cross-border payments, as well as its impact and challenges on cross-border transactions.

CBDC features programmability and real-time settlement, which are expected to enhance the efficiency and security of cross-border payments CPMI (2020). For example, CBDC can enable real-time settlement, avoiding the high costs, inefficiency, and uncertainty associated with traditional cross-border payments. CBDC can also use smart contracts for automated supervision Sklaroff (2017), improving the effectiveness of anti-money laundering and counter-terrorism financing efforts. However, the technical implementation of CBDC needs to consider issues such as data security, privacy protection, and coordinating regulatory frameworks and technical standards across different countries.

CBDC's traceability and inclusivity features may have a profound impact on cross-border payments. It could alter existing payment structures and market dynamics, driving competition and innovation in the payment market and affecting the survival and development of traditional cross-border payment service providers. Additionally, CBDC could facilitate the cross-border transmission of monetary policy, enhancing financial stability and economic integration. However, the implementation of CBDC faces challenges, such as coordinating regulatory and legal frameworks across different countries, resolving technical issues related to cross-border clearing and settlement, and ensuring the system's security and stability.

The application of CBDC in cross-border payments also needs to consider its synergy with other digital currencies and payment tools. CBDC can be combined with blockchain technology to enhance the traceability and security of cross-border payments. Moreover, CBDC can be integrated with mobile payment tools like Alipay and WeChat Pay to expand payment scenarios and increase convenience. However, the relationship between CBDC and other digital currencies and payment tools may also bring competition and substitution, requiring effective regulation and coordination.

Furthermore, the application of CBDC in cross-border payments needs to fully consider the differences and demands of different countries and regions. There are significant variations in regulatory frameworks, technical standards, payment markets, and financial systems across different countries and regions, and the application of CBDC needs to be tailored accordingly and jointly discussed with other countries for cooperation.

CBDC can also provide central banks with more direct monetary policy tools, increasing the transparency and effectiveness of monetary policy. Here, we provide a dynamic equilibrium model to analyze the impact of CBDC on monetary policy, the banking system, and financial stability. The model primarily includes three variables: households, enterprises, and the government. Households represent consumers and labor forces, enterprises refer to production sectors and banks, and the government includes the central bank and the finance department.

When considering the impact of CBDC on monetary policy, the dynamic general equilibrium model can simulate the supply and demand of CBDC and consider its monetary transmission mechanism. The model can also examine the substitution relationship between CBDC and other monetary tools and whether the introduction of CBDC would alter the structure and operation of the monetary market. Through these simulations, the potential impact of CBDC promotion on monetary policy objectives, such as inflation rate and economic growth rate, can be evaluated.

Regarding the impact on the banking system, the dynamic general equilibrium model can simulate the proportion of substitute deposits for CBDC and consider whether the real-time settlement feature of CBDC would change the structure and efficiency of banking operations. Additionally, the model can assess the impact of CBDC on the stability and regulatory framework of the banking system, as well as the possibility of capital flow and competition.

When considering the impact of CBDC on financial stability, the dynamic general equilibrium model can examine the substitution relationship between CBDC and existing payment tools and the privacy protection and security issues of CBDC. Additionally, the model can evaluate whether the promotion of CBDC would alter the structure and stability of financial markets, including payment market competition, the promotion of financial innovation, and risk allocation.

Finally, we analyze the development of central bank digital currencies from the perspective of global financial capitalism. After the subprime crisis, people began to question whether the existing financial system and monetary system are suitable for the modern economy. We provide a preliminary multinational analysis to explore the technical characteristics, financial stability impact, implementation prospects, international cooperation, and standardization of CBDCs in different countries.

Firstly, different countries have conducted research and practices on the technical characteristics of CBDC, mainly based on regulatory requirements and technological capabilities Fan (2020). China's Digital Yuan adopts a centralized design, with banks acting as intermediaries for issuance and transactions. On the other hand, Sweden's e-krona employs a decentralized design, utilizing distributed ledger technology for issuance and transactions. Moreover, countries are concerned with CBDC's technical design in payment tools, security mechanisms, and data privacy protection.

Secondly, countries are also concerned about the impact of CBDC on financial stability Auer and Boehme (2020). CBDC features such as traceability, inclusivity, and flexibility may influence financial stability. For instance, CBDC may lead to the loss of bank deposits, affecting the stability of the banking system. At the same time, CBDC may promote competition in the payment market, driving financial innovation, and financial inclusion. Countries need to carefully assess the potential impacts of CBDC based on their financial systems and regulatory frameworks.

Thirdly, countries have discussed the prospects of CBDC implementation. Despite some progress in various countries regarding CBDC, there are still many challenges in its implementation. For instance, how to ensure the security and privacy of CBDC, how to coordinate the interests of various financial markets, and how to meet consumer demands. Therefore, countries need to develop detailed implementation plans and gradually advance through pilot projects and other means.

Finally, international cooperation and standardization of CBDCs are also significant concerns. As research and practice on CBDCs deepen, countries need to strengthen cooperation and coordination to avoid isolation and incompatibility between different CBDCs. Additionally, international standardization of CBDC is crucial to ensure interoperability and mutual trust of CBDCs. International standardization organizations have already started to formulate international standards for CBDCs, but challenges remain due to the different technological characteristics and practices of CBDCs in different countries.

In conclusion, with the continuous expansion of the global financial market and the rapid development of the digital economy, CBDC has the potential to become a new form of the financial system, providing new opportunities for the development of global financial capitalism. The development of CBDC is expected to promote cross-border trade and investment and may become a major way of financial transactions in the future. Additionally, CBDC's development will drive the advancement of the digital economy and accelerate the integration of the digital economy with the real economy. Thus, the emergence of CBDC offers new opportunities for financial capitalism and is likely to drive the development of the global economy in the future.

References

Auer, R., & Boehme, R. (2020). The technology of retail central bank digital currency. BIS Quarterly Review.

Auer R, Cornelli G, & Frost J. (2020), "Rise of the central bank digital currencies: drivers, approaches and technologies" BIS Working Papers[No.880]

Bech, M., & Garratt, R. (2017). Central bank cryptocurrencies. BIS Quarterly Review.

Bindseil, U. (2020). Tiered CBDC and the financial system. European Central Bank Working Paper No. 2351.

CPMI (2020). Central bank digital currencies: foundational principles and core features. Bank for International Settlements.

Fan, Y. (2020). China's central bank digital currency. In Handbook of Digital Finance and Financial Inclusion. Academic Press.

Kumhof, M., & Noone, C. (2018). Central bank digital currencies—design principles and balance sheet implications. Bank of England Staff Working Paper No. 725.

Sklaroff, J. M. (2017). Smart contracts and the cost of inclusion. Yale Journal on Regulation, 35, 207.

Chapter 7
Digital Finance and the International Monetary System

7.1 Overview of Digital Finance and the International Monetary System

With the rapid development of the digital economy, the relationship between digital finance and the international monetary system has become a focal point in the global financial landscape. The rise of digital finance has brought about innovative ways of cross-border payments and settlements, accelerating the convenience of global trade and investment, while also driving adjustments and evolution in the international monetary system. The emergence of digital finance will significantly change the landscape of the international monetary system and pose new challenges to central banks' roles, policies, and regulatory frameworks.

One of the most typical cases is the significant impact of the rise of digital finance and blockchain technology on the international monetary system and the role of central banks. The rise of digital finance has made financial transactions more efficient and convenient, while also giving birth to new forms of currency, such as cryptocurrencies and digital assets. Blockchain technology has provided technical support for decentralized digital currencies, further promoting the development and popularization of digital currencies.

In this context, central banks face new challenges and opportunities in their roles and responsibilities. As the entities responsible for currency issuance and regulation, central banks need to actively respond to the development of digital finance and blockchain technology, promote the innovation and application of digital currencies and distributed ledger technology, and ensure the safety and stability of the financial market.

Firstly, central banks need to strengthen the regulation and risk control of digital currencies to ensure their safe and stable operation. Compared to traditional currencies, digital currencies carry higher risks and volatility. Central banks need to formulate corresponding regulatory policies and security measures to deal with the instability and uncertainty of the digital currency market.

Z. Liu and W. Hou, *Digital Finance*, https://doi.org/10.1007/978-981-99-7305-7_7

Secondly, central banks need to promote the innovation and application of digital currencies and distributed ledger technology. The rise of digital currencies and blockchain technology provides central banks with new means of currency issuance and regulation. Central banks should actively explore the application of digital currencies and distributed ledger technology in payment settlements, cross-border payments, and other fields, promoting the integration and innovation of digital currencies and blockchain technology with the traditional financial market.

Lastly, central banks also need to actively participate in the construction and development of the international monetary system, promoting the application and development of digital currencies and blockchain technology on a global scale.

In addition, the trend of digitization and technological advancements has brought new challenges and opportunities to the international monetary system. With the rise of digital currencies and blockchain technology, significant changes are occurring in the way financial markets conduct transactions and settlements. This not only impacts the development of the international monetary system but also has profound effects on countries' monetary policies and financial stability.

Firstly, the trend of digitization and technological advancements has made cross-border payments and settlements more efficient and convenient. This presents an opportunity for the international monetary system Carney (2019) as it can promote trade and investment between countries and further drive the process of globalization. However, digitization also poses challenges to the traditional monetary system. For instance, traditional monetary policies and financial regulatory models may struggle to adapt to the development of digital currencies and blockchain technology, leading to increased volatility and instability in financial markets.

Secondly, the trend of digitization and technological advancements intensifies currency competition. With the rise of cryptocurrencies and digital currencies, the monopoly position of traditional monetary systems is being challenged Bordo and Levin (2017), and the dynamics of currency competition are changing. This not only affects the formulation and implementation of monetary policies but also has an impact on the stability of the international monetary system.

Next, let's analyze and discuss the role of digital finance in promoting inclusive growth using China as an example.

As a developing country, China has played a significant role in promoting inclusive growth through digital finance. The development of digital finance in China can be traced back to 2004 when services like mobile payments and e-commerce started to emerge. With the continuous advancement of internet and communication technologies, the application scope of digital finance in China has expanded. For instance, in 2013, the People's Bank of China introduced the Payment and Clearing Association, establishing interbank payment and clearing systems, providing the infrastructure for the development of digital finance. In 2014, China launched the "Internet Plus" action plan, further driving the growth of digital finance.

China's policy framework for digital finance mainly includes three aspects: regulatory policies, market policies, and industrial policies.

Regarding regulatory policies, the Chinese government is committed to establishing a regulatory mechanism for digital finance to strengthen supervision over the digital financial market. This involves formulating and improving regulations for digital finance, clarifying regulatory responsibilities and authorities, and enhancing supervision and inspection of digital financial institutions and platforms to ensure the security and stability of digital financial activities.

In terms of market policies, the Chinese government actively promotes the development and innovation of the digital finance market. This includes strengthening market supervision to prevent financial risks and maintain market order, fostering research and application of digital financial technology to promote the development of financial technology, and encouraging digital financial institutions and platforms to provide diversified financial services to enhance consumer experiences and protect consumer rights.

Regarding industrial policies, the Chinese government supports the growth and expansion of digital financial enterprises. This involves providing policy support and tax incentives, creating an environment for digital financial enterprises to start and grow their businesses Ahlstrom et al. (2018), enhancing talent development and technological innovation to improve the quality of digital financial services, and promoting the integration of digital finance and the real economy to drive the industrialization of digital finance.

The role of digital finance in promoting inclusive growth in China is manifested in several aspects:

Firstly, digital finance can improve the coverage and accessibility of financial services. China has a vast geographical area, and some remote areas have limited access to traditional financial services. Through the application of the internet and communication technologies, digital finance can overcome spatial limitations and provide online financial services, enabling more people to access financial services and promoting financial inclusion.

Secondly, digital finance can facilitate financing for small and micro-enterprises. The traditional financial system provides relatively limited support for financing small and micro-enterprises. Digital finance, by establishing risk assessment models based on big data and artificial intelligence, can lower financing barriers, increase the feasibility of financing for small and micro-enterprises, stimulate their development, and promote economic growth and employment.

Thirdly, digital finance can enhance financial literacy and knowledge dissemination among consumers. Many Chinese residents lack knowledge and experience in the financial field, making them vulnerable to financial fraud and scams. Digital finance can provide financial education and training, increase financial knowledge and skills, improve consumer financial literacy, and help individuals better understand and manage their personal finances, reducing financial risks.

Fourthly, digital finance can improve the efficiency and cost-effectiveness of financial services. In the traditional financial system, many financial service processes are cumbersome, inefficient, and costly. Through automation and digitization, digital finance can enhance the efficiency of financial services, reduce financial service costs, making financial services more affordable and accessible to a broader population.

However, digital finance in promoting inclusive growth also faces several challenges.

One of the main challenges is the digital divide. In China, the digital divide exists between urban and rural areas, different regions, and different population groups. Due to uneven levels of digital technology adoption, some regions and populations are unable to fully enjoy the convenience and opportunities brought by digital finance.

Another challenge is the risk associated with digital finance. Digital finance relies heavily on technology and information, leading to risks such as data security, privacy protection, and cyber-attacks. Additionally, the innovation and rapid development of digital finance also bring certain risks, such as market risk, operational risk, and regulatory risk.

As the digital economy continues to develop and expand, digital finance will become an essential driving force for China's economic growth. The government needs to take more measures to strengthen digital finance regulation, support the development of digital financial enterprises, bridge the digital divide, and enhance financial knowledge dissemination to better leverage the role of digital finance in promoting inclusive growth.

Apart from China, other developing countries have also experienced similar influences, such as Indonesia.

Indonesia's development of digital finance has gone through different stages. In 2007, mobile network operators such as Indosat, Telkomsel, and XL Axiata started offering mobile financial services. However, due to the lack of regulation and infrastructure support, the growth of these services was limited. It was not until 2014 when the Central Bank of Indonesia (BI) launched the "Indonesia Payment System 2025" plan that digital finance began to truly develop in Indonesia. This plan aimed to strengthen regulation, enhance financial inclusion, and promote digital payments, among other objectives.

Indonesia's policy framework for digital finance mainly includes regulatory policies, market policies, and industrial policies. Regulatory policies involve establishing a regulatory mechanism for digital finance, improving regulations, and ensuring the security of digital finance. Market policies focus on enhancing market supervision and promoting digital finance innovation. Industrial policies support the development of digital finance enterprises and improving the quality of digital financial services.

The application scope of digital finance in Indonesia continues to expand and is manifested in several aspects:

Firstly, digital finance can promote financial inclusion. Indonesia has a large population and vast geographical diversity, making it challenging for financial services to reach certain areas. The application of digital finance through mobile devices and the internet can provide financial services to residents in remote areas, increasing the accessibility and coverage of financial services.

Secondly, digital finance can facilitate financing for small and micro-enterprises. Small and micro-enterprises are essential components of the Indonesian economy but often face difficulties in obtaining financing. Digital finance can assess risks using big data and artificial intelligence, thereby reducing financing barriers and providing more accessible and flexible financing channels for these enterprises. P2P lending platforms in Indonesia, such as KoinWorks and Modalku, have utilized digital financial technology to support small and micro-enterprises in obtaining financing more conveniently.

Thirdly, digital finance can promote individual financial management. With the continuous promotion of digital payments and financial products, digital finance has become an important channel for individuals to manage their finances and investments. Digital financial services in Indonesia have covered digital payments, digital banking, digital investments, among other areas, providing individuals with convenient and diverse financial products and services. Through mobile applications, individuals can manage their finances, investments, and personal finances more efficiently.

However, the application of digital finance in Indonesia also faces challenges. Firstly, the digital divide persists, and some regions and population groups are unable to fully benefit from the convenience of digital finance. Secondly, data security and privacy protection need to be emphasized to safeguard users' personal information and funds. Additionally, financial knowledge dissemination and education need to be strengthened to ensure individuals can correctly understand and use digital financial products and services.

Through the analysis above, it is evident that digital financial innovation is an essential means of promoting financial services' accessibility in developing countries. By innovating digital finance, the cost and barriers of financial services can be reduced, thereby promoting financial inclusion and economic development.

Digital financial innovation includes mobile payments, electronic currency, online lending, and other technologies and applications, which have had a significant impact on the informal economy in developing countries. The informal economy has long been a problem in developing countries, involving economic activities conducted outside the legal framework and difficult to regulate and manage. Digital financial innovation may accelerate the transition of the informal economy to the formal economy, but it may also have some negative effects on the informal economy. For example, digital financial innovation may lead to the disappearance of the informal economy, causing some individuals engaged in informal economic activities to lose their sources of income. Therefore, to promote the promotion and application of digital finance in developing countries, some policy measures need to be taken.

Firstly, it is essential to establish relevant laws and regulations to regulate the development of digital financial innovation Zetzsche et al. (2017). These regulations should cover various aspects of digital finance, including payments, lending, investments, etc., to ensure the safety and stability of digital financial innovation and prevent criminals from using digital finance for illegal activities.

Secondly, there is a need to strengthen the supervision and management of digital finance Akinola et al. (2020). Despite the cost and barrier reduction of financial services through digital finance, there are also certain risks and uncertainties associated with it.

Thirdly, it is crucial to increase the penetration rate of digital finance. Currently, rural and remote areas in many developing countries have a low penetration rate of digital finance. To promote digital finance, measures such as optimizing network coverage and providing popularization training should be implemented to enable more people to understand and use digital financial services.

Fourthly, enhancing the customization and personalization of digital financial services is essential. Many residents in developing countries still face challenges in meeting their financial service needs, such as small and micro-enterprises without collateral and individuals with poor credit records. Digital financial innovation can develop more personalized and customized financial products to provide more suitable financial services for these individuals.

Lastly, it is vital to strengthen the coordination and integration between digital financial innovation and the informal economy. Digital financial innovation can help the informal economy gradually transition into the formal economy by innovating financial service models and improving the quality of financial services. At the same time, the informal economy can better integrate into the formal economic system with the support and assistance of digital finance.

Through the above analysis, it can be seen that digital finance has many impacts on international financial development. From the perspective of international politics, the following considerations arise:

(1) The redistribution of power in the international monetary system: Traditionally, the dominant position in the international monetary system is held by developed countries such as the United States, Europe, and Japan. However, with the rise of digital financial technology, financial institutions and technology companies from emerging economies are playing increasingly important roles, elevating their status and influence in the international monetary system.
(2) Digital financial technology enhances the stability of the international monetary system: The traditional international monetary system faces various risks and challenges, such as foreign exchange fluctuations, capital flows, and financial crises. Nevertheless, digital financial technology provides faster, more transparent, and safer payment and settlement methods, reducing intermediate links and risks, thus improving the stability of the international monetary system.
(3) Intensified competition in the international monetary system: Digital financial technology provides emerging economies with more opportunities to challenge the status of traditional currencies. Some emerging economies have begun to explore issuing their digital currencies to enhance their position and competitiveness in the international monetary system. This intensifies competition within the international monetary system, possibly challenging the dominance of traditional currencies.
(4) Increased difficulty in coordinating international monetary policies due to digital financial technology: Digital financial technology makes cross-border transactions easier and quicker; however, different countries' monetary policies may have different impacts, such as exchange rates, inflation, and interest rates. This increases the difficulty in coordinating international monetary policies, potentially posing greater challenges to international economic cooperation.
(5) Challenges to currency sovereignty posed by digital financial technology: The development of digital currencies and blockchain technology makes

cross-border transactions more convenient, potentially challenging traditional currency sovereignty. Some countries may feel threatened in their currency sovereignty and take measures to protect their interests, leading to disputes and conflicts in international monetary policies, further exacerbating international political instability.

In conclusion, digital finance has a broad and profound impact on international financial development, involving significant issues related to the power structure, stability, competition, coordination difficulty, and currency sovereignty in the international monetary system. These factors will deeply affect and challenge international politics and economics.

7.2 Digital Finance and Cross-Border Payments

Digital finance and cross-border payments are two essential components of today's global economy. As the global economy continues to develop and globalization accelerates, cross-border payments have become a crucial means for international trade and investment. The rapid development and widespread adoption of digital financial technology also provide more opportunities and challenges for cross-border payments. This chapter will explore the relationship between digital finance and cross-border payments and their impact on the global economy.

From the perspective of the impact of digital finance on cross-border payments, digital currencies and blockchain technology offer more efficient, secure, and convenient cross-border payment solutions. The characteristics of these technologies, including decentralization, real-time settlement, and anti-counterfeiting features, make cross-border payments faster, more transparent, and more trustworthy, reducing intermediaries and associated costs. Additionally, the proliferation of digital payment methods such as mobile payments and cloud payments further simplifies the cross-border payment process, making it more convenient and flexible, and promoting the accelerated development of cross-border trade and investment.

However, the application of digital financial technology also faces some challenges and risks. The primary challenge is the regulatory issues surrounding digital currencies and blockchain technology. Due to their decentralized nature, regulating digital currencies and blockchain technology is relatively difficult and can be prone to illegal activities and money laundering. Additionally, the widespread adoption of digital financial technology in cross-border payments also faces issues related to payment security, privacy protection, and compliance.

From the perspective of the impact of cross-border payments on digital finance, the expansion of the cross-border payment market and increased competition stimulate innovation and optimization of digital financial technology. Faced with the growing demand for cross-border payments, digital financial technology is continuously evolving to provide more efficient and secure solutions. Next-generation digital currencies and digital identity authentication technology can effectively improve the efficiency and security of cross-border payments, driving further development of digital financial technology.

However, the competition and inequality in the cross-border payment market also bring some challenges to the development of digital financial technology. Large payment institutions and banks hold a significant share in the cross-border payment market, creating competitive pressure for small payment institutions and emerging digital financial enterprises. They may face difficulties entering the market and lack of resources. Additionally, the digital payment infrastructure and regulatory capabilities in some developing countries and regions are relatively weak, affecting the efficiency and security of cross-border payments and limiting the development of digital financial technology in these areas.

To promote the healthy development of digital financial technology in cross-border payments, some measures need to be taken. Firstly, promoting fair competition and market openness to provide more opportunities and support for small payment institutions and emerging digital financial enterprises to drive market diversification and innovation. Secondly, strengthening international cooperation to enhance the digital payment infrastructure and regulatory capabilities of developing countries and regions to improve the efficiency and security of cross-border payments. Additionally, enhanced information sharing and technology exchange can promote cooperation and innovation of digital financial technology on a global scale, collectively driving the development of cross-border payments.

With technological advancements, digital finance and cross-border payments are continuously evolving. Next, we will analyze relevant issues from three aspects: technology architecture, technological innovation, and technological applications.

Firstly, there are various technological architectures Tapscott and Tapscott (2016) and implementation methods for digital finance and cross-border payments. Among them, blockchain technology is a new type of distributed ledger technology that enables decentralized transactions and information storage, ensuring data security and transparency. Additionally, technologies such as artificial intelligence, cloud computing, big data, and the Internet of Things are widely applied in the fields of digital finance and cross-border payments. The application of these technologies makes digital finance and cross-border payments more convenient, efficient, and secure.

Secondly, technological innovation in digital finance and cross-border payments is mainly manifested in the following aspects Narayanan et al. (2016). Firstly, the emergence of digital currencies has changed the traditional payment methods of fiat currencies, promoting the convenience and globalization of cross-border payments. Secondly, smart contract technology allows parties in cross-border payments to complete transactions more rapidly and transparently, significantly shortening the payment cycle. Additionally, the application of artificial intelligence technology also makes payment monitoring more intelligent, effectively reducing payment risks.

The application of digital finance and cross-border payments poses several challenges to risk management and regulation for financial institutions. In fact, with the acceleration of globalization and the development of digital technology, international cross-border payments have become an essential part of global economic activities.

However, due to involving multiple currencies, payment methods, and legal systems of different countries, international cross-border payments face many challenges in terms of policy and regulation.

The policies and regulatory mechanisms of international cross-border payments involve multiple levels and regulatory agencies Ahern (2015) of various countries. For example, international organizations such as the International Monetary Fund (IMF), the Bank for International Settlements (BIS), the Financial Stability Board (FSB), play important roles in the policies and regulation of cross-border payments. Additionally, central banks and financial regulatory agencies of various countries are responsible for regulating their own cross-border payment business.

However, due to involving multiple countries' legal systems, there are differences in cross-border payment regulations among nations, making it a challenge to achieve international regulatory coordination and uniformity. Additionally, the rapid development and innovation of technology may render existing regulatory mechanisms inadequate in adapting to new business models and technologies in digital finance and cross-border payments. Finally, issues such as malicious activities, money laundering, and cybercrime pose challenges to the regulation of cross-border payments.

To address the issues and challenges in international cross-border payment regulation, countries and international organizations have adopted various cooperative and coordination approaches. One common approach is the establishment of international cross-border payment regulatory bodies, such as the European Union's Payment Services Directive (PSD2), the Asia–Pacific Economic Cooperation (APEC) Cross-Border Payment Guidelines, etc. These institutions promote the development of the international cross-border payment market and coordination of regulation by setting up cross-border payment rules, technical standards, and regulatory requirements. Another approach involves adopting international standards and frameworks, such as the International Monetary Fund's (IMF) cross-border payment standards, the Bank for International Settlements' (BIS) payment standards, and the Financial Stability Board's (FSB) digital financial regulation framework. These international standards and frameworks provide common regulatory principles and guidelines for regulatory agencies in different countries, facilitating the development of the international cross-border payment market and regulatory coordination.

Furthermore, international cooperation in the regulation of digital finance and cross-border payments can also be achieved through information sharing, regulatory sandboxes, and regulatory cooperation. Information sharing can help regulatory agencies in different countries better understand the dynamics and risks of the international cross-border payment market, thereby strengthening regulatory coordination. Regulatory sandboxes provide a testing ground for innovative digital finance and cross-border payment companies, promoting innovation while maintaining a balance with regulation. Regulatory cooperation fosters mutual trust and collaboration among regulatory agencies in different countries, enabling better responses to risks and challenges in the cross-border payment market.

It is evident that the regulatory mechanism for digital finance and cross-border payments needs to balance financial innovation and risk control. To achieve this goal, regulatory mechanisms can start from the following aspects:

(1) Develop appropriate regulatory policies and rules to promote the development and innovation of digital finance and cross-border payments. For example, the European Union's Payment Services Directive (PSD2) sets regulatory requirements that third-party payment service providers must comply with, thereby promoting the development of the European digital finance and cross-border payment market.
(2) Establish a comprehensive risk assessment and monitoring mechanism to promptly identify and address market risks. For instance, regulatory agencies can use technologies such as big data and artificial intelligence to monitor and issue warnings about the cross-border payment market, thereby identifying market risks and issues in a timely manner.
(3) Establish effective cooperation mechanisms to enhance communication and collaboration among regulatory agencies. For example, regulatory agencies can establish cross-border payment regulatory liaison mechanisms to jointly address risks and challenges in the cross-border payment market.

In conclusion, digital finance and cross-border payments are indispensable components of the global economy. Digital financial technology provides more efficient, secure, and convenient solutions for cross-border payments while facing challenges in regulation and risk. The development of cross-border payments also drives innovation and optimization of digital financial technology, but it also encounters market competition and inequality issues. To better promote the development of digital finance and cross-border payments, further international cooperation and regulation are needed to break down geographical and institutional barriers and foster a sound development of digital finance and cross-border payments.

7.3 Challenges and Opportunities of Digital Finance and the International Monetary System

With the development of digital technology, digital finance is becoming an integral part of the global financial system. However, the security of digital financial technology and transaction data is a pressing concern, and the issuance and operation of digital currencies also require adherence to certain technological and security standards.

Next, we will analyze these issues and explore the impact of continuous innovation in digital financial technology on data security.

Firstly, how can we ensure the security of digital financial technology and transaction data?

To ensure the security of digital financial technology and transaction data, the following measures can be taken:

(1) Establish robust digital finance regulatory mechanisms and legal frameworks. Regulatory mechanisms should adapt to the development of digital finance, encompassing areas such as digital currencies, encryption technologies, and decentralized exchanges. Simultaneously, legal frameworks need to keep pace, regulating issues like smart contracts, data privacy, and cybersecurity, to provide strong legal safeguards for digital finance.
(2) Adopt advanced encryption technologies and security measures. Blockchain technology can provide decentralized and trustless security, safeguarding the integrity and authenticity of transaction data. Digital finance platforms need to implement multi-layered authentication, data encryption, and firewall technologies to strengthen the protection of user data and transaction information, preventing unauthorized access and data breaches.
(3) Establish comprehensive risk management mechanisms. Digital finance platforms should develop robust risk management mechanisms, including anti-money laundering and anti-terrorism financing measures, to identify and mitigate the risks of illicit activities using digital finance. Additionally, enhanced risk assessment and monitoring can promptly detect and address potential risks, ensuring the secure and stable operation of digital finance.

Secondly, what technological and security standards do digital currency issuance and exchanges need to meet?

Generally, digital currency issuance and exchanges need to adhere to the following technological and security standards:

(1) Digital currencies need to adopt advanced encryption technologies to ensure the security and anonymity of transactions. Moreover, digital currencies should possess high scalability to support large-scale transactions.
(2) Digital currency exchanges require high availability and stability to handle the challenges of high concurrency transactions. These exchanges need to employ advanced technology architectures, such as distributed systems, fault tolerance mechanisms, load balancing, and high-speed caching, to ensure their reliability and performance.
(3) Digital currency exchanges need to implement multi-layered security measures, including identity authentication, access control, data encryption, and security audits, to safeguard the security and privacy of digital currency transactions.

Thirdly, how does continuous innovation in digital financial technology impact data security?

As technology advances, digital financial technology becomes increasingly complex and involves larger amounts of data. Therefore, continuous innovation in digital financial technology impacts data security in the following ways:

(1) The introduction of new technologies brings forth more security threats Zohar (2015). As digital financial technology continuously innovates, new security

vulnerabilities and attack methods also emerge, such as smart contract vulnerabilities and zero-day exploits. To address these threats, digital finance platforms need to strengthen security assessments and vulnerability scans of new technologies and promptly patch vulnerabilities to enhance system security.

(2) The increase in data volume poses higher data risks for digital finance platforms. Digital financial technology involves handling large amounts of sensitive data, such as transaction data and user information. To protect this data from leaks and misuse, digital finance platforms need to employ more advanced data encryption and security audit technologies to ensure data confidentiality and integrity.

(3) Continuous innovation in digital financial technology also brings solutions and opportunities Narayanan et al. (2016). For instance, new technologies like blockchain and smart contracts can enhance the security and reliability of digital finance platforms. The decentralized nature of blockchain provides a trust mechanism that prevents tampering of transactions. Smart contract technology automates contract execution, reducing potential human errors and fraudulent activities.

In recent years, digital finance has become a significant trend in the financial industry. However, the instability of the international monetary system has an impact on the development of digital finance.

Firstly, how does the instability of the international monetary system affect the development of digital finance?

The instability of the international monetary system mainly includes economic fluctuations, exchange rate fluctuations, and financial market risks. It manifests in the following ways:

(1) The unstable international monetary system affects the digital currency market. The instability of the monetary system may lead to exchange rate fluctuations and inflation issues, thus affecting the price volatility and performance of digital currencies. The value of digital currencies is influenced by the stability of the monetary system. Therefore, an unstable international monetary system may increase the volatility of the digital currency market, subjecting investors to greater risks and uncertainties.

(2) The unstable monetary system may trigger financial market instability. The volatility of financial markets directly impacts the performance and user confidence in digital financial markets. An unstable international monetary system may lead to turmoil in financial markets, including stock markets, foreign exchange markets, and bond markets, which can have a cascading effect on the digital finance market. This may cause a decline in investor confidence, reduced investment activity, and adversely affect the development and innovation of digital finance.

(3) The unstable monetary system may raise investors' risk awareness. In the digital finance market, investors' risk awareness and confidence are significant factors influencing market development. An unstable international monetary system may cause investors to be concerned about risks, leading to increased caution and conservatism. Investors may pay more attention to risk management and

asset protection, reducing their participation and willingness to invest in the digital finance market, which could hinder its development.

Next, let's discuss the impact of international monetary policies on the development and use of digital finance.

International monetary policies directly relate to the development and use of digital finance, manifesting in the following aspects:

(1) The degree of monetary policy looseness or tightness directly affects the financing costs and difficulties in the digital financial market. The looseness or tightness of monetary policy directly impacts the digital financial lending market, thereby affecting the financing costs and difficulties in digital finance. When monetary policy is loose, with lower interest rates and abundant funds, it benefits the development and innovation of digital finance. Conversely, if monetary policy tightens, with rising interest rates and a shortage of funds, it will increase the financing costs and difficulties in digital finance.
(2) The direction of monetary policy affects the development and use of the digital finance market. The direction of monetary policy includes the coordination and cooperation between fiscal and monetary policies, influencing economic development, inflation levels, exchange rate trends, and other factors, which in turn affect the development of the digital finance market. For example, if monetary policy is loose, and fiscal expenditures increase, it will promote economic growth and market activity, driving the development of the digital finance market. However, if monetary policy tends to tighten, and fiscal policy is restrictive, it may lead to economic slowdown, negatively affecting the digital finance market.
(3) International monetary policies also have a significant impact on the use of digital finance. Cross-border payment and remittance services rely on the support and coordination of international monetary policies; otherwise, issues such as payment restrictions and exchange rate fluctuations may arise, affecting the application and development of digital finance in the international market. The stability and coordination of international monetary policies play an important role in the convenience and security of cross-border payments and provide the necessary environment and support for the internationalization of digital finance.

Lastly, let's discuss how to formulate effective digital financial regulatory policies to balance regulation and market demands.

Digital financial regulatory policies need to strike a balance between regulation and market demands, avoiding risks resulting from either excessive regulation or inadequate regulation. To achieve this, consideration can be given to the following aspects:

(1) Establishing a sound regulatory mechanism: Formulate clear laws, regulations, and policy frameworks for digital finance to ensure its legal and compliant operation. Establish effective entry mechanisms, risk assessment mechanisms,

and information disclosure mechanisms for digital financial enterprises to ensure healthy market development.

(2) Technological and intelligent supervision: Strengthen the regulatory capacity of digital finance using advanced technologies such as artificial intelligence and big data. Through intelligent supervision and data analysis, achieve comprehensive and precise regulation, enhancing regulatory efficiency and effectiveness.
(3) Transparency and fairness: Ensure transparency and fairness in digital financial regulation by establishing open and transparent regulatory mechanisms. Regulatory agencies should exercise their duties impartially and publicly release regulatory information to increase market participants' confidence and recognition in the regulatory process.
(4) Strengthen international cooperation: Enhance international cooperation and coordination in digital financial regulation to jointly address cross-border risks and challenges. Establish cooperative mechanisms to share regulatory experience and information, promoting global integration of digital financial regulation.
(5) Innovative regulatory approaches: Encourage regulatory agencies to adopt innovative regulatory approaches, such as regulatory sandboxes, to provide new digital financial enterprises with pilot and testing environments, fostering technological innovation and market development. Additionally, regulatory agencies should continuously innovate regulatory tools and methods to keep up with the changing needs of digital finance.
(6) Emphasize risk management and compliance requirements: Digital financial enterprises should establish robust risk management and compliance systems, strictly adhering to regulatory requirements and standards. Strengthen internal controls to prevent risks and violations, ensuring the safety and stability of the digital financial market.

In general, the instability of the international monetary system, international monetary policies, and digital financial regulatory policies will all have significant impacts on the development and use of digital finance.

The emergence of digital currencies and digital finance has brought new opportunities and challenges to the traditional financial system. The convenience and efficiency of digital currencies can promote financial innovation and progress while also posing challenges to the traditional financial system.

First, let's examine the impact of digital currencies and digital finance on the financial system and the economy.

Here is a summary of some key aspects of the impact of digital currencies:

(1) Digital currencies enable fast peer-to-peer payments without the need for intermediaries, thus enhancing payment efficiency and speed. Compared to traditional bank transfers or cash payments, digital currency transactions have shorter confirmation times and can achieve real-time settlements, especially advantageous in international cross-border payments.

(2) The development of digital currencies helps reduce the use of cash. Traditional cash payment methods come with a range of issues such as security risks, inconvenience in carrying, and easy loss. The emergence of digital currencies provides a convenient, secure, and contactless payment method, reducing reliance on cash and lowering the cash management costs for banks.
(3) The anonymity of digital currencies can protect users' privacy. Digital currency accounts typically use encryption technology to secure user identity and transaction data, allowing users to have more control over their personal privacy and reducing the risk of personal information leakage.

However, the development of digital currencies also poses some challenges to the financial system and the economy.

(1) The lack of regulation and legal framework is the first major challenge. The unique and global nature of digital currencies makes it difficult for traditional financial regulatory mechanisms to adapt to their developmental needs. Therefore, regulatory authorities need to actively study and formulate appropriate regulatory policies to ensure the healthy development of the digital currency market. This includes regulatory requirements for various participants such as digital currency trading platforms, digital wallet providers, and digital asset management institutions, as well as provisions for protecting user rights and data privacy.
(2) The stability of digital currencies is an important challenge. Due to the relative novelty and instability of the digital currency market, digital currencies' prices can fluctuate significantly. This affects their storage and transaction value and may increase risks for users and investors. To address this issue, the concept of stablecoins has been introduced, which are pegged to certain assets or currencies to maintain relatively stable value.
(3) The adoption rate of digital currencies needs to be further increased. Currently, the use of digital currencies is relatively limited and has not yet been widely adopted globally. This limitation could be due to technical challenges, legal restrictions, and lack of user education, among other factors. To promote the adoption and use of digital currencies, it is necessary to strengthen user education, increase public awareness and trust in digital currencies, and provide user-friendly digital currency trading and storage tools.

The emergence of digital finance has also brought about a series of transformations to the financial system and the economy.

(1) The advent of digital finance has accelerated the digital transformation of the financial industry. By applying innovative technologies and business models such as mobile payments, electronic banking, and digital securities trading, digital finance has improved the efficiency and quality of financial services, making financial services more accessible and convenient. This benefits both individuals and businesses in their financial activities and provides financial institutions with broader development opportunities.

(2) The development of digital finance has accselerated the speed of fund circulation, promoting economic development and growth. Through the convenience of digital payments and electronic transactions, the transfer and settlement of funds have significantly sped up, reducing transaction costs and time, and promoting business activities' dynamism. This is of vital importance in driving economic growth, facilitating trade, and promoting investment.
(3) The development of digital finance also helps reduce financial risks. Digital financial transactions and risk management tools provide more accurate and timely data, enabling financial institutions to better identify, assess, and manage risks. The application of digital technology can enhance the precision and efficiency of risk management, reducing risks exposure in the financial system.
(4) The development of digital finance provides more convenient financial services for the general public. Through digital financial tools such as mobile payments and internet banking, people can conduct various financial transactions, such as transfers, payments, and shopping, anytime and anywhere. This offers individuals and businesses more choices and convenience, increases financial inclusivity, and promotes the popularization of financial services.

However, the development of digital finance also poses some challenges to the financial system and the economy.

(1) Security risks in digital finance are a significant concern. With the development of digital finance, cybersecurity and data privacy have become focal points of attention. Digital financial platforms need to strengthen security measures, employing advanced technologies and encryption methods to prevent security threats like hacking attacks, data leaks, and identity theft. Additionally, user education and awareness are crucial aspects in preventing security risks.
(2) Credit risks on digital financial platforms need effective management and control. The operation and transactions on digital financial platforms rely on trust and cooperation from users. Therefore, these platforms need to establish effective risk management mechanisms, including customer identity verification, credit assessment, anti-fraud measures, etc., to reduce the impact of credit risks on the platform.
(3) The degree of popularization of digital finance also needs to be further increased. Although digital finance is widely used in many developed countries, its adoption rate remains relatively low in some developing countries and regions. This may be limited by factors such as infrastructure, financial education, and regulations. Therefore, efforts are needed to promote awareness and understanding of digital finance and develop corresponding policies and measures to encourage its wider adoption and application.

Next, let's discuss the impact of digital finance and the international monetary system on economic globalization and financial stability.

Digital finance, as a crucial aspect of the digital transformation of the financial industry, has profoundly affected the provision and consumption of financial services. Meanwhile, the international monetary system plays a critical role in the process of global economic and financial integration.

Firstly, digital finance has a profound impact on economic globalization. The development of digital finance has made financial transactions more convenient, fast, and secure, significantly reducing the costs of international trade and investment transactions and accelerating the circulation of funds. Digital finance enables easier cross-border payments, reduces exchange rate risks, and enhances the reliability and security of cross-border trade. It also promotes international investment and cross-border financing, making the global financial market more interconnected.

However, the development of digital finance also presents some challenges and risks related to cross-border business complexity and varying regulatory standards. It can lead to challenges in regulation and compliance, which may have adverse consequences. Therefore, international cooperation and the establishment of standards become even more critical to ensure the orderly development and risk management of digital finance. Additionally, digital finance can be exploited by criminals, increasing financial security risks. Hence, it requires strengthened security measures and awareness to address issues such as cyber threats, data privacy breaches, and financial crimes, protecting users and the financial system's security.

Secondly, the international monetary system's impact on economic globalization and financial stability should not be overlooked. The international monetary system serves as the foundation of global economic development and directly influences the development of global financial markets and economic globalization. One of the main characteristics of the international monetary system is currency liquidity and exchange rate systems, with currency liquidity being a key factor affecting financial stability. An excess or lack of currency liquidity can have negative effects on global financial markets, such as currency depreciation, inflation, and debt crises.

The impact of digital finance and the international monetary system on economic globalization and financial stability can be observed in several aspects:

(1) The development of digital finance indeed contributes to facilitating cross-border transactions and investments. The efficiency and low-cost characteristics of digital finance reduce the costs of cross-border transactions and investments, accelerate fund flow, and promote the development of global trade and investment. Furthermore, the convenient cross-border payment methods provided by digital finance also help to mitigate exchange rate risks, enhancing the reliability and security of cross-border trade.
(2) The transformation of digital finance and the international monetary system does present new challenges and demands for international financial governance. The rapid development of digital finance and the introduction of new technologies put pressure on regulatory authorities, necessitating continuous adjustments and improvements to regulatory standards to keep up with digital finance's evolution. Similarly, the transformation of the international monetary system requires international cooperation and coordination to address issues like cross-border capital flows and exchange rate stability. Therefore, global financial governance needs to enhance cooperation, establish more robust regulatory mechanisms and institutional systems to adapt to the changes brought about by digital finance and the international monetary system.

(3) The transformation of digital finance and the international monetary system indeed impacts financial stability. The development of digital finance and the changes in the international monetary system may lead to market volatility and risks, requiring enhanced monitoring and early warning systems for financial stability. Additionally, the transformation of digital finance and the international monetary system can also influence the implementation and adjustments of monetary policies, necessitating stable and coordinated financial policies to maintain financial stability.

Now, let's examine how digital finance and the international monetary system affect global wealth inequality and financial inclusion.

Digital finance, through its technological advancements in improving the efficiency and accessibility of financial services, is believed to contribute to global financial inclusion. On the other hand, the international monetary system serves as the foundation for global economic development and financial stability, which also plays a crucial role in global wealth inequality. When discussing the impact of digital finance on financial inclusion, we can explore the following aspects:

(1) Widening access to financial services through the proliferation of digital finance technology. The rise of mobile payments, internet lending, digital currencies, and other digital finance technologies has made financial transactions more convenient, rapid, and reduced barriers to financial transactions. These technologies offer new financial options to population segments that traditional financial institutions have difficulty reaching, such as rural areas, impoverished regions, and sparsely populated areas. Through digital finance technology, these populations can enjoy the convenience and opportunities provided by traditional financial services, thereby enhancing financial inclusion.
(2) Encouraging financial service innovation and diversification. Traditional financial institutions' service models and products are often limited, but the application of digital finance technology injects new vitality into financial services. Through technologies like the internet, blockchain, and artificial intelligence, digital finance platforms can offer more personalized and diverse financial products and services to meet the needs of different demographics. This innovation and diversification expand the coverage of financial services and promote higher financial inclusion.

However, the development of digital finance also faces certain challenges and risks concerning global wealth inequality and financial inclusion.

(1) The issue of the digital divide persists. Despite the widespread application of digital finance technology, there are still regions and population groups where digital technology adoption remains insufficient. The digital divide might result from factors such as education, technological literacy, and infrastructure limitations, restricting some populations' access to digital financial services. Addressing the digital divide requires efforts in enhancing digital education, increasing technological literacy, and improving infrastructure development.

(2) The security and privacy concerns of digital finance need attention. Digital finance involves a vast amount of personal and financial information, exposing it to security risks during information transmission, storage, and processing. Security issues like hacking, data breaches, and identity theft can lead to severe losses for individuals and financial institutions. Therefore, digital finance platforms and related entities must strengthen security measures, including data encryption, identity verification, and security audits, to ensure the safety of user information and funds.
(3) The regulation and legal frameworks for digital finance need to keep pace with its development. The rapid growth of digital finance poses new challenges to traditional financial regulations, requiring regulatory authorities to adjust policies and legal frameworks promptly to ensure the safe and stable development of digital finance. Regulatory bodies should strengthen supervision of digital finance platforms and services, including compliance checks, risk assessments, and market monitoring, to protect user rights and maintain the stable operation of the financial system.

The impact of the international monetary system on global wealth inequality is also complex. Let's further discuss its effects, covering stability, inequality, financial crises, and economic recessions:

(1) The stability of the international monetary system is crucial for global economic development. Stable monetary policies and exchange rates promote global trade and investment, supporting economic growth, job creation, and improved living standards, thus reducing wealth inequality to some extent.

However, the international monetary system also exhibits certain flaws and inequities. The monetary policies of some developed countries may have adverse effects on the economies of developing countries. For instance, devaluation policies in developed countries could reduce the export competitiveness of developing countries, thereby exacerbating global wealth inequality. Additionally, there is inequality within the international monetary system, with a few developed countries possessing significant influence and decision-making power, while developing countries have relatively weaker representation, potentially further exacerbating global wealth inequality.

(2) The instability of the international monetary system can lead to financial crises and economic recessions, which in turn affect global wealth inequality. Financial crises and economic recessions often cause severe economic losses, particularly impacting vulnerable groups and impoverished regions. During such crises and recessions, the poverty rate may increase, and the wealthy and economically strong nations are more likely to recover and benefit from the situation, thus intensifying global wealth inequality.

To address these issues, international cooperation and reforms in regulatory mechanisms are necessary to ensure the stability and fairness of the international monetary system. Additionally, providing development aid, promoting economic diversification, and enhancing financial inclusivity are crucial measures in efforts to reduce global wealth inequality. Furthermore, promoting a more balanced and inclusive global economic growth model to mitigate economic inequalities is also a crucial direction.

To narrow the global wealth gap and enhance financial inclusion, various measures need to be taken.

(1) Strengthen regulation of digital finance technology: Ensuring the compliance and security of digital finance technology to prevent its misuse and illegal activities. Regulatory authorities should establish robust frameworks, formulate relevant rules and standards, and enhance monitoring and enforcement efforts.
(2) Promote the adoption of digital finance technology in impoverished regions: By providing inclusive financial services, ensure that digital finance technology reaches a broader population, especially those traditionally underserved by financial institutions. This can be achieved through the establishment of digital finance infrastructure, widespread financial education, and support for financial innovation.
(3) Support the development of financial systems in developing countries: Developing countries often face weak financial infrastructure and limited financial service capabilities. The international community should increase support to developing countries by providing funding, technology, and knowledge transfer to promote the development of their financial markets and enhance financial inclusion.
(4) Improve the inequality within the international monetary system: The dominance of developed country currencies and the vulnerability of currencies in developing countries are issues within the international monetary system. To reduce the wealth gap, measures should be taken to improve these inequalities, such as increasing the international use of currencies from developing countries and providing more equitable and reasonable monetary policies to offer better development opportunities to these nations.

It can be observed that with the development of digital finance, the transformation of digital finance and the international monetary system has garnered significant attention concerning global wealth inequality and financial inclusion. This transformation has the potential to promote financial inclusion and reduce the wealth gap, but it may also exacerbate wealth disparities and financial exclusion.

On one hand, the development of digital finance can promote financial inclusion and reduce the wealth gap. Digital finance can provide financial services to populations that traditional finance has difficulty reaching, such as individuals without bank accounts or credit history, allowing them to access the benefits of financial services. The widespread adoption of digital finance technology can expand the coverage of financial services, enabling more people to participate in economic activities and promote economic development while reducing the wealth gap.

On the other hand, the development of digital finance can also exacerbate wealth disparities and financial exclusion. Digital finance's progress requires certain technological and financial literacy, which some segments of the population may lack, preventing them from benefiting from the convenience of digital finance. Additionally, digital finance may bring about new risks and issues, such as cybersecurity and privacy concerns, which could disproportionately affect vulnerable groups. Therefore, promoting inclusivity is crucial in digital finance development, ensuring that everyone can equally benefit from its progress.

The impact of the transformation of the international monetary system on global wealth inequality and financial inclusion should not be underestimated either. The transformation of the international monetary system can provide more financial support to impoverished countries, promoting economic development and reducing the wealth gap. It is essential to focus on increasing representation and participation for weaker countries and institutions in the decision-making and rule-making processes within the international monetary system, to avoid exacerbating wealth disparities and inequality.

However, the transformation of the international monetary system can also lead to increased wealth disparities and financial exclusion. During the process of transformation, the interests of powerful countries and institutions may receive more protection, while weaker countries and institutions could face more challenges and risks. Therefore, international cooperation and coordination are necessary to ensure that the transformation of the international monetary system promotes sustainable global development and reduces the wealth gap.

In conclusion, the impact of the transformation of digital finance and the international monetary system on global wealth inequality and financial inclusion is complex. To achieve a more equitable and sustainable global economic development, countries need to enhance cooperation and coordination to jointly drive the transformation of digital finance and the international monetary system. This will ensure that these transformations better align with the needs of the global economy and society, providing more equitable and sustainable financial services for all individuals.

References

Ahern, D.M. (2015) , "Regulatory arbitrageina FinTech world: devising anoptimal EU regulatory response to crowd lending", Working Paper [No.24], European Banking Institute, Germany.

Ahlstrom, D, Cumming, D.J.andVismara, S. (2018). , "New methods of entrepreneurial firm financing: Fintech, crowd funding and corporate governance implications", Corporate Governance: An International Review, Vol.26No.5

Akinola, E. A., Ilo, B. M., & Osabuohien, E. S. (2020). *Digital finance and inclusiveness: Any trade-offs?*. Electronic Journal of Information Systems in Developing Countries, 86(5)

Bordo, M. D., & Levin, A. T. (2017). *Central bank digital currency and the future of monetary policy*. National Bureau of Economic Research, No. w23711.

Carney, M. (2019). The growing challenges for monetary policy in the current international monetary and financial system. Bank of England.

Narayanan, A., Bonneau, J., Felten, E., Miller, A., & Goldfeder, S. (2016). *Bitcoin and Cryptocurrency Technologies*. Princeton University Press.

Tapscott, D., & Tapscott, A. (2016). Blockchain revolution: How the technology behind bitcoin is changing money, business, and the world. Penguin.

Zetzsche, D. A., Buckley, R. P., Arner, D. W., & Barberis, J. (2017). *Regulating a revolution: From regulatory sandboxes to smart regulation.* Fordham Journal of Corporate & Financial Law, 23(1)
Zohar, A. (2015). *Bitcoin: Under the hood.* Communications of the ACM, 58(9)

Chapter 8
Cybersecurity and Data Privacy in Digital Finance

8.1 Overview of Cybersecurity and Data Privacy in Digital Finance

The digital finance industry has long faced challenges related to cybersecurity and data privacy. To address these issues, various security technologies have been adopted. Security technologies refer to technical measures taken to protect and defend systems and data to ensure their integrity, availability, and confidentiality. In the realm of digital finance, security technologies are widely applied, encompassing aspects such as network security, data security, identity authentication, encryption, and decryption.

Currently, many solutions have been proposed in financial services to tackle the challenges of privacy protection and cybersecurity. Below, we introduce three key technical directions: privacy-preserving data sharing methods based on game theory, privacy-preserving data methods based on federated learning, and privacy-preserving data collection and analysis technologies.

8.1.1 Privacy-Preserving Data Sharing Methods Based on Game Theory

Game theory is a mathematical tool used to study decision-making interactions and strategic choices among participants. In the context of data sharing, game theory can be applied to analyze the interests among participants and design rational data sharing strategies. The following are steps to implement such strategies:

Firstly, establish a data-sharing game model. Participants in the model can be users and data collectors. Each participant has their own strategy and interest objectives. Users can choose whether to share their data, while data collectors can decide how much to pay to acquire this data.

Z. Liu and W. Hou, *Digital Finance*, https://doi.org/10.1007/978-981-99-7305-7_8

Secondly, design reasonable incentive mechanisms. Participants in data sharing often consider their own interests. Therefore, an incentive mechanism needs to be designed to encourage data sharing. For example, rewards can be provided to users who share their data, or certain penalties can be imposed on users who are unwilling to share their data.

Finally, introduce privacy protection mechanisms. Protecting users' data privacy is crucial during the data sharing process. Therefore, privacy protection mechanisms need to be introduced to safeguard users' personal information. This may include using encryption technology, anonymization, or differential privacy techniques to protect user data privacy.

Although privacy-preserving data sharing methods based on game theory have promising applications in financial social networks, there are still challenges in practical implementation, such as balancing data sharing efficiency with data privacy protection. Future research should further explore how to incorporate considerations of fairness into the game model and investigate more intelligent privacy protection mechanisms to better address data privacy issues in financial social networks.

8.1.2 Privacy-Preserving Data Methods Based on Federated Learning

Federated learning, as a decentralized machine learning framework, has unique advantages and potential in addressing data privacy protection issues. It enables model training and updates to be performed on local devices, avoiding direct sharing of sensitive data, thereby providing an innovative approach to solving data privacy protection issues.

In federated learning, participants have their own local datasets, which often contain users' sensitive information. Therefore, data privacy becomes a key issue in federated learning. To address this, researchers have proposed various privacy protection methods, among which differential privacy is the most commonly used. The core idea of differential privacy is to add some noise during computation, making the change in output results insignificant for any individual data, thereby ensuring data privacy.

In addition to differential privacy, encryption technology is another essential means to encrypt and decrypt data, ensuring the security and integrity of data during transmission and storage. Data anonymization is another method that involves perturbing and transforming data to hide personal identities and sensitive information, protecting user privacy.

8.1.3 *Privacy-Preserving Data Collection and Analysis Technologies*

The core idea of privacy-preserving data collection and analysis technologies is to protect user privacy during data collection, transmission, and analysis processes. These technologies aim to ensure the confidentiality, integrity, and availability of personal data. Commonly used privacy protection technologies in practical applications include data encryption, data anonymization, and data aggregation measures.

Data encryption is a crucial privacy protection technology used to encrypt and decrypt data to ensure data security and integrity during transmission and storage. Common encryption methods include symmetric encryption and asymmetric encryption. Symmetric encryption uses the same key for data encryption and decryption, while asymmetric encryption uses public and private keys for encryption and decryption. These encryption methods can effectively protect data confidentiality and prevent unauthorized access and tampering.

Data anonymization refers to perturbing and transforming data to hide personal identities and sensitive information, protecting user privacy. Common data anonymization techniques include k-anonymity, l-diversity, and t-closeness. The core idea of k-anonymity is to obscure any individual data in a group of data, making it difficult for attackers to identify specific individuals. L-diversity achieves increased data dissimilarity by perturbing data in the dataset, increasing the difficulty of analysis for attackers. T-closeness limits the number of sensitive data contained in query results, thereby reducing the risk of sensitive information leakage.

Data aggregation involves combining dispersed datasets into a comprehensive result for data analysis and mining purposes. In the context of privacy-preserving data collection and analysis, the goal of data aggregation is to achieve effective data analysis while safeguarding user privacy. Common data aggregation techniques include differential privacy and aggregation algorithms. Differential privacy adds random noise to original data during computation to hide personal information and protect individual privacy. Aggregation algorithms combine data from multiple datasets to generate a comprehensive result while preserving user privacy.

In addition to the common privacy protection technologies mentioned above, there are some emerging technologies proposed to address more challenging privacy issues. For example, homomorphic encryption is a special encryption technique that allows computations to be performed on encrypted data, protecting data privacy. Secure multi-party computation is a collection of protocols and algorithms that enable multiple parties to perform computations without sharing their raw data and obtain the final computation result. Secure multi-party machine learning combines machine learning with secure multi-party computation to train and infer machine learning models while preserving data privacy.

Although these privacy-preserving data and analysis technologies hold great promise theoretically, they still face some issues and challenges in practical applications.

Firstly, privacy protection technologies may have an impact Li et al. (2007) on data quality. For instance, in k-anonymity, data is perturbed, which may result in losing some detailed information, affecting data accuracy and usability. Data distortion during data anonymization can lead to biased results and less accurate analyses.

Secondly, privacy protection technologies often require significant computational resources. For instance, in differential privacy, adding considerable random noise is necessary to protect personal information. This means complex calculations and noise injection during data processing, resulting in increased computational complexity and cost.

Moreover, privacy-preserving data collection and analysis technologies also face challenges Katal et al. (2013) in handling big data. Big data involves a massive volume of data, and for privacy protection technologies, data processing and storage issues need to be addressed. Processing big data may require distributed computing and storage systems with efficient, scalable, and secure features to handle the demands of large-scale data.

To address these problems and challenges, researchers are actively exploring new privacy-preserving data collection and analysis technologies. The following are some emerging privacy protection technologies and methods:

(1) Variants of Differential Privacy: While differential privacy is a crucial technology for protecting individual privacy, there are still some limitations in practical applications. To overcome these limitations, researchers have proposed variants of differential privacy, such as joint differential privacy, mutually exclusive differential privacy, and progressive differential privacy. These technologies provide individual privacy protection while having better computational efficiency and data quality.
(2) New Aggregation Algorithms: Aggregation algorithms play a critical role in privacy-preserving data analysis. Two common aggregation algorithms are multi-party computation and homomorphic encryption, which enable computations and aggregation without exposing individual data. These algorithms perform computations in the encrypted domain, preserving individual privacy and data confidentiality.
(3) Personalized Privacy Protection: Personalized privacy protection is a method tailored to different users' privacy needs and preferences. It provides customized privacy protection schemes for each user based on their preferences and risk tolerance. This approach can balance individual privacy requirements while considering data quality and usability.
(4) Context-Based Privacy Protection: Context-based privacy protection involves selecting the most suitable privacy protection scheme based on different application scenarios and requirements. Different datasets and application scenarios may have varying privacy protection requirements, so flexible selection and application of privacy protection technologies are needed. Context-based privacy protection maximizes the balance between privacy protection and data usability.

This chapter will explore the internal management mechanisms of digital financial institutions, their roles and limitations in network security and data privacy protection, and how to improve the internal management mechanisms of digital financial institutions to enhance network security and data privacy protection.

The internal management mechanisms of digital financial institutions refer to the management systems established by these institutions in various aspects of business operation and management, including rules and regulations, organizational structure, internal controls, and supervision systems. Specifically, digital financial institutions should establish sound risk management systems, internal control mechanisms, information security management systems, and data privacy protection systems, among others.

The role of internal management mechanisms in network security and data privacy protection in digital finance is multifaceted, including:

(1) Discovering and Preventing Network Security Threats and Risks Whitman and Mattord (2017): By establishing internal management mechanisms, digital financial institutions can timely detect and assess network security threats and risks. Internal management mechanisms should include security risk assessment, incident response, and disaster recovery plans to address various security threats, such as network attacks, malicious software, and data breaches. Through these mechanisms, digital financial institutions can quickly identify and respond to potential security issues, reducing the risk of attacks and losses.
(2) Controlling Internal Employees' Operations and Anomalies: Internal management mechanisms can regulate and monitor the operations of internal employees to prevent malicious behavior and abuse of privileges. By establishing strict access control and identity verification mechanisms, digital financial institutions can limit employees' access to sensitive data and system resources, ensuring data confidentiality and integrity. Additionally, through appropriate monitoring and reporting mechanisms, digital financial institutions can promptly detect and respond to anomalies in employee operations, including internal data leaks and abuse of privileges.
(3) Improving Operational Efficiency and Reducing Cost Risks Davenport (2013): Sound internal management mechanisms can improve the operational efficiency of digital financial institutions. By standardizing and optimizing business processes, digital financial institutions can collect, process, and analyze data more efficiently, providing faster and more accurate services. Moreover, internal management mechanisms also help reduce cost risks. By regulating and monitoring the use of internal resources, digital financial institutions can mitigate the risks of resource waste and abuse, achieving effective resource allocation and utilization.
(4) Enhancing Competitiveness and Reputation: Sound internal management mechanisms can enhance the competitiveness and reputation of digital financial institutions. Through effective network security and data privacy protection, digital financial institutions can earn the trust and loyalty of users, attracting more users and partners. Simultaneously, digital financial institutions can provide

more secure and stable services through effective internal management mechanisms, enhancing cooperation with partners and expanding their business scope and market share.

However, the limitations of internal management mechanisms in digital financial network security and data privacy protection are also significant and cannot be overlooked.

Firstly, internal management mechanisms alone cannot fully guarantee the security and privacy protection of digital financial institutions because security and privacy protection require a comprehensive system engineering approach. Internal management mechanisms are just one part of it, and they need to be combined with other measures and technologies to form a comprehensive security protection system. Digital financial institutions should adopt multi-level and multi-dimensional security measures, including technical measures, institutional measures, and organizational culture construction.

Secondly, the effectiveness and efficiency of internal management mechanisms rely on the active cooperation and execution of the internal employees of digital financial institutions. Even if sound security policies and control measures are established, there are still security risks and potential data leaks if employees do not comply with or execute them. Therefore, digital financial institutions need to strengthen employees' security education and training, raise awareness of security and data privacy protection, and reinforce their sense of responsibility and security behavior.

Lastly, the rapid development and changes in digital financial business present new challenges to internal management mechanisms. Digital financial institutions need to continuously update and improve their internal management mechanisms to adapt to new security threats and privacy protection requirements. With technological advancements and business expansions, new security vulnerabilities and risks continue to emerge. Therefore, digital financial institutions should stay attentive to the development of security technologies, promptly update security strategies and control measures, and strengthen their capabilities to respond to emerging threats.

To address the limitations of internal management mechanisms in network security and data privacy protection for digital financial institutions, we propose some improvement and enhancement suggestions:

(1) Establish a Culture of Comprehensive Participation in Security: Digital financial institutions should foster a culture of comprehensive participation in security, where all employees understand the importance of network security and data privacy protection and consider it their responsibility. This can be achieved through regular security training, internal communication, and incentive mechanisms.
(2) Strengthen Internal Supervision and Audit: Digital financial institutions should enhance supervision and audit of internal systems and devices to ensure the effective implementation of security measures. Internal supervision includes regular security checks, vulnerability scanning, compliance reviews, as well as monitoring and auditing of employee behavior and operations. These efforts

help identify and correct security vulnerabilities and non-compliant behaviors promptly, safeguarding network security and data privacy.

(3) Promote Technological Innovation and Compliance Development: Digital financial institutions should actively promote technological innovation and seek more advanced and effective security and privacy protection technologies. At the same time, institutions should maintain sensitivity and compliance with relevant laws, regulations, and regulatory requirements to ensure internal management mechanisms align with external norms.

(4) Enhance Cooperation with External Security Institutions: Digital financial institutions can establish partnerships with external security institutions to share information and intelligence, strengthen monitoring and prevention of security threats. Such collaborations provide digital financial institutions with professional security advice and support, enabling joint responses to network security challenges.

(5) Continuously Improve and Learn: Digital financial institutions should establish mechanisms for continuous improvement and learning, regularly evaluating the effectiveness of internal management mechanisms, and adjusting and optimizing them as needed. Through continuous improvement, digital financial institutions can constantly enhance their levels of network security and data privacy protection, adapting to ever-changing security threats and technological developments.

In conclusion, internal management mechanisms of digital financial institutions play a crucial role in ensuring network security and data privacy protection. Digital financial institutions should formulate comprehensive internal management systems, strengthen employees' security awareness and confidentiality consciousness, enhance supervision and management of internal systems and devices, and strengthen cooperation and coordination with external security institutions. By doing so, digital financial institutions can elevate their levels of network security and data privacy protection, making positive contributions to the development and stability of the digital financial market.

8.2 Data Protection Regulations and Data Sovereignty Issues

With the rapid development of digital finance, data protection has become a highly discussed topic. Sensitive information such as personal data and financial transaction data involved in digital finance needs to be protected. Therefore, the establishment and enforcement of data protection laws and regulations have become crucial.

Next, we will analyze the data protection laws and regulations in digital finance, the level of protection they provide for data protection, the shortcomings of these regulations, and potential solutions, as well as issues related to data sovereignty.

In the field of digital finance, one of the fundamental and crucial regulations is the Personal Information Protection Law. The purpose of this regulation is to safeguard the security and privacy of users' personal information and restrict the actions of digital financial institutions in collecting, using, storing, and transmitting personal information. Digital financial institutions must adhere to the principle of user consent, clearly inform users of the purpose and scope of personal information collection, and take necessary security measures to prevent personal information leakage, abuse, or unlawful collection.

In addition, the Data Security Law also applies to the digital finance industry, aiming to maintain data security and protect the legitimate rights and interests of digital financial institutions and users. According to this regulation, digital financial institutions must establish and implement data security management systems, adopt necessary technical and organizational measures to ensure data integrity, availability, and confidentiality. Digital financial institutions also need to establish data security incident emergency plans to promptly detect, report, and handle data security incidents, reducing losses and impacts.

Furthermore, the Cybersecurity Law and Financial Industry Regulation also have an impact on data protection in the digital finance industry. The Cybersecurity Law requires digital financial institutions to establish sound cybersecurity management systems, adopt technical and managerial measures to protect network security and prevent cyber attacks. The Financial Industry Regulation involves compliance supervision of digital financial institutions, including provisions related to data reporting, internal controls, risk management, etc., to ensure data security and compliance operations of digital financial institutions.

It can be seen that these regulations cover various types of institutions in the digital finance industry, such as P2P lending platforms, payment institutions, fintech companies, etc., ensuring the universality and applicability of data protection. The regulations provide clear provisions regarding data collection, use, protection, sharing, storage, and disposal, offering guidance and standardization for digital financial institutions.

Next, let's take the United States as an example to explore the development history and main legal systems of personal information protection laws and make a comparison with China's personal information protection legal system. Finally, we will propose improvement suggestions for China's personal information protection laws.

First, let's analyze the development history and main legal systems of personal information protection laws in the United States.

The development history of personal information protection laws in the United States can be traced back to the Privacy Act passed in 1974. This act established regulations on how federal government agencies should collect, use, and disclose personal information and granted citizens the right to access and correct their personal information. Subsequently, with the popularization of the internet and the rise of e-commerce, the collection and use of personal information became increasingly widespread, leading to the leakage and abuse of personal information. This prompted the U.S. government and industry organizations to begin formulating more comprehensive and specific laws for personal information protection. Currently, the U.S. personal information protection legal system includes several key legal systems:

1. Health insurance portability and accountability act (HIPAA) U.S. Department of Health & Human Services. (2003)
   HIPAA is a federal law aimed at protecting the privacy of medical information and healthcare workers. The law requires healthcare institutions to protect individuals' medical information, including medical history, medical records, prescription information, etc. It also sets standards and restrictions for the collection, use, and disclosure of this information.
2. Electronic communications privacy act (ECPA)
   ECPA is a federal law aimed at protecting the privacy of personal electronic communications and other online communications. The law stipulates standards and restrictions for the collection and monitoring of electronic emails and online communications, requiring law enforcement agencies to obtain appropriate authorization and search warrants to collect and monitor such communications.
3. Children's online privacy protection act (COPPA)
   COPPA is a federal law aimed at protecting the online privacy of children under 13. The law sets standards and restrictions for online service providers in the collection, use, and disclosure of children's personal information, requiring explicit authorization from parents or guardians before collecting and using children's personal information.
4. Data security and breach notification act (DSSA)
   DSSA is a federal law that sets standards and restrictions for notifying affected individuals after a data breach occurs. The law requires organizations affected by data breaches to notify affected individuals as soon as possible and provide necessary information and advice to help them guard against risks.
5. California consumer privacy act (CCPA) Hoofnagle et al. (2019)
   CCPA is a personal information protection law enacted in California, aimed at protecting consumers' personal information. The law establishes rules that businesses must follow regarding the collection, use, disclosure, and sale of consumers' personal information, granting consumers certain control and rights, such as access, deletion, and restriction of personal information.

In addition to the laws and regulations mentioned above, the United States also has other laws and regulations that play a crucial role in personal information protection. For example, the Gramm-Leach-Bliley Act (GLBA) is used to protect the privacy of financial information, and various state-level personal information protection laws, such as New York State Data Security Act in New York State.

It is important to note that the personal information protection legal system in the United States is relatively decentralized, lacking a comprehensive federal-level personal information protection law. As the digital era continues to develop and the importance of personal information protection increases, some states and federal agencies are working to strengthen and improve the laws and regulations related to personal information protection to ensure better protection of citizens' personal information.

Now let's compare the legal systems of personal information protection between the United States and China.

While there are some differences and deficiencies in the personal information protection legal systems of both the United States and China, they also have their respective advantages.

(1) Scope of Applicability: The United States' personal information protection legal system is primarily composed of federal and state laws, with varying standards and applicability between different states. This can result in digital platforms and companies conducting cross-state businesses having to comply with different legal requirements, increasing the complexity of legal compliance. In contrast, China's "Personal Information Protection Law" provides a unified legal framework for personal information protection nationwide, ensuring a more uniform and clear approach to the collection, use, and disclosure of personal information.
(2) Level of Legal Protection: The United States' personal information protection laws primarily focus on industries and specific sectors, leading to certain limitations in coverage and protection. On the other hand, China's "Personal Information Protection Law" is a more comprehensive and detailed legislation, clearly defining the principles, rights, and obligations related to personal information protection, providing higher legal protection for personal information.
(3) Enforcement: The enforcement of personal information protection laws in the United States is mainly shared by law enforcement agencies and industry organizations. However, the differences in legal standards and enforcement efficiency between different states result in inconsistent enforcement efforts. In China, the enforcement of personal information protection laws is primarily carried out by government departments and judicial institutions, leading to relatively unified and effective enforcement. In recent years, the Chinese government has strengthened the enforcement of personal information protection, imposing severe penalties and sanctions for violations of personal information protection laws.

Finally, we propose improvements to China's personal information protection laws.

In our country, the legal system for personal information protection is an important measure to safeguard citizens' personal information security and promote the construction of a digital society. Although China has already established the "Personal Information Protection Law" and achieved some results, there are still some problems and challenges in its practical implementation. Therefore, in order to further enhance the level of personal information protection, we need to take a series of possible improvement measures.

(1) Enhance the enforceability of the legal system: This requires strengthening the punishment for personal information leakage and abuse to ensure that illegal acts are effectively dealt with. By increasing the risks and costs of illegal

behavior, companies and individuals will attach greater importance to personal information protection, thereby effectively reducing the occurrence of illegal activities.

(2) Strengthen supervision and enforcement Bennett and Raab (2006): Establishing and improving personal information protection law enforcement agencies will enhance the supervision and punishment of illegal behavior by companies and individuals, ensuring the legal and standardized use and protection of personal information. Regulatory authorities should actively conduct inspections and impose serious penalties for violations to safeguard personal information security and privacy.
(3) Improve personal information protection standards Schwartz and Solove (2011): These standards should keep pace with new information technologies and application scenarios. Moreover, it is essential to align them with international standards to ensure that personal information protection complies with both international and domestic legal norms. By formulating and updating standards, the forward-looking and effectiveness of personal information protection can be enhanced, ensuring that personal information is not violated or abused.
(4) Strengthen regulation of cross-border data flows Kuner (2013): Cross-border data flow involves differences in laws and systems between different countries and regions. Therefore, it is necessary to establish a comprehensive cross-border data flow management mechanism, including the establishment of a personal information outbound security assessment mechanism, to ensure that cross-border data flows comply with the law and regulations and protect personal information's security and privacy.
(5) Enhance public education and awareness: By conducting publicity and educational activities, the public's awareness and knowledge of personal information protection can be raised, allowing them to better understand the importance of personal information protection and actively participate in it. Additionally, cultivating public awareness of monitoring personal information protection will create a social atmosphere of collective concern and participation, further promoting the development of personal information protection work.

Now let's turn our attention to data sovereignty protection in digital finance. Data sovereignty refers to the rights that individuals or organizations have over the data they generate, own, manage, and use. Under the concept of data sovereignty, data owners have the decision-making power over their data, including its use, sharing, storage, and destruction.

Data sovereignty has the following characteristics:

Independence: Data sovereignty emphasizes the data owners' independent decision-making power over their data. Data owners have the right to decide whether to share, use, store, destroy, or otherwise process their data. This independence allows data owners to autonomously manage and make decisions about their data according to their wishes and needs.

Inseparability: Data sovereignty is inseparable and includes data ownership and control. Data owners have complete control over their data, including access, usage, and processing. This inseparability ensures comprehensive protection of data owners' rights and interests.

Specificity: Data sovereignty has specificity, meaning data owners can choose to authorize others or organizations to use their data without affecting their ownership and control over the data. Data owners can reach agreements with other parties to authorize them to use the data, but they still retain ownership and decision-making power over the data.

Timeliness: Data sovereignty has a temporal aspect, allowing data owners to grant limited or long-term authorizations to their data as needed. Data owners can set data expiration periods or revoke previous authorizations to maintain control and decision-making power over their data.

Value: Data sovereignty has value, and as data accumulates and increases in value, data sovereignty also increases in value. By managing and utilizing data in a reasonable manner, data owners can generate economic, social, or personal value from the data. Protecting data sovereignty helps incentivize data owners to actively manage and develop the value potential of their data.

These characteristics together form the fundamental principles and requirements of data sovereignty, ensuring that data owners have legitimate rights and decision-making power over their data.

As China is the world's second-largest economy and a populous nation, data has become a core strategic resource for its national development. With continuous economic development and digital transformation in China, there is an inevitable increase in China's reliance on foreign technologies. While introducing foreign technologies can promote economic development and innovation in China, it also brings about technological dependence and security risks.

Foreign interference in China's data infrastructure is one of the significant challenges to China's data sovereignty and cybersecurity. Some foreign countries and companies attempt to gain access to sensitive and confidential data in China through various forms of interference and control, taking advantage of their technological and market advantages. Such interference and control pose potential threats to China's cybersecurity and data sovereignty. For example, foreign governments may use methods such as cyber-attacks and information warfare to obtain sensitive information from China, further exacerbating cybersecurity risks. Additionally, some foreign companies, holding monopolistic positions in the Chinese market, may pose potential threats to China's national security and economic development by controlling and analyzing Chinese data.

To address these issues, the Chinese government has implemented a series of measures to protect data sovereignty and cybersecurity. First, the Chinese government has strengthened the review and management of the introduction of foreign technologies to ensure compliance with national security and legal requirements. Through reviews and regulations, the Chinese government seeks to prevent security risks and data leaks. Second, the Chinese government actively promotes the development and innovation of local technologies to reduce reliance on foreign technologies. Moreover, the government has strengthened the protection of data and privacy, formulating a series of laws and regulations to safeguard individuals' and businesses' data security and privacy. These laws and regulations include the "Personal Information Protection Law," which requires companies to comply with relevant regulations when collecting, using, and processing personal information.

Furthermore, the Chinese government actively promotes international rules and standards for data sovereignty and cybersecurity to maintain the stability and order of global cybersecurity and data flow. China advocates the construction of an open, secure, and orderly digital world and uses international cooperation and multilateral mechanisms to promote the regulation and security of transnational data flow. The Chinese government cooperates with other countries and international organizations to strengthen information sharing, technology exchanges, and cybersecurity cooperation, jointly addressing transnational data interference and cybersecurity threats.

Protecting data sovereignty is the foundation for the development of digital finance, and in the future, digital finance should strengthen its efforts in data sovereignty protection.

Firstly, digital financial institutions should pay more attention to data sovereignty protection and incorporate it into their core values for data collection and usage. They should establish clear data usage policies and regulations, clarify data owners' rights, and ensure legal, transparent, and prudent use and sharing of data. Additionally, digital financial institutions should enhance the protection of personal information and data privacy, ensuring data security and confidentiality.

Secondly, digital financial institutions need to comply with relevant laws and regulations, including the "Personal Information Protection Law" and the "Data Security Law," to ensure the legitimacy and compliance of data sovereignty. They should establish sound internal control mechanisms, strengthen the examination and supervision of data usage behaviors, and prevent data misuse, leaks, or unauthorized access by third parties. Furthermore, digital financial institutions should conduct regular data security assessments and risk evaluations to promptly identify and address potential security risks and vulnerabilities.

In addition, technological innovation is also a crucial means of safeguarding data sovereignty. Digital financial institutions should actively promote technological research and development and explore advanced data protection technologies, such as encryption, blockchain, and secure multi-party computation. These technologies can provide a higher level of data security and privacy protection, offering strong support for data sovereignty protection.

Regarding data sovereignty protection, foreign experiences can offer valuable insights. For instance, the General Data Protection Regulation (GDPR) issued by the European Union in May 2018 has played a proactive role in personal data protection. The regulation sets a series of strict provisions, requiring companies to inform users clearly about the purposes of data collection and usage and provide transparency in data processing to protect user data sovereignty. The GDPR also imposes severe penalties for data breaches, leading to significant fines for non-compliant behavior. These measures effectively safeguard user data sovereignty and individual privacy, providing robust protection and guidance for the digital finance industry.

It is noteworthy that the enactment of the GDPR not only affects European countries but also has a global impact on companies and organizations worldwide. Many countries and regions have paid high attention to the GDPR and actively drawn lessons from it to strengthen the development of their own data protection laws and systems. This further promotes the global focus and concern on data sovereignty protection.

In summary, data sovereignty protection in digital finance is a critical topic, and digital financial institutions need to enhance data sovereignty protection in data collection and usage, comply with relevant laws and regulations, increase the transparency and controllability of data sovereignty, and strengthen scrutiny and supervision of data usage. Governments should also intensify the formulation and enforcement of relevant regulations, increase their emphasis on data sovereignty protection, and provide digital financial institutions with clear and robust legal support. Technological innovation is also a vital means to ensure data sovereignty protection, and digital financial institutions can enhance research and application of more advanced and effective data protection technologies. These measures will contribute to better safeguarding user data sovereignty and promoting the healthy development of the digital finance industry.

8.3 Challenges and Opportunities in Cybersecurity and Data Privacy in Digital Finance

As mentioned earlier, the rise of digital finance has brought many conveniences to the financial industry, but it also faces risks of cyber-attacks and data privacy breaches. These risks threaten the stability and development of digital finance systems and must be thoroughly studied and addressed. Next, we will explore the reasons, risks, and the challenges new technologies pose to cybersecurity and data privacy in the context of digital finance.

One of the primary security threats that digital finance faces is cyber-attacks. Cyber-attacks and data breaches have become one of the most significant threats to the digital finance industry. Between 2013 and 2017, the global financial services sector experienced over 6800 data breach incidents, resulting in economic losses exceeding $30 billion. Additionally, many digital finance platforms have vulnerabilities and security loopholes. For example, the Mt. Gox Bitcoin exchange platform suffered a $400 million loss after being hacked in 2014. Cyber-attacks can be categorized into three types: hacker attacks, including intrusion, viruses, Trojans, etc.; denial-of-service attacks, which render systems inaccessible by occupying their resources; and social engineering attacks, which exploit deception and manipulation to obtain information.

Cyber-attacks pose serious threats to the digital finance system, creating significant risks for financial institutions and users. These threats include:

Firstly, cyber-attacks can lead to system failures and service disruptions, severely impacting the normal operation of digital finance systems. Attackers may employ various methods such as Distributed Denial of Service (DDoS) attacks, malicious software, and viruses to target and penetrate digital finance systems, causing system crashes, data loss, or unavailability. In such situations, users may be unable to access and use financial services properly, resulting in significant inconvenience to user experience and business continuity.

Secondly, cyber-attacks can result in the leakage of personal information and sensitive data, posing a serious threat to users' privacy and security. Attackers may use techniques like hacking, phishing websites, and malicious software to obtain users' personal identification information, account passwords, credit card details, and other sensitive data. The leaked data could be used for identity theft, financial fraud, phishing, and other malicious activities, posing a significant risk to users' financial assets and personal safety.

Additionally, cyber-attacks can lead to an increase in fraud and deceptive activities, further damaging the stability and reputation of the financial system. Attackers may employ methods like phishing, fake websites, and fraudulent investment platforms to deceive users into providing personal information or engaging in illegal transactions. These fraudulent activities not only directly harm users' financial interests but also undermine the fairness and integrity of the financial market, reducing users' trust in the digital finance system.

Data privacy breaches are another major risk faced by the digital finance sector. More and more digital finance platforms have become increasingly aggressive in collecting and utilizing users' personal data. However, due to the complexity and sensitivity of digital finance, protecting data privacy has become more challenging. For instance, some digital finance platforms may have their users' data stolen by hackers and used for criminal activities. The reasons for data privacy breaches mainly include technical issues and human errors. Technical reasons encompass system vulnerabilities, inadequate security measures, and the like, while human reasons involve employee negligence, internal fraud, and so on.

The risks of data privacy breaches are primarily manifested in the following aspects:

Firstly, data leaks may lead to unauthorized individuals obtaining and misusing users' personal information, posing a threat to users' privacy and security. Sensitive data such as personal identification information, financial details, and transaction records may be stolen by hackers for identity theft, fraudulent activities, or other criminal acts. This can cause users financial losses and create personal trust crises.

Secondly, data leaks may harm the financial institutions' economic interests and reputation. Once users' data is exposed, financial institutions may face user complaints, refund requests, legal lawsuits, resulting in substantial compensations and reputational damage. Additionally, data leaks can lead to customer attrition and a decrease in market share, negatively impacting the financial institution's sustainable development.

Furthermore, data leaks can trigger legal and regulatory risks. Many countries and regions have established laws and regulations for personal data protection and privacy

Greenleaf (2017), setting strict requirements for financial institutions concerning data handling and protection. Should a data leak occur, financial institutions may face penalties and investigations from government regulatory agencies, or even class-action lawsuits filed by users.

In addition, new technologies in digital finance, such as blockchain and artificial intelligence (AI), play a significant role in improving financial efficiency and reducing costs. However, they also bring some challenges in terms of network security and data privacy. These challenges primarily include the following aspects.

Firstly, blockchain systems themselves face some potential security risks. For instance, there might be vulnerabilities in the coding and execution of smart contracts, which hackers could exploit to launch attacks, tamper with contracts, or steal assets. Additionally, nodes in the blockchain network could be subject to malicious attacks, leading to data leaks or disruptions in network services. Therefore, digital financial institutions adopting blockchain technology need to strengthen security audits, contract reviews, and network monitoring to mitigate potential risks.

Secondly, the complexity of AI algorithms and data privacy issues pose challenges. For example, AI algorithms may generate biases or discrimination, resulting in unfair decisions. To address this, digital financial institutions need to conduct fairness assessments and regulations on algorithms, ensuring data quality and diversity to minimize biases. Moreover, the collection and processing of personal data must comply strictly with relevant privacy regulations and guidelines to ensure the security and privacy of user data.

Furthermore, digital finance platforms' adoption of cloud computing and distributed ledger technology (DLT) also presents challenges in network security and data privacy.

Firstly, cloud computing brings new risks to network security. Since user data is stored in the cloud, improper security measures or attacks on cloud service providers could expose user data to the risk of leakage. Additionally, interruptions in cloud service provision could cause disruptions in the operation of digital finance platforms, greatly impacting users and business operations.

Secondly, DLT faces some challenges as well. For example, a 51% attack refers to when an attacker controls over half of the computing power in the network, enabling them to control the operations of the blockchain network. Vulnerabilities in smart contracts could also result in malicious actions and financial losses. To address these challenges, digital financial institutions need to enhance the security of the blockchain network, including implementing multi-signature authentication, selecting consensus algorithms, and establishing audit mechanisms. Additionally, strengthening audits and code reviews of smart contracts is a critical measure to ensure blockchain security.

Looking ahead, the security and privacy protection in the digital finance industry will be a crucial direction for future development. With the rapid growth of the digital economy, the digital finance sector faces increasingly complex challenges in network security and data privacy. Therefore, digital financial institutions need to adopt appropriate technological measures to safeguard users' digital assets and privacy information. For instance, strengthening data encryption and storage, establishing automated security mechanisms, and enhancing identity verification are essential steps. Moreover, digital financial institutions must continuously update their technological approaches to adapt to evolving security landscapes, such as advancements in AI technology and blockchain.

As a nascent industry, digital finance also requires continuous improvement and updates in regulations and oversight to address the ever-changing market environment and technological challenges. In this context, some pressing issues need resolution, including the adequacy of legal regulations in safeguarding network security and data privacy in digital finance, challenges in internal regulatory frameworks within the industry, and whether international standards can meet the demands of network security and data privacy in digital finance.

Firstly, there are still shortcomings in the legal regulations concerning network security and data privacy in the digital finance sector. The abundance of transactions and data within digital finance platforms could lead to security vulnerabilities and data breaches if regulatory measures are insufficient. Balancing customer information protection with business innovation is crucial in regulatory efforts for digital finance. However, the current regulatory agencies often face challenges like inadequate regulatory tools and the lack of unified standards, which affect their ability to effectively oversee digital finance platforms.

Secondly, challenges in internal regulatory frameworks within the digital finance industry revolve around striking a balance between innovation and oversight. Regulatory measures need to consider industry-specific factors such as customer trust, financial stability, and consumer protection, which may influence industry innovation and development. Additionally, the cross-border nature of digital finance platforms further complicates the regulatory landscape, requiring coordination among multiple countries and regions' legal regulations.

Lastly, there is significant attention on whether international standards can adequately address the network security and data privacy demands of digital finance. As the digital finance industry continues its globalization, establishing unified international standards becomes essential. These standards must account for the unique characteristics of the digital finance industry, including the application of emerging technologies such as virtual currencies, blockchain, and fintech. Furthermore, due to the cross-border nature of digital finance, international standards need to harmonize and coordinate legal regulations across various countries and regions while safeguarding network security and data privacy.

In conclusion, network security and data privacy protection in digital finance represent a global challenge that requires collaborative efforts from all stakeholders. The establishment of legal regulations, international standards, and active exploration by digital financial institutions provide crucial support and assurance to build a more secure, trusted, and stable digital finance ecosystem.

References

Bennett, C. J., & Raab, C. D. (2006). The governance of privacy: Policy instruments in global perspective. MIT press.

Davenport, T. H. (2013). Process Innovation: Reengineering Work Through Information Technology. Harvard Business Press.

Greenleaf, G. (2017). Global data privacy laws 2017: 120 national data privacy laws, including Indonesia and Turkey. Privacy Laws & Business International Report, 145.

Hoofnagle, C. J., van der Sloot, B., & Borgesius, F. Z. (2019). *The European Union general data protection regulation: What it is and what it means.* Information & Communications Technology Law, 28(1).

Katal, A., Wazid, M., & Goudar, R. H. (2013). *Big data: Issues, challenges, tools and good practices.* In 2013 Sixth International Conference on Contemporary Computing (IC3) (pp. 404–409). IEEE.

Kuner, C. (2013). *Transborder data flows and data privacy law.* Oxford University Press.

Li, N., Li, T., & Venkatasubramanian, S. (2007). *t-Closeness: Privacy beyond k-anonymity and l-diversity.* In 2007 IEEE 23rd International Conference on Data Engineering (pp. 106–115). IEEE.

Schwartz, P. M., & Solove, D. J. (2011). The PII problem: Privacy and a new concept of personally identifiable information. NYUL Rev., 86, 1814.

U.S. Department of Health & Human Services. (2003). *Summary of the HIPAA Privacy Rule.* HHS Office for Civil Rights.

Whitman, M. E., & Mattord, H. J. (2017). *Principles of Information Security.* Cengage Learning.

Chapter 9
Social and Environmental Impacts of Digital Finance

9.1 Overview of the Social and Environmental Impacts of Digital Finance

Digital finance refers to a new financial service model that utilizes information technology such as the internet and mobile communication to digitize, network, and smarten financial services. The emergence of digital finance has changed people's consumption and savings behavior, impacted financial inclusion and stability, and also transformed the job market and labor force.

Firstly, digital finance has altered people's consumption and savings behavior. With the widespread adoption of digital financial services like mobile payments and e-commerce, there has been a significant shift in how people consume goods and services and save their money. Let's explore this from both consumption and savings perspectives:

From the consumption perspective, the proliferation of digital finance technology has made consumption more convenient, diverse, and transparent. The widespread use of mobile payments, digital wallets, and other digital payment methods allows people to make purchases anytime, anywhere without the need for carrying cash. Additionally, digital finance has provided consumers with more choices, such as online shopping, sharing economy services, etc., making consumption more flexible and personalized. Consumers can access information like price comparisons and product reviews, enabling them to make more informed and rational decisions.

From the savings perspective, the development of digital finance has brought convenience and innovation to people's savings behavior. Through digital finance platforms, individuals can choose different savings and investment options such as fixed deposits, current accounts, wealth management products, etc., based on their financial needs and goals. The application of digital finance technology has also expanded investment opportunities, such as funds and stocks, allowing people to participate in a broader range of capital markets. Furthermore, the rise of digital banking has made savings operations more convenient, enabling people to perform

Z. Liu and W. Hou, *Digital Finance*, https://doi.org/10.1007/978-981-99-7305-7_9

transactions like deposits and withdrawals through mobile banking and online banking without physically visiting a bank branch.

Secondly, digital finance has impacted financial inclusion and stability Demirgüç-Kunt et al. (2015).

Digital finance has the potential to enhance financial inclusion, enabling more people to participate in the financial market. Its development has facilitated the design and accessibility of financial products, reducing market barriers and increasing the availability and affordability of financial services. For example, mobile payments and peer-to-peer (P2P) lending Yan et al. (2015) platforms provide convenient financial services, meeting the needs of diverse population segments, particularly those who have limited access to traditional financial services.

The impact of digital finance on financial stability is two-fold, both promoting stability and introducing risks. On one hand, digital finance can enhance market transparency and efficiency, reducing information asymmetry and transaction costs, which can contribute to financial market stability.

Finally, digital finance has also transformed the job market and labor force.

The rapid growth of digital finance has created a demand for technology and financial talents, providing new opportunities in the job market. At the same time, the emergence of digital finance has posed new challenges to traditional financial institutions. They need to adapt to the development of digital finance and enhance their competitiveness, leading to changes in the labor market.

Next, we will analyze the impact of digital finance on employment opportunities, work patterns, and skill requirements, exploring its effects on the job market and labor force.

Firstly, let's examine the changes in employment opportunities. The rapid development of digital finance has brought new opportunities and challenges to the job market. The digital finance industry involves various professional fields such as finance, computer science, data analysis, etc., leading to an increased demand for related talents. The employment growth rate in the digital finance sector significantly surpasses other industries, especially in the technology domain.

Moreover, the development of digital finance has created new job positions, such as blockchain engineers, data scientists, fintech product managers, etc., which are expected to become crucial career paths in the future.

However, there are also challenges in employment opportunities within the digital finance industry. The fast-paced transformation and technological advancements demand higher qualifications and capabilities from professionals. Additionally, the development of digital finance may impact employment in traditional finance sectors, as the application of automation technology may reduce the demand for certain traditional financial roles.

Furthermore, the development of digital finance has led to changes in work patterns, such as the rise of freelancers and remote work. The industry emphasizes technological innovation and flexibility, leading many companies to adopt a freelance model, allowing employees to organize their work time and space more flexibly. Remote work is also a prominent characteristic in the digital finance sector since many of its enterprises operate globally. Remote work reduces office costs, improves efficiency, and has a lower environmental impact, making it a growing trend in the digital finance industry.

Without a doubt, the development of digital finance requires professionals to acquire new skills and knowledge. For instance, fintech development demands expertise in financial products and technology, while data analysis requires knowledge of data science and statistics.

Moreover, professionals in the digital finance field need to possess innovation and problem-solving capabilities, as the industry undergoes rapid and frequent changes and innovations compared to traditional finance. Additionally, there is a higher demand for proficiency in English since digital finance is a global industry, requiring employees to communicate and collaborate with clients and partners from different countries and regions. However, the transfer of skills from traditional finance to digital finance has certain limitations. Due to the higher technical and data requirements in digital finance, professionals from traditional finance may need to relearn new skills and knowledge, which might require more time and effort.

Research indicates that the rapid development of digital finance has not only changed people's production and lifestyle but also had profound impacts on the environment and society.

Next, let's explore the impact of digital finance on environmental sustainability from three perspectives: carbon emissions and climate change, natural resource utilization and environmental protection, and the role of digital finance in promoting green financial innovation and sustainable development.

In terms of carbon emissions and climate change, the development of digital finance has brought new financial services and transaction methods, such as electronic payments, online finance, blockchain, etc., which can improve energy efficiency and reduce carbon emissions. For instance, electronic payments can replace traditional paper currency and credit cards, reducing energy consumption and carbon emissions associated with currency printing and logistics. Blockchain technology can establish decentralized energy trading platforms, promoting the dissemination and trading of renewable energy and carbon reduction through digital energy transactions and clearing. Digital finance can also facilitate carbon finance, including carbon trading and carbon funds, enabling the circulation and trading of carbon emission rights through financial instruments and market mechanisms to achieve carbon reduction goals. However, the development of digital finance may also have some negative impacts, such as an increase in energy consumption due to the widespread application of digital financial services, such as data centers and cloud computing.

Regarding natural resource utilization and environmental protection, the development of digital finance can promote effective natural resource utilization and environmental protection. For instance, digital finance can promote green financial products, such as green bonds and green credits, to support investments and financing for sustainable development and environmental protection-related projects. Digital finance can also facilitate sustainable consumption and production, such as achieving resource sharing and recycling through digitalized sharing economy models, reducing waste and pollution. Moreover, digital finance can enhance environmental information disclosure and regulation. Through digital technology and big data analysis, environmental monitoring and assessment can be implemented to improve the efficiency and accuracy of environmental regulation. However, the development of digital finance may also have negative impacts, such as increased generation of electronic waste and electronic waste, exacerbating resource waste and environmental pollution. Additionally, the governance and regulation of digital financial services need attention to avoid adverse impacts on natural resources and the environment.

In terms of the role of digital finance in promoting green financial innovation and sustainable development, the development of digital finance can assist traditional financial institutions in conducting green financial businesses, such as green bonds and green credits, as well as promoting financial products and services related to green investments and financing. Digital finance can also help traditional financial institutions achieve digital transformation, optimize financial processes, improve efficiency, and reduce resource waste. However, it may also bring negative consequences, such as digital divide and inequality, data privacy and security risks, technological risks and system vulnerabilities, financial risk transmission, and environmental impacts.

Finally, let's consider the issue of digital finance policies and regulatory environments and their impact on society and the environment, which is one of the current focal points of digital finance development.

First, let's assess the methods and standards for evaluating the impact of digital finance policies (Xiaochuan, 2019) and regulations on society and the environment.

The assessment methods and standards for the impact of digital finance policies and regulations on society and the environment should be comprehensive, scientific, and feasible. A comprehensive assessment should encompass multiple dimensions, including economic, social, and environmental aspects. The scientific assessment should be based on objective data and scientific methodologies, while the feasibility assessment should guide the formulation and implementation of policies and regulations.

The evaluation criteria should include the following aspects:

(1) Economic benefits: The development of digital finance should lead to economic benefits, such as improved financial efficiency, reduced financial costs, and promoted economic growth.
(2) Social benefits: The development of digital finance should promote social equity, enhance social welfare, and strengthen social security.
(3) Environmental benefits: The development of digital finance should reduce resource consumption, lower environmental pollution, and promote sustainable development.

Next, let's discuss the specific impacts of digital finance policies and regulations on society and the environment.

(1) Impact on Financial Stability and Risk Management: The rapid development of digital finance poses new challenges to financial risk management and stability. Policies and regulations should focus on formulating corresponding measures to ensure the stability and controllable risks of financial markets.

(2) Impact on Consumer Rights: The rapid development of digital finance brings more choices and convenience for consumers but also raises new issues such as information leaks and fraud. Policies and regulations should protect consumers' legitimate rights and interests by strengthening data protection and fraud prevention.
(3) Impact on Impoverished Regions and Micro-enterprises: Digital finance can provide more convenient financing channels for impoverished regions and micro-enterprises, promoting economic development and social progress. Policies and regulations should encourage innovation and application of digital finance services in these areas while strengthening supervision and protection.
(4) Impact on the Environment: The development of digital finance can reduce resource waste and environmental pollution through reducing physical transactions, optimizing production and consumption methods, and promoting green investments. Policies and regulations should encourage the application of digital finance services in environmental protection while supervising and evaluating the industry's environmental awareness and practices.

Finally, we propose the following suggestions for improving digital finance policies and regulations:

(1) Strengthen the Scientificity and Effectiveness of Supervision: Digital finance supervision should employ scientific methods and tools, enhancing accuracy and efficiency through regulatory technology, and improving coordination and cooperation among regulatory bodies to enhance overall effectiveness.
(2) Promote Innovation and Application of Digital Financial Services: Policies and regulations should encourage greater progress in the innovation and application of digital financial services, especially in impoverished regions and environmental protection, while strengthening supervision and protection of these services.
(3) Protect Consumer Rights and Data Security: Policies and regulations should strengthen the protection of consumer rights and data security, crack down on violations, and increase consumer awareness and prevention of digital financial risks.
(4) Promote Deep Integration of Digital Finance with the Real Economy: Digital finance should deeply integrate with the real economy, promoting the widespread application and promotion of digital financial services in the real economy while strengthening supervision and guidance of this integration.

In summary, digital finance policies and regulations have far-reaching impacts on society and the environment, necessitating a balance between innovation and risk management, promoting financial inclusivity and sustainable development, protecting data privacy and security, and reducing the digital divide and social inequality. Achieving these goals requires collaborative efforts from governments, regulatory agencies, and the financial industry to develop appropriate policy and regulatory frameworks that align the development of digital finance with the interests of society and the environment.

9.2 Sustainable Finance and Green Investment

Sustainable development has become a globally significant issue, and financial institutions play a crucial role in this endeavor. The funding, technology, and expertise provided by financial institutions are key resources for promoting sustainable development. Next, we will delve into the role of financial institutions in sustainable finance and the application of financial instruments to advance sustainable development.

Firstly, let's examine the role of financial institutions in sustainable finance.

Financial institutions are major suppliers of funds and significant participants in the market. They can promote sustainable development through the following means:

Providing Financial Support: Financial institutions can offer financing support for sustainable development, ensuring funding for the implementation of sustainable projects.

Risk Management: Financial institutions can reduce risks associated with sustainable development projects through risk management measures, such as insurance and risk diversification, safeguarding the implementation of sustainable projects.

Information Disclosure: Financial institutions can promote public awareness and understanding of sustainable development by disclosing information related to sustainability to investors and the general public.

Compliance and Ethical Standards: By adhering to relevant compliance and ethical standards, financial institutions protect the interests of investors and the public while driving sustainable development.

Next, let's explore the application of financial instruments.

Financial instruments are tools used by financial institutions to manage risks and provide funding support. They can also be utilized to promote sustainable development. Here are some common financial instruments:

Green Bonds: Green bonds are used to finance sustainable projects. Companies issuing green bonds must comply with sustainability standards, and the raised funds must be dedicated to the development of sustainable projects. These projects are typically related to environmental protection and renewable energy, among other fields.

Sustainable Bonds: Similar to green bonds, sustainable bonds are used to finance sustainable projects, but their scope is broader. In addition to environmental sustainability, sustainable bonds also consider social and governance aspects. Therefore, the use of funds from sustainable bonds can cover various areas, such as environmental protection, social responsibility, and community development.

Socially Responsible Investing (SRI): SRI is an investment approach where financial institutions consider social and environmental factors in their investment decisions to achieve sustainable development goals. SRI not only focuses on sustainable projects but also emphasizes aspects such as corporate governance and social responsibility. This investment approach aims to promote sustainable development and achieve balanced economic, social, and environmental development.

Green Loans: Green loans are specialized loans used to finance sustainable projects. Similar to green bonds, the use of funds from green loans must comply with specific sustainability standards. This loan format provides financial support for sustainable projects, facilitating the implementation of sustainable development.

Green investment refers to investments in environmentally friendly and sustainable projects and enterprises to promote economic development while protecting the environment. We will explore the development and market competitiveness of green investment from the following aspects.

9.2.1 Policies and Regulations Driving Green Investment Development[1]

The development of green investment is reliant on support and promotion from policies and regulations. Some major policies and regulations include:

The Paris Agreement: In 2015, 195 countries signed the Paris Agreement, aiming to limit global warming to within 2°C. The agreement requires countries to take action against climate change, including promoting sustainable development and reducing carbon emissions. This provides a global policy framework and goals for green investment.

Government Procurement Policies: Government procurement policies refer to policies where governments consider environmental and social impacts when procuring goods and services. Many countries and regions have adopted relevant policies, requiring governments to prioritize environmentally friendly products and services in their procurement processes, thus promoting the development of the green economy.

Green Finance Guidelines: International financial institutions and regulatory bodies have released green finance guidelines, providing standards and guidelines for green investment. These guidelines include defining the criteria for green projects, risk management, and reporting requirements, providing guidance and references for investors and increasing the comparability and transparency of green investment.

Tax Incentive Policies: Some countries and regions have implemented tax incentive policies to encourage investment in environmentally friendly and sustainable development fields. These policies may include tax reductions, exemptions, or other measures to lower the cost of green investment, increase return on investment, and enhance its attractiveness.

[1] Ehlers and Packer (2017)

9.2.2 Market Size and Growth Trends of Green Investment in Different Countries and Regions

With the increasing global environmental awareness, green investment has become a global trend. The following are some key aspects to explore the market size and growth trends of green investment in different countries and regions:

Europe European Commission (2020): Europe is one of the most developed green investment markets. According to data from the European Environment Agency, the green investment market in Europe has reached 1.5 trillion euros and is expected to continue growing in the coming years. EU member countries are increasing their investments in renewable energy, energy efficiency, sustainable cities, and other areas. The EU has also introduced a series of regulations and policies, such as the European Green Deal and carbon emissions trading, to encourage the development of green investment.

United States Weber and Feltmate (2016): The green investment market in the United States is also rapidly expanding. According to data from the U.S. Energy Information Administration, renewable energy capacity in the U.S. has already exceeded 10%. The U.S. government has implemented a series of green economic policies to encourage investments in renewable energy and energy-saving technologies. For example, policies like production tax credits and investment tax credits provide support for the development of renewable energy.

China: China is one of the largest green investment markets globally. The scale of China's green finance market has already exceeded 10 trillion RMB. The Chinese government has introduced a series of policies and measures to encourage investment in green areas such as renewable energy and environmental protection industries. For instance, China's "Thirteenth Five-Year Plan" sets the goal of "green, low-carbon, and circular development," encouraging investments in green energy and environmental protection.

Other Countries and Regions IFC (2018): Apart from Europe, the United States, and China, the green investment market in other countries and regions is also continuously developing. For example, the renewable energy markets in countries such as India, Brazil, and Australia are also growing. The Australian government has launched an energy transition plan with the goal of achieving 50% renewable energy capacity. The Japanese government has also introduced various policies to encourage investment in renewable energy, energy-saving, and emission reduction to achieve low-carbon and environmentally friendly development. These initiatives provide broader development space and opportunities for green investment in these countries and regions.

As global environmental awareness continues to strengthen, green investment has become a global trend. We will explore the market competition and key participants in green investment from the following aspects.

The market competition in grween investment primarily involves the following aspects:

Financial Institutions: Financial institutions play a significant role in the green investment market. Banks, insurance companies, fund management firms, and other financial institutions have introduced various green financial products, such as green bonds and green loans, providing financing channels and funding support for green investment.

Enterprises: Enterprises are core participants in the green investment market. More and more companies are recognizing the importance of environmental protection and increasing their investments in green initiatives. Companies are investing in areas such as renewable energy, energy efficiency, and sustainable cities, driving the development of the green industry through innovative technologies and business models.

Government: Governments are crucial drivers in the green investment market. They introduce a series of regulations and policies to encourage investments in green areas. Policies like tax incentives for green bonds and carbon emissions trading provide policy support and incentives for green investment.

The main participants in the green investment market include the following aspects:

Financial Institutions: Within financial institutions, European banks are the largest issuers of green bonds. Institutions like SEB in Sweden, BNP Paribas in France, and ING in the Netherlands are major players. In the United States, Goldman Sachs and Citibank are major underwriters of green bonds. Additionally, Chinese banks like Bank of China, Agricultural Bank of China, and China Construction Bank have also introduced green bond products.

Enterprises: Renewable energy companies are key players in green investment among enterprises. Companies like First Solar in the United States, L'Oréal in Europe, and State Power Investment Corporation in China are continuously increasing their investments in renewable energy. Moreover, some large multinational corporations are driving development in sustainable development and environmental protection, such as Apple, Google, and Coca-Cola.

Government: In terms of government participation, green investment is most mature in Europe, where the European Union and its member countries have proposed a series of green initiatives and policies, such as the European Green Deal and the EU Green Finance Plan. In Asia, the Chinese government is also actively promoting green investment, implementing carbon emissions trading markets and constructing renewable energy power bases.

As mentioned earlier, green investment is an investment approach that promotes economic development and environmental protection, but its risk factors cannot be ignored compared to traditional investment. Next, we will discuss risk mitigation in green investment from the following three aspects: risk factors, return evaluation, and portfolio management.

9.2.2.1 Risk Factors and Measurement of Green Investment

Policy Risk: Policy changes can affect the returns and market demand for green investment. Policy uncertainty makes green investment more unpredictable and unstable.

Technology Risk: Green technologies are still in a stage of continuous development and improvement, and their maturity and reliability are not yet high enough. Therefore, the unreliability and maturity of green technologies are important risks in green investment.

Market Risk: The green investment market is still relatively small, and the demand for green products and services is still in its early stages. The resulting market instability and increased competition are also important risk factors in green investment.

Environmental Risk: Environmental issues such as pollution and climate change can also have a negative impact on green investment. For example, extreme weather and natural disasters may cause damage to green facilities and infrastructure.

How to Measure these Risks?

As the risk factors of green investment are diverse, various measurement methods are needed to better assess their risks. These methods include:

Environmental, Social, and Governance (ESG) Rating: This is a method used to measure the environmental, social, and governance risks of companies. By evaluating factors such as environmental protection, social responsibility, and corporate governance, one can better understand the risks and green nature of the company.

Carbon Emission Calculation: This is a method used to measure the carbon emissions of companies and portfolios. By calculating carbon emissions, one can better understand the environmental level and green nature of companies and portfolios.

Green Standards Certification: This is a method used to measure the green nature of green investment products and projects. Through green standards certification, one can better understand the authenticity and environmental friendliness of green investment products and projects.

9.2.2.2 Return Evaluation of Green Investment[2]

The return evaluation of green investment needs to consider its environmental, social, and economic benefits. Compared to traditional investment, the return evaluation of green investment needs to consider more factors. Here are some common methods for evaluating the return of green investment:

Energy and Carbon Emission Cost-Benefit Analysis: This is a method to compare the cost-effectiveness of traditional and green investment. Energy and carbon emission cost-benefit analysis can evaluate the environmental and social impacts and economic returns of green investment.

[2] Zerbib (2019)

Green Investment Portfolio Return: This is a method to evaluate the return of green investment portfolios by comparing them with the return of traditional investment portfolios.

Socially Responsible Investment Return: This is a method that considers the social responsibility and environmental impact of green investment. Socially responsible investment return can compare the social and environmental impacts and returns of traditional and green investment.

9.2.2.3 Portfolio Management of Green Investment

Portfolio management of green investment needs to consider environmental and social responsibility factors of the investment portfolio. Below are some common methods for managing green investment portfolios:

Selecting Green Securities: Choosing securities that meet green certification standards is a common method for managing green investment portfolios. By selecting green securities, the environmental level and green nature of the investment portfolio can be enhanced.

Portfolio ESG Evaluation: Portfolio ESG evaluation is a method that comprehensively considers the environmental, social, and governance factors of the investment portfolio. Through portfolio ESG evaluation, one can better understand the risks and green nature of the investment portfolio.

Green Bonds: Green bonds refer to bonds used to finance environmental and sustainable development projects, and their market size is rapidly growing. Especially in Europe, green bonds have played an important role in financing renewable energy projects.

In summary, green investment is an investment approach that promotes economic development and environmental protection. Although its returns may be relatively unstable, through measuring its risk factors and return evaluation, one can better manage its investment portfolio and thereby increase its long-term returns and environmental nature.

9.3 Inclusive Digital Finance: A New Paradigm for Developing Countries

The development of digital financial technology has attracted widespread attention globally, especially in developing countries. In this chapter, we will discuss the challenges and opportunities faced by digital finance from different perspectives, with a focus on its application and impact in developing countries.

Specifically, we will explore the importance of digital finance for financial inclusion and poverty alleviation, and how it promotes financial inclusion and poverty reduction by lowering the cost of financial services and expanding their coverage.

Firstly, digital financial technology is of great significance for financial inclusion in developing countries. In these countries, many people are unable to access traditional financial services due to geographical, economic, or social reasons. However, the popularity of digital financial technology provides them with new ways to access financial services. Through digital financial tools such as mobile payments, e-wallets, and internet finance, people can easily carry out operations such as payments, transfers, and financing without the need for traditional bank accounts or physical access to institutions. This convenience and flexibility improve financial inclusion, enabling more people to participate in the formal financial system, helping them achieve financial stability and economic growth.

Secondly, digital financial technology has the potential to reduce poverty. Poverty is prevalent in developing countries, and digital financial technology can provide more opportunities and resources for impoverished populations. Through digital financial services, they can more easily access small loans, savings, and insurance, supporting their entrepreneurship and economic activities. Additionally, digital financial technology can provide targeted financial education and counseling, helping impoverished populations improve their financial management capabilities and economic decision-making. Through these means, digital financial technology is expected to help impoverished populations escape poverty and achieve sustainable economic development.

However, the promotion of digital financial technology in developing countries faces numerous challenges. Firstly, the digital divide is a major obstacle to the widespread adoption of digital financial services. Many people in developing countries lack the digital skills and related equipment to fully utilize digital financial services. Therefore, governments, financial institutions, and society as a whole need to work together to provide digital education and training, promote the widespread adoption of digital devices and internet access, in order to reduce the digital divide and improve people's digital literacy.

Next, we take India as an example to explore the application and opportunities of digital finance in developing countries, analyzing its impact on India's economy and society.

India, as a developing country with a relatively lower level of economic development, has made significant progress in digital financial services. This achievement is attributed to the government's active support and a series of policies and measures launched, such as financial inclusion projects and the development of financial service infrastructure. Additionally, India's digital financial service market is quite active, covering areas like mobile payments, digital currency, and internet finance, forming mature business models and market competition patterns.

The development of digital financial services brings many opportunities to India. Firstly, digital financial services can enhance financial inclusion, providing more convenient and flexible financial services to hundreds of millions of people in India. Through digital financial services, rural residents and micro, small, and medium-sized enterprises in India can more easily access loans and financing, promoting their economic development and growth. Digital financial services can also improve the efficiency of financial services, reduce transaction costs, and boost economic activity and liquidity.

Secondly, the development of digital financial services can raise India's level of digitization. As the world's second-most populous country, India's adoption rate of digital financial services is not yet high. However, with the development and promotion of digital financial services, India's level of digitization has been improving. Digital financial services can provide more intelligent and convenient management methods for Indian enterprises, lower production and transaction costs, improve efficiency, and promote economic development.

The development of digital financial services also brings some challenges.

Firstly, the issue of the digital divide in India still exists, which means that the level of technology adoption varies among different regions and population groups. This imbalance restricts the universality and coverage of digital financial services. Solving the digital divide requires strengthening infrastructure construction, providing digital technology training and education, and ensuring the ease of use and accessibility of digital services.

Secondly, the security and stability of digital financial service platforms are essential safeguards for the promotion of digital financial services. As digital financial services expand, data privacy and security become critical issues. Establishing a sound digital security system is key to ensuring the sustainable development of digital financial services. This requires implementing effective security measures, including encryption technology, identity verification, and security certification, to protect users' personal and financial information from improper access and abuse.

Additionally, the rapid development of digital financial services may lead to lagging financial regulation, resulting in potential risks and instability. In terms of the regulation of digital financial services, the government and regulatory agencies need to strengthen regulatory capabilities and formulate regulations to ensure the transparency, stability, and fair competition of the digital financial market. Regulatory agencies should also closely monitor the innovation and development of digital financial services, promptly respond to potential risks and issues.

Next, we will explore the practical application and development opportunities of digital finance on the African continent.

Firstly, the universality of digital financial services can enhance financial inclusion GSMA (2019), allowing more people to access financial services. Many rural and remote areas in Africa have large populations, but traditional financial service institutions have low coverage in these areas. However, through digital financial services, people can use tools such as mobile devices to access financial services without the need to reach urban areas or have traditional bank accounts. This provides a wider range of financial access channels for those outside the traditional financial system.

Secondly, digital financial services play a driving role in economic growth in Africa. Africa has a large number of small businesses and individual operators who often face financing difficulties. Digital financial services provide more convenient and innovative financing methods, such as crowdfunding and micro-loans through digital platforms. This financing approach not only helps small businesses obtain financial support but also promotes business innovation and economic growth.

Additionally, the widespread adoption of digital financial services can promote the development of related industries, such as mobile device manufacturers and digital payment platforms, bringing more opportunities and benefits to the local economy.

Although the development of digital financial services in Africa brings many benefits, there are also some challenges. Firstly, the digital divide is a significant obstacle to the universality of digital financial services. Many regions in Africa lack the digital skills and related equipment, preventing them from using digital financial services. Secondly, the security issues of digital financial services also need attention. In areas such as digital payments and internet finance, security threats cannot be ignored. Digital financial service providers need to strengthen security measures to prevent risks such as fraud and data breaches, ensuring the safety of users' funds and personal information.

Additionally, the widespread adoption of digital financial services in Africa also needs to address some cultural and social issues. In some areas, people are accustomed to using cash for transactions and have reservations about forms of financial services like digital payments and e-wallets. Digital financial service providers need to understand the local culture and social background, find effective ways to promote and popularize their services, and encourage more people to accept and use digital financial services.

In conclusion, the application and opportunities of digital financial services in Africa are enormous. Digital financial services can enhance financial inclusion, promote economic growth, address financing difficulties for micro-enterprises and individuals, and drive the development of related industries. However, the development of digital financial services in Africa also faces challenges such as the digital divide, security issues, and cultural-social considerations, requiring joint efforts from relevant stakeholders to address them.

Next, let's focus on the situation in Latin America, which is a region with vast development prospects but also experiences financial inequality. The emergence of digital financial services offers an opportunity to address this issue, and the adoption of digital financial services in the Latin American region continues to increase.

Firstly, the widespread adoption of digital financial services in Latin America is of significant importance for enhancing financial inclusion. The region has a large population of impoverished individuals and microenterprises that often lack access to traditional financial services. However, digital financial services provide convenient financial support through means such as mobile devices, enabling these individuals to access the financial services they need. The relatively lower cost of digital financial services makes them more affordable and aligned with the consumption habits of the middle and lower-income populations, resulting in increased acceptance and usage, thus further enhancing financial inclusion.

Secondly, digital financial services can also promote economic growth in the Latin American region. The area is home to numerous small and medium-sized enterprises and individual operators who face financing difficulties, which restricts their development and growth. Digital financial services offer more convenient and flexible financing options, such as micro-loans and financing platforms, helping these enterprises and individuals obtain the necessary funds, thereby fostering their economic development. Furthermore, the widespread adoption of digital financial services can drive the development of related industries, such as mobile device manufacturers and digital payment platforms, creating more job opportunities and economic benefits locally.

However, the development of digital financial services also faces some challenges. Firstly, the digital divide is a major obstacle to the widespread adoption of digital financial services. Many populations in Latin America lack the skills and access to digital technology, making it difficult for them to use digital financial services. Secondly, the security issues of digital financial services need attention. In areas such as digital payments and internet finance, security risks are high, and users' funds and personal information are vulnerable to threats. To safeguard users' property and privacy, it is essential to establish robust regulatory and risk control mechanisms, strengthening security measures for digital financial services.

Moreover, the widespread adoption of digital financial services may lead to the decline of traditional financial institutions and an increase in unemployment rates. Many traditional financial institutions may face challenges in digital transformation and need to accelerate their pace to remain competitive. However, this may also lead to the closure of some traditional financial institutions and job losses, among other issues.

The development of digital financial services is significant for the Latin American region as it can enhance financial inclusion and promote economic growth. However, the challenges of the digital divide, security risks, and traditional financial institutions need attention. To maximize the potential of digital financial services, the Latin American region should accelerate its digital transformation, address the digital divide, strengthen regulatory and risk control mechanisms, and also focus on the transformation and employment issues of traditional financial institutions, achieving the coordinated development of digital and traditional finance.

In conclusion, the widespread adoption of digital financial technology in developing countries has become a trend, and its impact on financial inclusion and economic growth is gaining attention. Next, we will explore the role and opportunities of digital finance in developing countries.

Firstly, digital financial technology has a significant role and opportunities for developing countries. As the financial markets in developing countries are still immature, the coverage of services provided by traditional financial institutions is relatively low. Digital financial technology can fill the gap in financial services, offering a broader range of financial services and promoting financial inclusion.

The role of digital financial technology in financial inclusion mainly includes the following aspects:

Firstly, digital financial technology can lower the cost of financial services and expand their coverage Arner et al. (2015). Traditional financial institutions require substantial human and physical resources to establish branches and hire personnel, resulting in high administrative costs for financial services. In contrast, the operating costs of digital financial service platforms are relatively low. The popularization of digital financial technology can effectively reduce the cost of financial services and increase their coverage, providing financial services to those who lack bank accounts or credit records.

Secondly, digital financial technology can enhance the efficiency and risk management capabilities of financial institutions, thereby providing better financial services for the poor. Through data analysis and risk management models, digital financial technology can provide more accurate and comprehensive risk assessments for financial institutions, improving the efficiency of credit approval and reducing the cost of credit, thus offering better financial support for the poor. In addition, the application of digital financial technology can speed up the response time of financial services, improve customer experience, and further enhance customer loyalty.

Thirdly, digital financial technology can provide users with more convenient financial services. Digital financial services allow users to conduct transactions and inquiries anytime, anywhere, reducing the constraints of time and location on financial services. This is particularly important for the impoverished populations in some regions who may face challenges such as lack of transportation, credit records, and identity verification. Digital financial services can help them overcome these barriers and access more convenient financial services.

In addition to promoting financial inclusion, digital financial technology can also boost economic growth. Digital financial technology can offer more financing opportunities for microenterprises and farmers, supporting their development and growth. These enterprises often face financing difficulties and high costs, but digital financial technology can provide more accurate and comprehensive credit assessments through risk management models and data analysis, thereby reducing the cost of financing and promoting their development and growth, ultimately driving economic growth.

Moreover, by improving the efficiency of payments and settlements and reducing transaction costs, digital financial technology can also enhance economic activity and liquidity. Digital payment platforms enable people to complete transactions more quickly and conveniently, improving transaction efficiency and reducing transaction costs, thus promoting economic activity and liquidity.

However, the widespread adoption of digital financial service platforms faces challenges such as the digital divide and lack of skills. Many regions in developing countries lack infrastructure, education, and technological support, making the digital divide prominent and hindering the widespread adoption and application of digital financial technology in these areas.

In conclusion, digital financial technology has vast prospects and a promoting role in developing countries. It can fill the gap in financial services, enhance financial inclusion, promote economic growth, and improve liquidity. However, it also faces challenges such as digital security and the digital divide. Governments and financial institutions need to actively promote the widespread adoption and application of digital financial technology, establish sound technical support and regulatory systems, increase public awareness and acceptance of digital finance, and create a better environment for the development of digital financial technology. Only through joint efforts can we fully leverage the significant role of digital financial technology in promoting economic development in developing countries.

References

Arner, D. W., Barberis, J. N., & Buckley, R. P. (2015). The evolution of fintech: a new post-crisis paradigm? Georgetown Journal of International Law, 47, 1271.

European Commission (2020). The European Green Deal Investment Plan and Just Transition Mechanism.

Demirgüç-Kunt, A., Klapper, L., Singer, D., & Van Oudheusden, P. (2015). The Global Findex Database 2014: Measuring Financial Inclusion around the World. World Bank Policy Research Working Paper, (7255).

Ehlers, T., & Packer, F. (2017). Green bond finance and certification. BIS Quarterly Review.

GSMA. (2019). State of the Industry Report on Mobile Money. GSMA.

IFC (2018). Climate Investment Opportunities in Emerging Markets. International Finance Corporation.

Weber, O., & Feltmate, B. (2016). Sustainable Banking: Managing the Social and Environmental Impact of Financial Institutions. University of Toronto Press.

Zhou Xiaochuan. The Interaction between Information Technology and Financial Policy [J]. China Finance, 2019 (15)

Yan, J, Yu, W.andZhao, J.L.(2015), “How signaling and search costs affect information asymmetry in P2P lending: the economics of big data”, Financial Innovation, Vol.1, No.1

Zerbib, O.D. (2019). The effect of pro-environmental preferences on bond prices: Evidence from green bonds. Journal of Banking & Finance, 98

Chapter 10
The Future of Digital Finance and Fintech

10.1 Digital Finance and FinTech

With the continuous advancement of technology, digital finance and FinTech have become important topics in the financial industry, and they complement each other. Digital finance uses digital and internet technologies to digitize and smartify financial operations, providing more efficient and convenient financial services. FinTech, on the other hand, leverages technology to drive innovation and improvement in financial services, aiming to enhance the efficiency and quality of financial services.

Firstly, the development of digital finance relies on the support of FinTech. The progress of FinTech provides technical support and innovative ideas for digital finance. For example, the application of technologies such as artificial intelligence, big data, and blockchain Larios-Hernández (2017) offers robust support to digital finance. These technologies can enhance the efficiency and quality of financial services, reduce financial risks, and promote financial innovation.

Secondly, the development of digital finance also propels the advancement of FinTech. The application of digital finance presents new opportunities for the development of FinTech, as digital finance requires constant innovation and improvement in FinTech. For instance, the development of digital currencies requires the support of blockchain technology, and the growth of robo-advisors relies on artificial intelligence and big data.

Digital finance and FinTech have a mutually beneficial and interdependent relationship. The development of digital finance necessitates the support of FinTech, while the progress of FinTech also relies on the application of digital finance. Combining the two can improve the efficiency and quality of financial services, reduce financial risks, and drive financial innovation. The development of digital finance and FinTech brings more opportunities and challenges to the financial industry.

Due to their close relationship, this book's final chapter will discuss topics related to FinTech, serving as a summary and reflection of the entire book. In this section, we

Z. Liu and W. Hou, *Digital Finance*, https://doi.org/10.1007/978-981-99-7305-7_10

will mainly discuss the definition, evolution, and impact of FinTech on the financial industry.

FinTech refers to the use of digital technology, artificial intelligence, big data, blockchain, and other technological means to innovate and optimize financial services, improve financial business processes, and enhance risk management capabilities, constituting a new type of financial business model. The emergence of FinTech is rooted in the digital transformation Frost et al. (2019) of the financial industry and the widespread adoption of internet technology. It has not only changed the business models and competitive landscape of the financial industry but also profoundly influenced consumers' financial behaviors and socio-economic development.

The evolution Zavolokina et al. (2016) of FinTech can be divided into three stages, each with different characteristics and development focuses.

The first stage is the "post-crisis era" after the 2008 financial crisis, during which FinTech companies began to emerge, primarily focusing on payment, lending, and investment areas. These companies provided more convenient and efficient financial services through innovative technologies and business models. For example, PayPal, as the first successful online payment platform, LendingClub, as a pioneer in P2P lending platforms, and Wealthfront, as a digital wealth management platform, all achieved significant success during this stage.

The second stage is the "innovation era" from 2010 to 2015. During this period, FinTech companies expanded into more areas, such as insurance, wealth management, and digital currencies. With technological advancements and changing user demands, FinTech companies continued to innovate and improve, offering more choices and conveniences for financial services. For example, Lemonade, an online insurance company, provided simplified and transparent insurance services through digital processes and intelligent risk assessments. Betterment, a digital investment platform, offered low-cost and personalized investment portfolios through algorithms and automation. Coinbase, a digital currency exchange, promoted the development and application of digital currencies.

The third stage is the "maturity era" from 2015 to the present. In this stage, FinTech companies gradually became significant participants in the financial industry, cooperating or competing with traditional financial institutions. The innovation and growth of FinTech companies attracted the attention of traditional financial institutions and prompted them to actively seek cooperation with FinTech companies. For example, Ant Financial, as China's largest FinTech company, changed China's payment habits through its digital payment platform Alipay and established cooperative relationships with traditional banks. Square, a mobile payment and business services company, transformed the payment methods of small businesses through its innovative payment solutions. Revolut, a digital bank and payment company, provided global payment and remittance services, competing with traditional banks.

These three stages demonstrate the rapid development and evolving trends of the FinTech industry. The rise of FinTech has brought new vitality and innovation to the financial industry, driving the digital transformation of financial services.

As we mentioned earlier in our article, the most significant impact of digital finance or FinTech is on financial inclusion. Looking at the development of FinTech in developing countries or regions from a global perspective, we can understand the changes it brings to various areas, including financial inclusion.

Case 1: The Impact of FinTech on Financial Inclusion in Mexico

The FinTech industry in Mexico has become an integral part of the country's financial services. Statistics show that approximately 60% of adults cannot access credit, and only about 27% of the population has a bank account, creating an unequal situation that adversely affects economic growth and social stability.

With the widespread adoption of FinTech in Mexico, numerous innovative financial products and services have emerged, playing a positive role in promoting financial inclusion. The introduction of new FinTech services such as mobile payments, virtual credit cards, and online lending has provided convenience and opportunities for those who have difficulty accessing traditional financial institutions. The presence and development of FinTech companies significantly improved Mexico's financial inclusion index.

In addition to providing convenient financial services, FinTech also contributes to promoting financial literacy. Many FinTech companies offer online financial knowledge and educational courses to help consumers understand financial products and services, thereby enhancing their financial literacy. Furthermore, FinTech provides more secure and efficient solutions for Mexico's financial services through digital technology and intelligent algorithms. FinTech companies can better manage risks, improve the efficiency and security of financial services, and provide a more reliable and sustainable foundation for the development of financial services in Mexico.

However, the FinTech industry in Mexico also faces some challenges. Firstly, FinTech companies need to overcome regulatory and legal barriers to ensure the legitimacy and reliability of their services. Secondly, FinTech companies need to continuously improve their technological and managerial capabilities to adapt to market competition and changing customer demands. Technological innovation and talent development will be essential support for the industry's development.

Case 2: The Development of FinTech in Sub-Saharan Africa

Next, let's look at the development of FinTech in the Sub-Saharan Africa region. The rapid development of FinTech in Sub-Saharan Africa is driving financial inclusion and economic growth in the region. Governments and the private sector in this area have been investing in FinTech to promote financial inclusion and sustainable development. Mobile payments are one of the main focuses of FinTech in this region, providing a convenient payment method for residents in areas with limited access to traditional financial services. Mobile payment applications such as M-Pesa, MTN Mobile Money, and Airtel Money have achieved significant success in the region. At the same time, the development of FinTech has also raised the level of financial inclusion in the region by reducing costs and improving efficiency, making financial services more accessible and convenient. Start-ups and financial institutions have met the needs of a broader range of consumers by developing new products and services such as microloans, mobile banking, and insurance.

In the Sub-Saharan Africa region, the development of FinTech mainly focuses on digital payments, lending, insurance, and investments. Digital payments, as one of the essential directions of FinTech, provide a convenient payment method, especially for those without bank accounts. Mobile payment applications enable payments through mobile apps or SMS, with M-Pesa being one of the most successful examples in Kenya. The lending market is also gradually developing in the Sub-Saharan Africa region, where many people seek alternative options due to the lack of access to traditional bank loans. P2P lending platforms like RainFin and Branch have become popular choices. Insurance is another critical area of FinTech development, as traditional insurance costs are relatively high, and new insurtech companies offer more flexible and affordable insurance products, such as Bima and AllLife. The investment market is also starting to grow, with emerging investment tech companies providing more flexible and convenient investment options, such as EasyEquities and Abacus.

However, the development of FinTech in the Sub-Saharan Africa region also faces some challenges. The lack of digital infrastructure and financial infrastructure is the main bottleneck for FinTech development. Many areas lack high-speed internet and digital payment infrastructure, limiting the spread of FinTech. Uncertainty in the regulatory and legal environment also hinders FinTech development. The lack of unified regulatory standards poses challenges of regulatory uncertainty and high compliance costs for many FinTech companies. Additionally, digital security and privacy issues are challenges for FinTech development, requiring cooperation between governments and the private sector to address.

Case 3: The Development of FinTech in Southeast Asia

Lastly, let's take a look at the development of FinTech in Southeast Asia. With the advent of the digital era, FinTech in Southeast Asia has rapidly developed and gradually become a significant driving force in the region's financial services sector.

Firstly, the FinTech industry in Southeast Asia has achieved significant results. Numerous emerging companies and startups have emerged, providing consumers with diversified financial services through advanced technology and innovative business models, such as payments, lending, investment, insurance, and more. Traditional financial institutions have also begun to actively explore FinTech to enhance service quality and efficiency. Furthermore, both governments and the private sector widely support the development of FinTech in Southeast Asia. Governments have formulated a series of policies and measures to encourage and promote the innovation and application of FinTech. For example, many countries encourage banks and financial institutions to collaborate with FinTech companies to improve the quality and accessibility of financial services. At the same time, promoting the use of mobile payments and electronic currency is also part of the digital financial services promotion plan in many countries. The private sector is also investing heavily in FinTech and developing new products and services.

Secondly, the development of FinTech in Southeast Asia shows clear trends. With the popularity of mobile internet and digital payments, more and more people are starting to access and use FinTech services. Emerging technologies such as blockchain, artificial intelligence, and big data are also widely applied in financial services, providing more possibilities for FinTech innovation. The FinTech industry in Southeast Asia mainly focuses on areas such as mobile payments, digital currencies, and digital lending. Mobile payments have become one of the essential financial technology services in the region, allowing consumers to easily transfer money and make payments through mobile payment applications. Digital currencies have also gained extensive applications in several countries in the region. The development of digital lending helps improve the level of financial inclusion, especially in areas with limited access to traditional financial services.

However, the development of FinTech in Southeast Asia also faces some challenges. The incomplete digital and financial infrastructure is the main bottleneck for FinTech development. Many areas lack high-speed internet and digital payment infrastructure, limiting the popularity of FinTech. Uncertainty in the regulatory and legal environment also constrains FinTech's development. The lack of unified regulatory standards poses challenges in terms of regulatory uncertainty and high compliance costs for many FinTech companies.

In summary, the FinTech industry in developing countries or regions is growing rapidly, creating opportunities for enhancing financial inclusion and driving economic growth. However, the development of this industry requires concerted efforts from governments and the private sector to promote the construction of digital infrastructure and establish more unified regulatory standards, thereby fostering the healthy development of the FinTech industry. Additionally, FinTech companies need to strengthen risk management and data privacy protection to build consumer trust and protect consumer rights.

10.2 The Impact of FinTech: A Case Study of India and China

In recent years, India's FinTech landscape has been undergoing a digital revolution. The emergence of new technologies such as blockchain and artificial intelligence is changing the delivery of financial services, making them more efficient, convenient, and secure. The application of these new technologies is driving the rapid rise of FinTech companies in India, offering various financial services, including payments, lending, investments, and insurance.

In India, payments are one of the primary businesses of FinTech companies. The digital payment market in India is growing rapidly and is expected to reach \$1.2 trillion by 2023. This growth is mainly attributed to the government's digital initiatives, such as the Digital India program and the Unified Payments Interface (UPI). Besides payments, lending is another significant business for Indian FinTech companies. The lending market in India is growing rapidly and is projected to reach \$2.5 trillion by 2023. This growth is driven by India's digital initiatives and innovative products by FinTech companies, such as P2P lending platforms and digital credit scoring, making lending more convenient and efficient.

In the investment sector, Indian FinTech companies are also innovating continuously. They offer various investment products such as stocks, funds, and insurance. Among these, AI-based investment advisory services are becoming increasingly popular. These services use AI algorithms to analyze market data and portfolios to provide more accurate investment advice. The application of these new technologies is driving the rapid development of Indian FinTech companies.

Regarding the regulatory environment, Indian FinTech companies do face some challenges. The financial regulatory authorities in India have relatively strict supervision of FinTech companies, which may have some impact on their development. Regulatory authorities are committed to ensuring the compliance, risk management, and consumer protection aspects of FinTech companies. While the purpose of regulation is to ensure the stability and security of the financial system, overly burdensome regulations and procedures may hinder innovation and development. Additionally, India's data protection laws also impose some requirements on data handling and privacy protection for FinTech companies. Data protection laws aim to safeguard the privacy and security of personal data, limiting the freedom of FinTech companies in data collection, storage, and processing. Although these regulations are intended to protect individual privacy rights, FinTech companies also need to comply with the relevant legal requirements while seeking innovative solutions in data security and privacy protection. These challenges require FinTech companies to cooperate with traditional financial institutions and the government to jointly promote the development of FinTech.

Regarding major participants, India's FinTech landscape mainly consists of FinTech companies, traditional financial institutions, and the government. FinTech companies are the main drivers of India's FinTech landscape, meeting consumer demands through innovative products and services. Traditional financial institutions are also actively participating in the FinTech industry, enhancing their digital capabilities through collaborations with FinTech companies. The government promotes the development of FinTech through digital initiatives and regulatory policies.

Next, let's explore the impact of FinTech on financial inclusion in India.

Firstly, the development of FinTech has made financial services more accessible in India Chakravorti (2017), especially in rural areas. In the past, financial services in India were mainly concentrated in urban areas, with relatively fewer financial services available in rural areas. However, with the promotion of FinTech, more financial services are entering rural areas, significantly improving financial inclusion. This is crucial for a diverse and populous country like India. The development of mobile payments and internet financial services enables people living in remote areas to conduct financial transactions easily. The development of digital financial services, such as digital currencies and online banking accounts, makes financial services more accessible to more people in India.

Secondly, the development of FinTech has made financial services in India more convenient. In the past, Indian financial services mainly relied on traditional banking businesses, requiring customers to visit banks in person for transactions. However, the rise of FinTech has changed this situation, introducing convenient methods such as mobile payments and online banking, greatly improving the efficiency and convenience of financial services. Customers can conduct financial transactions anytime and anywhere through mobile devices without the need to visit a physical bank, saving time and effort. FinTech innovations have also improved the quality and scope of financial services, allowing more people to access high-quality financial services. For example, FinTech companies use smart contracts and blockchain technology to provide faster, transparent, and secure transaction methods, increasing the convenience and reliability of financial services.

Thirdly, the development of FinTech has made financial services in India safer. In the past, Indian financial services faced issues such as information leaks and fraud, with customers' fund security not effectively guaranteed. However, with the development of FinTech, digital technologies such as blockchain are widely applied in the financial services sector, providing better protection for customer fund security. Blockchain technology ensures the transparency and tamper-proof nature of transactions through distributed ledgers and smart contracts, reducing financial fraud and risks. At the same time, security measures such as encryption technology and identity authentication enhance the protection of customer data.

In conclusion, India's FinTech landscape is undergoing a digital revolution. With the emergence of new technologies and continuous innovation by FinTech companies, the financial services industry will become more efficient, convenient, and secure. However, FinTech companies still face challenges such as regulation and data protection. Therefore, FinTech companies need to cooperate with traditional financial institutions and the government to jointly promote the development of FinTech.

Continuing on, let's look at the situation in China. With the rapid development of FinTech in China, more and more people are paying attention to its impact on financial inclusion in the country. Researchers have found that the impact of FinTech on financial inclusion in China is significant.

China's financial services industry has witnessed a revolutionary transformation. Traditional financial services have limitations when dealing with issues such as lack of identification or poor credit records. However, the development of FinTech has provided better financial inclusion for these populations. China's mobile payment and internet finance markets are leading globally, especially in developing economies, where the role of FinTech is even more pronounced. For example, mobile payment applications like WeChat Pay and Alipay have become the primary payment methods in China, making mobile payment accessible to almost all residents.

In addition to driving the development of new financial services, FinTech is also improving traditional financial services. Traditional financial services often require customers to visit banks or other financial institutions in person, which can be time-consuming and costly. However, FinTech makes this process more convenient as customers can access their accounts, make transfers, and pay bills directly through mobile devices. This convenience and efficiency make financial services more accessible, particularly for low-income individuals. Moreover, traditional financial institutions often demand extensive information from customers for risk assessment and credit approval. However, with the development of FinTech, more and more new financial service providers are adopting new technologies to assess customer credit and risk, such as utilizing big data and artificial intelligence. These applications enable more accurate credit assessment, reducing the likelihood of risks and fraud, thus providing more people with opportunities to access financial services.

Furthermore, the rapid development of FinTech has significantly improved inclusive finance in China:

The rapid development of FinTech has brought significant opportunities and improvements to inclusive finance in China. Traditional financial institutions often cater only to customers with good credit records and substantial assets. However, FinTech companies, through the application of technologies like big data analysis and artificial intelligence, can more accurately assess customers' credit records and risks, thus providing financial services opportunities to a broader population. For instance, mobile payment platforms like Alipay and WeChat Pay have become indispensable parts of daily life for Chinese people, offering convenient payment methods to a vast number of consumers.

Furthermore, the development of FinTech has greatly enhanced the efficiency of inclusive finance. Traditional financial institutions' services often require customers to visit bank counters or ATMs for transactions, while FinTech companies can provide online services through the internet and mobile devices, significantly improving service efficiency. For example, utilizing internet and artificial intelligence technology, small loan companies can expedite the review and approval process, providing customers with faster and more convenient loan services.

Simultaneously, the development of FinTech has also reduced the cost of inclusive finance. Traditional financial institutions often require significant human and material resources for their services, while FinTech companies achieve automation and intelligence through technological means, lowering service costs. For instance, by utilizing blockchain technology, financial institutions can achieve more secure and efficient transactions and settlements, thereby reducing transaction costs.

In conclusion, the impact of FinTech on financial inclusion in China is significant. FinTech promotes the development of financial inclusion by increasing the accessibility, reducing the cost, and improving the quality of financial services.

Next, we will conduct a comparative analysis of the development and impact of FinTech in India and China.

Factors such as market size, regulatory environment, and major participants are essential factors influencing FinTech development. In the FinTech landscape of India and China, these factors show some similarities and differences.

Firstly, in terms of market size, the FinTech market in China is relatively large Zhang and Chen (2019). As one of the most populous countries in the world, China has a vast market potential. The mobile payment market in China has reached 45 trillion RMB, far exceeding India's 1.8 trillion Indian rupees. This reflects the relatively higher scale and maturity of the FinTech market in China.

Secondly, regarding the regulatory environment, the Chinese government's regulation of FinTech is relatively strict. The Chinese government has introduced a series of policies and normative documents to regulate and address risks in the internet finance sector. In comparison, the regulation of FinTech in India is relatively lenient, but it also faces some issues. India's "Digital India" program once promoted the development of FinTech, but inadequate regulation has led to problems with some FinTech companies.

Thirdly, in terms of major participants Arner et al. (2016), the Chinese FinTech market is mainly dominated by technology companies. Tech giants such as Alibaba and Tencent play important roles in the Chinese FinTech market. In contrast, in India, startup companies such as Paytm and PhonePe dominate the FinTech market.

To sum up the FinTech situation in India and China, we can draw some preliminary conclusions:

The impact of FinTech on inclusive finance in both India and China is significant. Inclusive finance aims to provide affordable, secure, and reliable financial services to low-income populations, and it is an important goal for governments and financial institutions. The emergence and rapid development of FinTech provide unprecedented opportunities and challenges for achieving inclusive finance.

In both India and China, FinTech companies have provided more convenient, secure, and low-cost financial services for low-income individuals through innovative products and services. Products such as mobile payments and e-wallets have become deeply ingrained in daily life, becoming an essential part of everyday transactions. These products not only simplify the payment process and enhance security and convenience but also enable more people to access financial services, whether in urban or rural areas.

Furthermore, FinTech companies have offered more flexible and tailored financial services for low-income individuals through innovative credit assessment models and micro-loan products. Traditional financial services often rely on conventional credit evaluation methods, while FinTech employs technologies such as big data analysis and artificial intelligence to more accurately assess customer credit and risks, thereby providing them with financing support. This innovative financial service not only enhances the financing capabilities of low-income individuals but also promotes the development and innovation of small and micro-enterprises, driving economic growth and social stability.

However, FinTech has also brought some challenges to inclusive finance. With the development of FinTech, some traditional financial services may gradually become obsolete, potentially causing inconvenience for some individuals. Additionally, issues such as digital security and privacy protection need attention and resolution. Therefore, while promoting the development of FinTech, governments and financial institutions need to establish sound regulatory policies and regulations to ensure that FinTech advances within a safe and reliable framework. Strengthening public education and training on FinTech, enhancing digital literacy and application capabilities, can help people better utilize FinTech services while reducing potential risks and uncertainties.

In summary, India and China exhibit some differences and common characteristics in the development of FinTech. The difference in market size reflects China's leading position in the FinTech field, but India is also rapidly catching up. Differences in regulatory environments result in varying government policies and regulatory requirements. The disparity in key participants indicates differences in the composition and driving force of FinTech companies. Governments, financial institutions, and FinTech companies need to collaborate to promote the development of FinTech, improve inclusive finance levels, and achieve mutual economic and social prosperity.

10.3 The Economic Perspective of FinTech Development

From an economic perspective, the essence of FinTech lies in technological innovation and business model innovation to reduce the cost of financial services, improve the efficiency and innovation of financial services, and promote financial inclusion and stability.

Firstly, FinTech can reduce the cost of financial services. Traditional financial institutions have high operating costs, including labor, rent, and information technology. FinTech companies can lower operating costs and increase efficiency through digitization, automation, and intelligence. For example, blockchain technology can achieve decentralized transactions and settlements, reducing intermediary involvement and transaction costs. Meanwhile, artificial intelligence and big data analysis can achieve precise risk control and customer profiling, reducing credit and fraud risks, and lowering operating costs.

Secondly, FinTech can enhance the efficiency and innovation of financial services. Traditional financial institutions often have complex service processes that require customers to visit counters, consuming time and effort. FinTech companies can provide online and intelligent services through technologies such as mobile internet, cloud computing, and the Internet of Things, improving efficiency and user experience. For instance, mobile payments and electronic banking enable anytime and anywhere transactions and transfers. Peer-to-peer lending and crowdfunding Langley and Leyshon (2017) platforms facilitate personal and small business financing, while virtual currencies and digital asset trading platforms promote asset digitization and liquidity. For example, electronic payments reduce cash circulation, thereby reducing operational costs, and blockchain technology enables decentralized transactions and smart contracts, reducing intermediate steps and trust costs.

Lastly, FinTech can promote financial inclusion and stability. Traditional financial institutions primarily serve large enterprises and high-net-worth clients, providing limited services to ordinary people and small businesses. FinTech companies can expand the coverage of financial services through digital and inclusive service models, promoting financial inclusion. For example, mobile payments and electronic banking enable rural and remote residents to access convenient financial services, while peer-to-peer lending and crowdfunding platforms provide financing channels for small and micro-enterprises, promoting entrepreneurship and employment. Additionally, FinTech can lower financial risks and promote financial stability through intelligent risk control and supervision.

In the future, the development of FinTech will witness a more diverse and intelligent trend.

Firstly, FinTech will extend its application to more fields, expanding its scope beyond widely used areas such as mobile payments and peer-to-peer lending. It will encompass insurance technology, wealth management technology, blockchain finance, and other domains. Insurance technology will provide more accurate insurance products and pricing strategies through data analysis and intelligent risk assessment. Wealth management technology will offer personalized wealth management services to investors using robo-advisors and automated investment tools. Blockchain technology will enhance financial transaction transparency and security, providing more efficient settlement and asset management solutions.

Secondly, FinTech will focus on intelligent service models, utilizing technologies like artificial intelligence, machine learning, and natural language processing to offer more personalized and intelligent financial services to users. Artificial intelligence will play a crucial role in the financial industry, enabling deep learning and big data analysis for precise risk assessment, customer profiling, and predictive modeling to provide customized financial solutions. Intelligent robots and virtual assistants will become integral parts of financial services, engaging in smart conversations and interactions with users through natural language processing and sentiment analysis, providing personalized financial advice and support.

Furthermore, let's discuss the relationship between FinTech, big data, and banking.

As FinTech and big data continue to advance, the banking industry is facing unprecedented opportunities and challenges. The emergence of FinTech has made banking services more convenient, efficient, and also opened up more space for innovation. Big data provides banks with more data support, helping them better understand customer needs and improve service quality. However, these new technologies also bring some issues that require banks to strengthen security measures and data management.

Firstly, FinTech brings more opportunities Batiz-Lazo and Wood (2018) to the banking industry. Emerging technologies like mobile payments and internet finance expand the service scope of banks, allowing customers to conduct banking transactions more conveniently. Additionally, applications of intelligent robo-advisors and blockchain technology provide innovative spaces, enabling banks to offer more intelligent and personalized services. These technological advancements allow banks to better meet customer needs and improve customer satisfaction.

Secondly, FinTech also presents challenges Arner et al. (2016). With the rapid development of internet finance, traditional banks face increasingly fierce competition. Traditional banks need constant innovation to remain competitive and attract more customers. Additionally, FinTech introduces security risks. Threats such as cyber-attacks and data breaches pose challenges to the banking industry, requiring banks to strengthen security measures to protect customers' funds and personal information.

Big data, on the other hand, provides more data support for the banking industry. Through the analysis of customer data, banks can better understand customer needs and provide more personalized services. At the same time, big data helps banks manage risks more effectively. For example, analyzing market data can forecast market trends and increase investment returns. These data analysis techniques enable banks to better understand customer needs and market changes, enhancing operational efficiency and profitability.

However, the application of big data also presents some issues. Firstly, data quality and accuracy need to be ensured. Banks must guarantee the sources and accuracy of data to avoid making decisions based on erroneous information. Secondly, data security is a significant concern, preventing data leaks and misuse. Banks need to strengthen data management and security measures to protect customer funds and personal information.

Now, let's explore the interesting relationship between FinTech, regulatory arbitrage, and shadow banking. Some studies have found that FinTech can promote the rise of shadow banking through regulatory arbitrage, which may negatively impact financial stability.

Regulatory arbitrage refers to financial institutions using regulatory loopholes or differences to adjust business structures, asset allocations, and other methods to evade regulatory requirements and achieve higher profits. Shadow banking refers to financial institutions that operate outside traditional banking regulations, engaging in activities similar to banking, but not subject to the same regulatory scrutiny.

The rapid development of FinTech offers more opportunities and space for regulatory arbitrage and shadow banking. On the one hand, the innovative and digital nature of FinTech allows financial institutions to evade traditional banking regulations by adjusting business structures and asset allocations. For example, some FinTech companies can use innovative business models and technologies to bypass traditional banking regulations, thereby gaining higher profits. On the other hand, the development of FinTech also provides more opportunities for the growth of shadow banking. Utilizing the internet and FinTech platforms, shadow banking can raise funds more flexibly and efficiently and engage in investment and financing activities.

However, the rise of regulatory arbitrage and shadow banking also brings risks and challenges. Firstly, regulatory arbitrage may lead to increased risk exposure and systemic risk for financial institutions. By evading regulatory requirements, financial institutions may increase leverage, thus raising financial risk. Secondly, the business model and risk management mechanisms of shadow banking are relatively immature, which may cause risk events and negatively impact financial markets and the economy. Additionally, the development of FinTech may also impact traditional financial institutions, increasing market instability risks.

To address the risks posed by regulatory arbitrage and shadow banking, regulatory authorities need to strengthen supervision and monitoring of the FinTech sector to ensure the stable operation of the financial market. Regulatory agencies should proactively keep pace with FinTech development, refine regulatory rules and systems, and guard against the emergence of financial risks. At the same time, FinTech companies and shadow banking entities should also enhance their risk management and compliance capabilities to ensure the safety and stability of their business activities.

Apart from the role of regulatory authorities, financial institutions should strengthen internal controls and risk management to ensure the safety and compliance of their business activities. They need to establish robust risk management systems, including risk identification, assessment, and monitoring, as well as effective internal control measures. Furthermore, enhancing personnel training and education to improve employees' awareness of compliance requirements and adherence is crucial.

As emerging players, FinTech companies also need to strengthen their compliance management, adhere to regulatory requirements and laws. They should establish comprehensive compliance systems, including compliance policies, procedures, and processes, and employ professional compliance personnel. Additionally, actively participating in industry self-regulatory organizations, enhancing industry cooperation, and information sharing are essential to promote industry standards and healthy development.

In addition to the efforts of regulatory authorities, financial institutions, and FinTech companies, the public also needs to enhance their awareness of FinTech and data security to protect personal information and fund safety. This can be achieved through increasing awareness of personal information protection, choosing secure and reliable FinTech products and services, and regularly updating and strengthening passwords, among other measures.

Lastly, let's analyze the impact of FinTech from a macroeconomic perspective.

The emergence of FinTech has profound implications for the macroeconomy, as it not only changes the way the financial industry operates but also presents challenges and opportunities for the financial system, monetary policy, and fiscal policy.

Firstly, the rise of FinTech has brought significant changes to the financial system. Traditional financial institutions face competition pressure from FinTech companies, compelling them to innovate and improve, providing more convenient, efficient, and cost-effective financial services. This competition promotes the transformation and upgrading of financial institutions and expands the coverage of financial services, driving the development and innovation of the financial system.

Secondly, the rise of FinTech has implications for monetary policy. Traditional monetary policy tools may no longer be suitable for the emerging FinTech environment. The development of FinTech alters the transmission mechanism of money, such as using digital currencies and mobile payments to facilitate faster and more convenient fund flow. This poses challenges to the effectiveness of monetary policy and decision-makers, requiring timely adjustments to policy tools and strategies to ensure the effectiveness of monetary policy.

Lastly, FinTech also impacts fiscal policy. The development of FinTech improves the efficiency and accuracy of fiscal policy execution. Through FinTech means, the government can better identify and target specific groups' needs, providing targeted fiscal support. Additionally, the development of FinTech also creates new sources of fiscal revenue for the government, such as issuing and trading digital currencies, providing new opportunities for fiscal revenue and expenditure balance.

However, the development of FinTech also poses challenges.

Firstly, the rapid development of FinTech may increase financial market instability. The introduction of new technologies and business models may trigger market shocks and risk contagion. For example, the application of virtual currencies and blockchain technology may lead to price fluctuations and market uncertainty. In such cases, policymakers need to strengthen regulation and risk management to ensure the stability and healthy development of financial markets.

Secondly, the development of FinTech may exacerbate financial inequality. While FinTech can provide financial services to more people, there exist digital divides and information asymmetry. Some individuals may not enjoy the convenience brought by FinTech, while others may excessively rely on FinTech, leading to greater exposure to risks. Policymakers need to take measures to safeguard consumer rights and interests, strengthen financial education and promote inclusive finance to ensure that the development of FinTech benefits a wider population.

In addition to the above challenges, the development of FinTech may also face issues of data security and privacy protection. A large amount of personal and transaction data is collected and processed by FinTech companies, and if not properly protected, it may be at risk of data breaches and misuse. Policymakers and FinTech companies need to enhance data security management to ensure the privacy and security of user data.

In conclusion, the impact of FinTech on macroeconomic stability is multifaceted, bringing both challenges and opportunities Batiz-Lazo and Wood (2018). Policymakers need to timely adjust policy tools and strategies to adapt to the development trends of FinTech, promoting the healthy development of the financial industry and stable economic growth. Meanwhile, FinTech companies also need to strengthen their risk management and compliance capabilities to ensure the stability and healthy development of financial markets.

The financial industry is undergoing a revolutionary transformation. However, this transformation also brings some potential risks, especially regarding its impact on financial stability. Let's explore the impact of FinTech on financial stability and propose some measures to address it.

Firstly, the development of FinTech makes financial markets more transparent and efficient. By using technologies such as artificial intelligence, big data, and blockchain, financial institutions can process transactions, assess risks, and monitor market dynamics more quickly. However, this efficiency may also lead to increased market volatility, posing a threat to financial stability. In other words, one of the reasons FinTech can enhance financial stability is that it contributes to improving the efficiency and security of financial services. For example, FinTech can help financial institutions reduce risks by providing better risk management and regulatory tools. Additionally, FinTech can increase market transparency and liquidity, thereby reducing market uncertainty and risk.

Secondly, the development of FinTech also brings new risks. For example, the emergence of new financial products like virtual currencies and Initial Coin Offerings (ICOs) may trigger market fluctuations and investor trust crises. Additionally, since the application of FinTech requires the collection of a large amount of personal data, data privacy and security become significant concerns. If this data is attacked or misused by hackers, it can negatively impact financial stability.

To address these risks, a series of measures need to be taken. Firstly, regulatory authorities need to strengthen supervision of FinTech, ensuring its legality and security. Secondly, financial institutions need to enhance data privacy and security protection, preventing data leaks and misuse. Additionally, financial institutions also need to strengthen risk assessment and monitoring of new financial products to timely detect and respond to potential risks.

In summary, the development of FinTech has both positive and negative effects on financial stability. To maximize its positive impact, a series of measures need to be taken to address its potential risks. Only in this way can FinTech become a significant force driving economic growth and promoting financial stability.

References

Arner, D. W., Barberis, J., & Buckley, R. P. (2016). *The evolution of fintech: A new post-crisis paradigm?* Georgetown Journal of International Law, 47(4)

Batiz-Lazo, B., & Wood, D. (2018). *Digital banking: Opportunities and challenges.* Computers in Human Behavior, 90

Chakravorti, B. (2017). *The FinTech opportunity in India.* Thunderbird International Business Review, 59(1)

Frost, J., Gambacorta, L., Huang, Y., Shin, H. S., & Zbinden, P. (2019). BigTech and the changing structure of financial intermediation. BIS Working Papers

Langley, P. and Leyshon, A. (2017) , "Capitalizing on the crowd: the monetary and financial ecologies of crowd funding", Environment and Planning A, Vol.49No.5

Larios-Hernández, G.J. (2017) , "Blockchain entrepreneur ship opportunity in the practices of the unbanked", Business Horizons

Zavolokina, L., Dolata, M., & Schwabe, G. (2016, September). FinTech transformation: How IT-enabled innovations shape the financial sector. In European Conference on Information Systems (ECIS).

Zhang, J., & Chen, Y. (2019). The growth of fintech in China: Causes and potential risks. International Economics and Economic Policy, 16(2)

MIX
Papier aus verantwortungsvollen Quellen
Paper from responsible sources
FSC® C105338

If you have any concerns about our products,
you can contact us on
ProductSafety@springernature.com

In case Publisher is established outside the EU,
the EU authorized representative is:
Springer Nature Customer Service Center GmbH
Europaplatz 3, 69115 Heidelberg, Germany

Printed by Libri Plureos GmbH
in Hamburg, Germany